Medical Education

Developing a curriculum
for practice

Contents

List of abbreviations

BERA	British Educational Research Association
BMJ	*British Medical Journal*
CEO	Chief Executive Officer
CMO	Chief Medical Officer
CR–UK	Cancer Research–UK
CT scan	Computerized Tomography scan
CV	Curricula Vitae
DoH	Department of Health
EWTD	European Working Time Directive
F1	Foundation Year One
F2	Foundation Year Two
GMC	General Medical Council
GP	General Practitioner
ITU	Intensive Treatment Unit
M and M	Morbidity and Mortality (conference)
MMC	*Modernising Medical Careers*
NHS	National Health Service
PBL	Problem-based learning
PGMDE	Post Graduate Medical and Dental Education
PMETB	Postgraduate Medical Education and Training Board
PRHO	Pre-registration House Officer
RCS Eng	Royal College of Surgeons of England
R, D and D	Research, Development and Diffusion
RITA	Record of In-Training Assessment
SCP	Surgical Care Practitioner
SCOPME	Standing Committee on Postgraduate Medical and Dental Education
SHA	Strategic Health Authority
SHO	Senior House Officer
SpR	Specialist Registrar
STA	Specialist Training Authority

Acknowledgements

We acknowledge with grateful thanks the permission of Professor Michael Golby and Dr Allan Parrott to quote extensively from their monograph (Golby and Parrott 1999), and also particularly for being permitted to reproduce their table: 'Three basic assumptions of the positivist and non positivist paradigms' which we use as Table 10.1.

We are also particularly grateful to Linda de Cossart (co-author with Della Fish) and Nikki Bramhill on behalf of tfm Publishing Ltd, for allowing us to quote extensively from Chapters 6 and 7 of de Cossart and Fish (2005) (and to use this work here in Chapters 6 and 8); and to reproduce from Chapter 7 'The elements of clinical thinking' (offered here as Figure 5.1); from Chapter 9 'A map of practice knowledge for professionals generally' (offered here at Figure 6.1); and from Chapter 3 the 'Summary of the ideas of Habermas' (offered here as Table 3.3).

We thank also our contributors to Chapter 4: Patrizia Capozzi (surgical SHO); Linda de Cossart (consultant surgeon); Cath Fazey (senior theatre sister); and Rosie Lusznat (consultant in old age psychiatry) for allowing us to become privy to the finer details of a piece of their practice and their thoughts on it.

Finally, but by no means as the least significant, we express our appreciation to our Trojan-like proof-readers, Jean Douglas and Evelyn Usher who once again have helped us to prepare for the publisher a text about whose prose style and accuracy we could be confident. Any mistakes are assuredly ours and not theirs.

Readers are asked to note that the ideas contained in this publication are our own and are by no means necessarily shared by any of the institutions for which we work.

About the authors

Colin Coles is an educationist who has been working in medical education for over 30 years. He has extensive experience in curriculum design, evaluation and development in undergraduate and postgraduate medical education, as well as in continuing professional development. He publishes widely, is an international conference speaker, advises professional organizations on educational matters, and runs developmental educational workshops in medical education within the UK and overseas. He collaborated with Della Fish in their previous book together, *Developing Professional Judgement in Health Care* (Fish and Coles 1998). He holds a personal chair in the School of Education at the University of Winchester, where he co-founded a masters degree in education for medical practitioners.

Della Fish is a practising teacher, teacher educator, and curriculum designer and developer. She worked in Teacher Education for 25 years, but alongside this, from the early 1980s, she supported occupational therapy staff in designing new diploma and degree programmes, and was rapidly drawn into working with a wide range of health care professionals. A developing passion for the challenge of providing education in clinical settings led her, in 1994, to extend this work into a full-time consultancy which supports educators in almost every health care profession. She began work in medical education as an educational adviser to South Thames Deanery in 1999 and worked for the Royal College of Surgeons of England, as they developed the draft curriculum for SHOs in surgery from 2001 to 2004. Her three books (Fish and Twinn 1997; Fish and Coles 1998; and Fish 1998), focused on teaching and learning in clinical settings. With Linda de Cossart she published *Cultivating a Thinking Surgeon* (de Cossart and Fish 2005). Della is Professor of Education (postgraduate medicine) at King's College, London.

Introduction

Our reasons for writing this book

We believe that initiatives in the early years of the twenty-first century to develop postgraduate medical education in the UK, under the title *Modernising Medical Careers*, have merits and provide considerable possibilities for growth. We believe particularly that the move to locate the education of doctors (including their assessment) in the practice setting is vitally important. However, the scheme urgently needs a more coherent, articulated curriculum framework, and a sounder educational underpinning, than it currently has in the *Curriculum for the Foundation Years in Postgraduate Education and Training* (**Department of Health** DoH 2005b). Indeed, we fear that both it, and all other versions of curriculum design for postgraduate medicine as they emerge in the early years of the twenty-first century, will short-change an entire professional generation of doctors in respect of their true educational entitlement. This is because we believe that, in its current and now definitive form the *Curriculum for the Foundation Years* is in danger of setting an inappropriate example for other postgraduate curricula, which will soon begin to emerge as this decade progresses.

Our task in this book therefore is to provide readers with the principles, processes, components and understanding that are necessary to build and to develop postgraduate medical curricula which will guide sound education in the practice setting and which will be robust and rigorous. In short, we outline here the basis for gaining expertise in the practice of curriculum design and development in postgraduate medical education.

Our main focus

Our focus is on postgraduate medicine and its context within the UK (and particularly hospital medicine rather than primary care), because it is a unique case of curriculum development which shares principles with such developments in other countries, but which nonetheless is based upon and provides for a context that is particular. Equivalences can be substantiated between curricula in different countries, but each context is different and the detail cannot therefore be generalized.

Readership

We believe that readers across a wide spectrum of medical education will find this book useful. We offer it to those designing such curricula, those entrusted with their introduction and management, those whose teaching, learning and assessment processes are shaped by them, and those whose lives are influenced by the kinds of doctors that emerge from them. We also believe that our book will be useful for those on masters degree courses which focus on medical education in particular or education for the health care professions more generally.

The structure of the book

The structure of the book is shaped in three parts. Part 1 outlines the urgent problems that are currently developing in respect of curriculum design and development for medical education. Part 2 focuses on what designers of a curriculum for medical education need to know, to discover and to decide about. Part 3 focuses on curriculum development.

The key issues addressed in Parts 1 and 2

Following the review of the current urgent problems in curriculum design which we offer in the only chapter of Part 1, we seek in Part 2 first to equip readers with a professional understanding of the practice of curriculum design and then of sound educational practice. Thereafter, we take chapter by chapter each of the key problematic issues upon which curriculum designers need to deliberate, and about which they need to come to a wise judgement. For each of these we provide a wide range of rich evidence, drawn from the practice setting, which sharply illuminates its complexities. This is designed to fuel the deliberative processes in which the design team must engage if their curriculum design is to support robust education both 'in' and 'for' the realities of the clinical setting.

 The kinds of problematic issues we address here arise from the following important questions, which we believe are currently being overlooked or ignored. They are each tackled in a separate chapter in order to provide step-by-step explorations of each area that curriculum developers for postgraduate medical education need to investigate and come to an informed view about.

- What are the principles, processes, components and logic of curriculum design as a practice (Chapter 2)?
- What unifies the disparate activities of teaching (in its general sense) into a sound educational practice (Chapter 3)?
- What kind of practitioner should such a curriculum be developing, and how might this shape the education offered in its name (Chapter 3)?
- What values underlie the day-to-day medical practice of individuals? What values should a curriculum for professional practice in medicine be based upon and also, what values should it promote (Chapter 4)?
- What is the real *nature* of the professional practice setting in which the educational programme will be enacted and for which it is a preparation, and how should this affect the details of the curriculum (Chapter 5)?
- What forms of knowledge underpin medical practice; what should be taught, learnt and assessed in the practical setting by postgraduate doctors; and how should this be expressed in the curriculum (Chapter 6)?
- What kinds of expertise should a postgraduate doctor learn before being appointed as a specialist? How do doctors acquire such kinds of expertise? And how can we design a curriculum that attends to these (Chapter 7)?
- How might we assess in the clinical setting the acquisition of such kinds of expertise by a postgraduate doctor in training, and what kind of framework would be appropriate to support the chosen assessment process (Chapter 8)?
- What are the other managerial and procedural matters about which a definitive curriculum must provide details, and how should curriculum designers attend to these (Chapter 9)?

Part 2 thus supports the design team's *complex deliberations and wise judgements about the problematic issues* of professional education in general, and postgraduate medical education in particular. (Such issues include framing the educational aims, and shaping the approaches to and relationships of teaching, learning and assessment.) At the end of Part 2, we illustrate, in Chapter 9, how these wise judgements will then provide the necessary basis for *resolving the more simple procedural decisions* which, in order to make it a 'live' success, must structure the curriculum enacted at the local level. Being matters about the management of the programme, these procedural decisions (like the criteria for recruitment, the regulations for progression and the required processes for quality assurance) must follow rather than lead the educational ones. Sadly, in amateur approaches to curriculum design where there is no understanding of where to begin, procedural decisions are often tackled first, as being easiest. Indeed, they are sometimes the only things tackled apart from assessment, because they are most easily recognized as needing attention. This distorts the professional practice of education into an enterprise which provides nothing educationally worthwhile but merely seeks to feed the needs of management.

To support readers who seek to design a rigorous curriculum for *education* in postgraduate medicine, we have provided key questions about the design of such a curriculum at the head of all relevant chapters in Part 2, and have attended to the implications for such designers at the end of these chapters.

The focus in Part 3

Having explored design issues in Part 2, we focus in Part 3 on evaluating a curriculum, on the principles of change which those who implement a curriculum need to understand, and on the development of the curriculum locally and the implications of this at both deanery and national levels. This may be of particular importance for those seeking to develop and reshape the *foundation curriculum framework*, but will be of equal significance to anyone involved in enacting any curriculum in the clinical setting within postgraduate medicine or in other fields of health care education.

In Part 3 then we first examine the processes endemic to good curriculum evaluation (Chapter 10). This chapter marks the pivotal centre of the book, being in one sense the end of the design process and the start of the developmental one, and thus could have found its place equally at the end of Part 2. However, on balance we decided to use it to spearhead the developmental section.

Following this, Chapter 11 explores the difficulties and constraints of introducing educational change as another means of setting the context for curriculum development. In Chapter 12 we advocate the idea of starting with the educational practice at local level and illustrate and explore this in detail. Here we suggest developing at intermediate (deanery) level, a curriculum to support teachers and learners in implementing the local programme. In leaving until the end of the chapter comments about the refinement of the national framework we suggest a reconfiguring of its nature and purpose to support work at the local level. We then refer readers back to the beginning of the book to indicate the essentially cyclical nature of design and development. In all this, we recognize emphatically the importance in the UK context of the role of the **Postgraduate Medical Education and Training Board** (PMETB), or a similar body in other settings, in among other things accrediting and quality assuring the whole enterprise.

The inevitably fragmenting result of focusing on the detail

From the above it will be apparent that, in order to explore the detail of the curriculum, we have disconnected its components in a somewhat arbitrary way which does no justice to their complex interrelationships. For example, we have separated assessment from teaching and learning (as its most closely related activities) and from all other elements that relate to assessment and make up the whole curriculum. We have also treated knowing, thinking and doing in the same way, focusing on them in one place and on the values that drive them in another. This is an inevitable result of trying to provide a volume of evidence and ideas about each component. All we can do to mitigate this is to urge readers to recognize that the whole curriculum is more than the sum of its parts, and to experience this at first hand by engaging in the practice of curriculum design and development (which like all practices can only be learnt by doing).

The key challenges we highlight

Many of the themes within the book revolve around a range of dangers to which curriculum designers can easily fall prey. These are:

1   The temptation to ignore the fundamental role of values which underlie all curriculum design and development issues, and which are the driving force of sound education.
2   The complex and uncertain nature of postgraduate practice in medicine which will tempt designers to invent a simplified version of it rather than try to do justice to its realities.
3   The creeping assault of management discourse in reference to matters educational, so that curriculum designers are seduced into using inappropriate terminology which in turn leads to a distortion of the whole enterprise of education. (An example is the pressure to see assessment as first and foremost a management 'tool' rather than understanding that it is part of educational practice and will lack validity in all areas if this is not recognized.)
4   The assumption that the components of practice in postgraduate medicine will all 'cash out' into simple and visible behaviour, so that designers fall into the trap of shaping the curriculum around the visible elements of practice at the expense of the invisible ones (like professional judgement, which is what makes professionals what they are, but which cannot be 'seen', developed and assessed merely through observation).
5   The crassness of the current western world view that quality can be couched in quantitative terms, with the result that curriculum designers are seduced into emphasizing the significance of numbers and thus depicting as trivial the expertise of professionals.
6   The damage done by the postmodernist view that we no longer need experts in anything, thus apparently rendering it unnecessary to bring into the design process those with an expertise in the field of knowledge which shapes this book.

On a more positive note, we particularly seek to illuminate the expertise which characterizes the practice of professionals and particularly doctors in the clinical setting. Any curriculum for medical practice needs to foster this, but the challenge in doing so is to do justice to its complexity. We provide a basis for starting this by making explicit much of the tacit and implicit knowledge, thinking and understanding that underlies the activities of such practitioners.

Most particularly, we highlight professional, personal and educational values as the most significant driving force for all involved whether they are aware of them or not. Our view is that education for professionals must particularly focus on these matters and that a curriculum which guides such education must find ways of promoting values as important, of ensuring that learners and teachers examine them, and encouraging the investigation of practice as a way of cultivating them in the learner. We believe that in this, the teacher's daily practice and the conduct of all who work with the learner are the most powerful pedagogic influences. This means that everyone in the practice setting is a teacher of and has educational responsibilities for postgraduate doctors, not only in that setting, but in terms of knowing the curriculum, contributing to it and understanding its philosophy.

We would simply add that curriculum design is a practice in its own right, and like all practices, it is best learnt by engaging in it and reflecting on that engagement. Its activities involve alternating between developing a theoretical understanding, deliberating about complex issues, becoming involved in relevant action, and keeping all three under critical review.

Our moral obligations as curriculum designers

It takes time to develop expertise in curriculum design and to refine and develop a new curriculum. Ensuring the soundness of all this is a solemn responsibility. These matters are not well understood by the public, the media and politicians, all of whom endlessly press the notion of expediency as an excuse for wanting everything immediately, for ignoring the advice of experts and for rushing to implement that which is not well thought through. And sometimes (as with a curriculum for a whole profession) this can lead at least to embarrassment if not catastrophe on a large scale. (Early versions of the National Curriculum for UK schoolchildren come to mind.)

A curriculum, then, has a profound influence on generations of learners and can even reshape the development of an entire profession (either deliberately or by default). We believe that it is therefore both the first and the final responsibility of curriculum designers and developers to stand firm against the calls for an expedient outcome, and the rhetoric of 'necessity' (which Pitt the Younger declared as: the plea for every infringement of human freedom, the argument of tyrants and the creed of slaves).

We believe that our moral responsibilities as curriculum designers and developers are threefold: to achieve the very best possible initial design in whatever time that requires; to develop it intelligently and in a systematic, educationally rigorous and appropriately-paced way in practice, by listening to the critiques of those engaged in implementing it; and then to refine, and keep under review, the initial overall design to support what is needed by those on the ground.

We believe above all that for postgraduate medical education in particular, we have to strive for excellence in these matters because the quality of any national curriculum framework, once in place, will profoundly influence the education offered to generations of doctors, and even shape the conduct of the entire medical profession and the health of the nation – for good or ill – for many years to come.

PART 1
Starting points

1 Developing rigorous curricula for medical practice in the twenty-first century: a matter of urgency

Introduction

Postgraduate medical education is an unusual enterprise and a special case of education, in that all doctors following graduation are required to continue to learn formally and to gain further qualifications relating to theory and practice, in order to practise in their specialty. This somewhat lengthy period spans the time between graduation from medical school to appointment as a specialist. This is a period in which doctors extend or consolidate their choice of specialist career, and that choice is from a wide range of specialties and sub-specialisms, many of which may not have formed part of the undergraduate curriculum. They thus need to gain both further theoretical understanding and considerable new practical expertise. This is also a time when doctors begin to take responsibility for patients while continuing to learn formally and formatively in the practice setting. Thus, compared with other health professions, doctors are required to pursue a far more extensive period of training following initial qualification. By necessity this requires extensive resources.

What is more, particularly in the UK, this period of preparation is truly 'postgraduate' in that it pursues the specialist education of doctors principally through academic means – courses, programmes of study, rigorous examinations – linked into the nation's systems of higher education. It requires scholarly understanding and not simply technical training (even though the postgraduates themselves are still traditionally referred to as 'trainees' and their teachers as 'trainers'). But it also requires rigorous learning within the clinical setting, during and as part of the service commitment. It is this aspect of postgraduate medical education, which is about *learning to practise*, that we specifically focus on throughout the book.

The practice of medicine, as we shall argue, is much more than a set of predetermined tasks carried out by highly trained technicians. In a word, it requires a particular form of 'expertise', and this will be a theme running through the book. The main challenge facing postgraduate medical education is the need to understand the nature of that expertise and how best to develop it.

To argue that medical practice requires considerable expertise is not to demean or denigrate the quality of the practice of other health professions. Theirs is not, in comparison with medicine, more technical or less rigorous. These professions have their own forms (and traditions) of practice which are different from those of medicine, and which require different educational provision.

Nor do we mean to imply that medical education should be entirely separate from that of other health professions. There is a strong case for elements of medical education being 'inter-professional', not least where this allows health professionals to understand the nature of their own practice and that of others (though this will not be a focus of this book). Nevertheless, traditionally, doctors have become the leaders of clinical teams. They have been the ones who are most responsible (and substantially accountable) for diagnosing conditions and prescribing treatments. It is true that increasingly other health professionals are taking on some of these roles but doctors still assume overall responsibility, and must continue to do so.

Our point is that medicine, perhaps like the legal profession rather than say nursing, requires a considerably extended period of deep learning through which to develop the expertise needed to respond to the demands of medicine. That is why we are treating postgraduate medical education here as a special case.

The overall problem that this book addresses

Having said all this, medicine generally, and especially its educational provision, is at something of a crossroads. Certainly in the UK and increasingly elsewhere in the world, huge developments are occurring that seriously challenge, and possibly threaten to undermine, the very fabric of the profession and the way in which doctors are educated. In a previous book (Fish and Coles 1998: 3) we spoke of the professions as being 'under siege'. We have seen nothing in the intervening period to lead us to change that view. Indeed, we now believe that postgraduate medical education itself is facing something of a crisis as is the reform of health care in the UK. We note that a number of influential figures are now seriously questioning the direction of current policies (Dyson 2003; Pollack 2004; Wass 2005; and Ribeiro in Sylvester 2005).

The UK government, as we shall shortly show, has recently initiated changes to postgraduate medical education that raise many educational questions. But we would rather not accept this development as inevitable and see its flaws inexorably gain ground. Rather, we consider now to be a unique moment to offer a robust critique of the proposed changes and particularly how they have been managed educationally, and to illustrate other and better ways forward. We do so by offering a reasoned, and we believe, well-founded and soundly-argued, educational perspective in which we consider the *educational* evidence and its implications. By this means we hope to offer all those involved in, or influenced and affected by, postgraduate medical education, the language and the understanding to ensure that the changes being introduced will take on and embody appropriately robust educational principles. We also hope to benefit future planning and policy-making, not just in postgraduate medical education but elsewhere in medicine and the other health care professions. And we believe that what we have to offer will be of value in places other than the UK, where medical and health care education are under review.

The aim of this book then is to address the central problem that we believe postgraduate medical education faces today – that curricula are being developed for education in the practice setting which have not been built from first principles and which lack sound educational underpinning. Our intention in this book is thus to inject some educational rigour into the processes of curriculum design and development.

Why postgraduate medical education?

Our reasons for focusing specifically and deliberately on postgraduate rather than undergraduate medical education are as follows.

First, we believe that the opportunity provided by the current government initiatives gives an impetus for change that, if channelled in what we would see as appropriate directions, could lead to significant and considerable gains not just for medical education but, as a result, for health care itself.

Next, we believe that the kinds of developments that we outline here can occur within a relatively short period of time. This is not so likely with undergraduate curricula, which in the UK have been the focus of much development over the past ten years or so following the publication and republication of *Tomorrow's Doctors* by the **General Medical Council** (GMC 1993). Undergraduate curricula are, naturally, located within the country's higher education system but universities work within a rather broader time dimension that fits uneasily with the shorter-term political imperatives of governments that are driving changes to postgraduate medical education. And these changes require urgent attention that cannot wait for a response that begins with undergraduate curricula and which might only slowly filter through into postgraduate medical education.

Further, changing an undergraduate medical curriculum is fraught with tensions and competing vested interests. Above all, universities deal (largely) with what in Chapter 6 we will refer to as 'propositional knowledge' (more commonly called 'facts') rather than the forms of knowledge which we will argue are needed for professional practice. Universities are largely in the business of teaching (and developing through research programmes) 'new' knowledge, which sometimes (wrongly in our view) is referred to as 'theory' – the knowledge of an expert as opposed to the knowledge of expertise. Their focus is much less on 'practice'.

In some ways this is perhaps rather surprising. The notion of 'academe' ought more properly be thought to focus attention on developing rigour, encouraging scholarly thinking and the pursuit of excellence, rather than teaching today's facts to tomorrow's doctors. It has been the convention in the UK, though in our view an educationally unhelpful tradition, to separate 'academic' and 'practical' teaching – a convention which is only now being reversed through the creation of technological universities. One consequence of this divisive history is that many medical graduates enter the profession often ill-prepared for, and with a view of medicine that is at odds with, the realities of medical practice. That is, they believe that: medicine is entirely 'scientific' and 'evidence based'; there is a solution to every problem; and that all solutions consist of the application of science to human suffering.

The evidence (from formal and informal studies as well as from our own observations and discussions), suggests that medical students are not as fully prepared as they might be by their undergraduate experiences to practise medicine as qualified doctors with any certainty or assurance on their first exposure to patients. It seems to us that medical students have been 'sold a myth' about medical practice, and that during their postgraduate years this myth has to be eradicated and replaced (in some cases not without a struggle) with a more appropriate perception of what the practice of medicine is actually concerned with.

In our view, designers of a curriculum for undergraduate medical education need to start from neutral first principles (as opposed to starting by defending current university theoretical territories and traditions). Thus, exactly like designers of postgraduate curricula, they need (as we show in Part 2 of this book) first to study critically the practice for which their curriculum is a preparation, and then to design a course which enables undergraduates to prepare for this. Such preparation would surely include the critical study of current medical practice as it is lived in the clinical setting (in all its complexity), to which should be brought the necessary theoretical components (in all their complexity) which prepare for and illuminate current practice and lay a foundation for future educational development. But this would require a deep change within the culture of higher education establishments – and development of postgraduate education cannot wait for that, and anyway perhaps should lead it.

So, in our view, the pursuit of curriculum development within undergraduate medical education is a much more long-term project than development within the postgraduate arena. Nevertheless, we believe that the development of a curriculum for practice in postgraduate medicine could lead to developments within the undergraduate curriculum through some kind of 'back flow', and that the changes brought about in this way would perhaps be more appropriate than some of the developments that have occurred in recent years. Not least of the reasons for this belief is that many of the teachers involved in postgraduate medical education are the same as those who teach medical students in the clinical years (and who we would hope might teach more about 'practice' in what is currently termed the 'pre-clinical' undergraduate curriculum).

This is not to say that changing the postgraduate curriculum will be easy or automatic. We have seen some hopeful signs that practising clinicians understand (perhaps more than some policy-makers) the nature of their practice and the knowledge that underpins it. Nevertheless, there will be the need for a culture change. This will, however, be by no means as extensive a change as would be required to change undergraduate medical education in the way we suggest.

Why now? Why is it urgent?

In this section we seek to show not only what the immediate problem is with postgraduate medical education in the UK, but also how it has arisen. Thus, first we offer the history and current context of the problem, as a basis for identifying the specifics of the problem in the practices of both medical education and curriculum design.

The context: *Modernising Medical Careers* (MMC)

In August 2002 the UK's Department of Health released for consultation a document written by the **Chief Medical Officer** (CMO), Professor Sir Liam Donaldson, entitled *Unfinished Business – Proposals for Reform of the Senior House Officer Grade* (DoH 2002). Following this, in February 2003 it published a policy statement, *Modernising Medical Careers* (DoH 2003), which confirmed its intention to introduce wide-ranging and radical changes not just for **Senior House Officers** (SHOs) but at all levels of postgraduate medical education.

Until then, medical graduates first undertook one year of training as **Pre-registration House Officers** (PRHOs), typically comprising two six-month clinical attachments, one in a medical and the other in a surgical specialty. At the end of that year, PRHOs gained full registration with the GMC, and were then able to practise more fully as doctors, for example in being fully able to prescribe medication. This was followed by an appointment as an SHO (roughly the equivalent of an intern in North America), and it was this grade that became the initial focus of the CMO's report.

Problems with the SHO grade had been well publicized for many years. Perhaps the most severe criticism was that these doctors had become known as 'the lost tribe' – lost partly because it was felt that many had unclear career plans but also because very little attention appeared to be given to their plight.

SHOs had become the 'workhorse' of the **National Health Service** (NHS), and comprised in fact over half of all doctors in training. But the problem with the grade was more than just the amount of service work they were expected to undertake: it reflected the enormously varied nature of their intended career pathways while in that grade.

Some SHOs, particularly those who were absolutely clear about their choice of career, took up posts to commence what was termed 'basic specialty training', which lasted perhaps three or four years, during which they would gain the relevant examinations (and perhaps research experience) that would lead them to obtaining an appointment as a **Specialist Registrar** (SpR). From then on they would continue with 'higher specialist training', lasting perhaps five or six years, following which they could apply for a hospital consultant post.

In the mid-1990s the SpR grade had been introduced to combine two previous training grades, those of Registrar and Senior Registrar. These changes were made by the previous CMO, Sir Kenneth Calman. At that time some people argued that this did only part of the business of reforming postgraduate medical education, as is reflected in the word 'unfinished' in the title of the following CMO's report. It was unfinished because it retained the separation of 'basic' and 'higher' specialist training in different career grades.

Other SHOs, particularly those who were less clear about their career intentions or perhaps were planning a career break (perhaps for domestic or family reasons), were particularly at risk. In his consultation paper *Unfinished Business* the CMO cited the following problems:

- lack of a coherent investment in the development of SHOs;
- poor job structure with half of SHO appointments being short-term and not part of a training rotation or programme;
- poorly planned training with no defined end-point;
- weak selection and appointment procedures;
- increasing workload;
- inadequate supervision, assessment, appraisal and career advice;
- 'basic specialist training' was too long and inadequately linked with 'higher specialist training'.

In fact, the CMO's report goes much further than reform of the SHO grade. In addition it also proposes:

. . . reform of the non-consultant career grades to effect a new and better link with the new training grades and to offer better career development for doctors in these grades. A further consequence of reform would be the introduction of new Foundation Programmes to span the existing Pre-Registration year and the current first year of SHO training. The object here is to give young doctors a structured grounding in the basics of their profession and to expose them to a wider range of experience before they make vital career choices.

(DoH 2002: 1)

The report foresees a modernized SHO grade as the platform for entry to shorter higher specialist training programmes which will see doctors in many specialties having opportunities to take up more generalist consultant posts at an earlier stage in their careers.

MMC, then, has very significant implications not just for the career path of doctors but perhaps more significantly for their postgraduate *education* at all levels and in all specialties.

A curriculum for the Foundation Programme

Following the publication of the policy statement in *MMC* (DoH 2003), the CMO established a UK strategy group 'to develop thinking' (DoH 2004: 1). This group presented its findings in March 2004 in a report entitled *MMC: The Next Steps*. This focuses particularly on the first two years of postgraduate medical education, to be called the Foundation Programme.

The CMO's consultation document *Unfinished Business* had proposed:

An integrated, planned two-year Foundation Programme of general training: the first year equating to the current pre-registration house officer year; the second (post-registration) year incorporating a generic first year of current SHO training . . . [This would] aim to imbue trainees with basic practical skills and competencies [*sic*] in medicine and will include: clinical skills; effective relationships with patients; high standards in clinical governance and safety; the use of evidence and data; communication; team working; multi-professional practice; time management and decision making and an effective understanding of the different settings in which medicine is practised.

(DoH 2002: 2)

The Next Steps suggested that the principles 'which will shape [the] development' of these programmes would be:

- trainee-centred;
- competency-assessed (*sic*);

- service-based;
- quality-assured;
- flexible;
- coached;
- structured and streamlined.

The report is concerned mainly with streamlining the careers of doctors, with filling low recruiting specialist areas, with being seen to do something at last for SHOs and finally with tying training into this enterprise. It is true that it speaks of the need for 'curriculum-based Programmes' to be developed 'which deliver an agreed set of competencies' (DoH 2004: 4). Indeed, the word 'curriculum' is frequently used in *The Next Steps*. But nowhere does the report say what is to be understood by the term or how such a curriculum might be developed.

Not daunted by (and quite probably entirely unaware of) this lack of definition, a group which had been working on a curriculum for intensive care took on the drafting of the document which would guide the training to be offered in the **Foundation Year Two** (F2). The group was quickly supplemented by representatives from all the Royal Colleges so that the core document became the responsibility of the Academy of the Medical Royal Colleges. The first version of that document appeared as the *Core Curriculum for the Foundation Years in Postgraduate Education and Training* in the Summer of 2003. Its major focus was on 'generic skills' and 'core requirement skills', and was derivative of the booklets produced by the Royal College of Physicians which describe the 'content of training in the disciplines relevant to general practice'. It listed the 'suggested learning opportunities' of clinical practice and then focused on the assessment of what it refers to as generic and core skills, on a nine point lickert-type scale.

Subsequently this document continued to be revised (refining the original ideas and adding a slightly broader view, but retaining its essential focus on 'content' and 'assessment' with little guidance about other elements of the curriculum), until it was sent out for consultation in November 2004. The Appendix to this book offers our critique of the details of the November 2004 version, which we submitted to government during the consultation period. Our major criticism was that the core document lacked any policy processes and regulatory framework such as is usually found within a curriculum document. These appeared in a separate policy document in January 2005 (just as the consultation period on the core curriculum drew to a close). The redraft of both the core and the policy documents appeared (still as drafts) in February 2005. Now entitled *Curriculum for the Foundation Years in Postgraduate Education and Training* the February 2005 draft attended to the need to differentiate between **Foundation Year One** (F1) and F2 doctors, and also added some details, for example, offering more information about the first year of the programme and removing the lickert scale in the assessment criteria. But these merely expanded the original. There was little structural change. The definitive version (DoH 2005b) was finally published at the beginning of April 2005, just before the general election in the UK. The main difference between it and the February draft was in layout and presentation rather than content. A new 'overview' was added, and some additional 'competences' (*sic*) appeared, but the structure was retained and no new sections added.

MMC has strengths. It brings to the national agenda, perhaps for the first time, the fact that postgraduate medical education requires attention. It also emphasizes, or rather re-emphasizes (as this has been repeatedly claimed for decades), that medical education must be seen as a continuum. However, it has started from the wrong end, being conceived of as firstly a management initiative, secondly as an educational one and only thirdly as about curriculum development. Indeed, we would argue that MMC has actually created problems for postgraduate medical education in the following four areas:

1   F2 was founded on a lack of recognition at the start of MMC that this initiative is a major educational enterprise, rather than just being about recruitment and retention, the management of posts and of medical careers and a way of resolving government problems about shortage areas in medicine. Thus was overlooked the importance of involving experts in curriculum design to provide a sound and rigorous basis for the enterprise. (Of course, had they done this, the process would have taken longer which no doubt they would have seen as unacceptable.)
2   As a result, the design of the core document was based upon limited educational understanding, lack of specialist language and lack of curriculum design expertise. Thus, a critique of the document reveals no principled approach to the practice of design, no rigour in the design processes or the choice of components, and no cohesive logic in the overall structure.
3   Furthermore, curricula already in existence for specialist training also lacked such expertise, and were seriously flawed in terms of logic, used inaccurate (as well as confusing and conflicting) educational terms, and contained misconceptions about the practices of curriculum design and development and about education itself. Thus, no prior expertise in curriculum design for medical education was immediately available to be drawn upon.
4   As a result there has been a yielding to the pressures of (most probably political) expediency, because of the absence of experience, and of the language and the arguments to defend the importance of sound curriculum development. And so there was no counter to the easy assumption that, being a simple common-sense matter of seizing a few ready-made

solutions from other countries and adjusting them minimally for UK medicine, curricula can be developed in a few days.

Ironically, this same lack of understanding is apparent too in the documents appearing from the newly established PMETB, which replaced the **Specialist Training Authority** (STA) as (among other things) the accrediting and quality assurance body for postgraduate medicine. The documents from PMETB appeared virtually in parallel to the various drafts of the foundation core documents and can be seen to be striving (not entirely successfully) to set out principles and standards which should underpin new medical postgraduate curricula, in respect of assessment (April 2003) and curriculum design (November 2004), yet which appear to have had little or no influence on what emerged.

The curriculum for the Surgical Care Practitioner (SCP)

A far better curriculum document, which we profoundly hope will influence future curriculum design, is *The Curriculum Framework for the Surgical Care Practitioner*, which the DoH launched for consultation in late March 2005 (DoH 2005a). This document exemplifies many of the qualities and details we commend in this book, although its logic in terms of design models is not entirely sound. It is clearly focused on education and specifies the curriculum model it is (mainly) based upon and whose headings it will use. It properly recognizes the managerial context, provides a section which sets out clearly the professional and educational values on which it is based, attends to the principles of teaching and learning, sees education as based on a learning partnership, and has clear educational aims (derived from an analysis of the SCPs role and the defining characteristics of learning in the practice setting), from which the rest of the curriculum logically follows. And although it erroneously refers to the elements of professional practice as 'competences', most of its language is properly educational, and it recognizes the significance of 'competence'. In short it is informed by knowledge about both education and curriculum design. Much (though not all) of this has clearly come from outside medical education.

Why then has the expertise of curriculum design (itself a postgraduate educational practice) never until now been developed inside postgraduate medicine? As we shall show, the climate has been against it. Indeed, even in heath care more generally and education itself in particular, the practice of curriculum design and development has, over the past two decades, been subjected to considerable distortion, as a result of government attempts to control and standardize professional practice. Thus the vision which should inspire educators for the professions to develop creative but rigorous curricula for each new generation of learning professionals has been lost in red tape and replaced by the quick-fix methods associated with political expediency and unsound generalizations.

Curriculum design: some problems

Expertise in the practice of curriculum design and development was widely available within the educational community and particularly in higher educa-tion until the advent of the National Curriculum in the early 1980s. (The activities of, or attempts at, curriculum design have to an extent been developed in other health care professions since that time, but not in medicine.) How-ever, its founding principles have been lost sight of during this process, because of the pressures to produce, as speedily as possible, safe and simple versions of professional education which conform to formulae constructed by civil servants to ensure maximum governmental control and minimum professional decision-making. (See also Wass, 2005.)

This has led to some very false ideas and assumptions about what is involved in curriculum design for health care which have influenced thinking generally, in health care more broadly and in medicine in particular, at both the policy and the local level.

Some current misconceptions

The following inaccurate and increasingly dangerous ideas are to be found as 'common-sense knowledge' in society generally; in the dictates and require-ments of government and particularly the DoH; among health care employ-ers and employees; and even in professional bodies specifically tasked with supporting the work of professionals. Though deeply and long held, they are at best problematic, and in some cases false and misleading. (It is interesting to note, and to some extent it gives us some optimism that this is just a phase that we are going through, that in the media as well as in academic and professional circles, the values on which many of these ideas are based have recently begun to come under public attack – see O'Neill 2002; Tallis 2004).

These false ideas include the following:

- professional practice is essentially a simple, unproblematic activity and will easily yield to simple rules;
- educational matters are similarly unproblematic and require mere com-mon sense;
- learning to practise in a profession involves learning skills on the job and theory in the classroom;
- skills learning is about simple repetition;
- skills make people competent and thus a 'competency-based' approach

to curriculum design is a wholly appropriate term for postgraduate medicine;

- the terms 'competence', 'competency' and 'competencies' – and even occasionally, as in the definitive curriculum for the Foundation Programme (DoH 2005b), the invented word 'competences' which in fact does not exist – all mean the same indisputably desirable thing – an able (meaning a technically proficient) practitioner;
- the quality of experience in professional practice is simply correlated to its amount ('more' automatically means 'better');
- professional education and development requires professionals to leave their practice setting and to study away from it 'in protected time';
- there is a simple, applicatory, relationship between theory and practice, and in quite straightforward terms, you learn the former and apply it to the latter;
- the role of the practitioner is thus simply to learn, and then apply theory in the practice setting;
- the role of researchers is to produce and shape that theory and provide the evidence for it;
- 'theory' is superior in value to practice (as shown in the emphasis placed on doctors' **Curricula Vitae** (CV) showing their publications rather than their clinical expertise);
- theory needs to be learnt prior to (as well as separate from) practice;
- 'education' (which in this impoverished context means 'training') is a simple means to the simple end of creating a worker with improved earning power, who will contribute better to the national economy (doctors are now referred to as 'workforce');
- the practice of professionals is not a moral concern, being no different from work in all other occupations, trades and industries, and should be treated like them, and seen as part of the exchange economy;
- given, then, that health care is like any other industry, quality in professional practice, and in the education for it, can only be achieved through some form of technical training, industrial forms of production and quality control.

We would also argue that, as a consequence, these ill-founded ideas have directly encouraged belief in the following false premises about curriculum design and development, which are rarely made explicit and thus are never questioned. These are:

- curriculum design and development are processes carried out by someone separate from the teacher (someone who must control professional activity) and, indeed, the teacher's role in curriculum design and development is merely to implement the handed-down design;

- professional educators must therefore follow a curriculum which is laid down by central government through its hired representatives;
- professional bodies must first set standards which a curriculum must then embody;
- standards are solid, concrete, immovable and absolute facts (except when they are from time to time 'raised' by those reporting to government);
- it is necessary to begin curriculum design by defining, and then placing within the programme, the essential theoretical knowledge, because this is what gives the educational programme its academic and public credibility, provides proper direction for practice and can be easily assessed;
- in undergraduate courses, any periods of practice required (as preparation to practise as a professional) should then be slotted into this corpus of knowledge, as and when they can;
- in postgraduate professional practice, most activities, processes and procedures can be learnt *simply*, that is by 'doing' repeatedly;
- the more repetition of processes to be learnt, the better the quality of the resulting practice (this is at odds with the notion that the most able learners are those who require the least repetition!);
- the educational credibility of any educational course can only be based upon the amount of theory which is taught;
- that which can be assessed by *academic means* should drive the content of the curriculum and the motivations of the learners;
- learners are there to take on the understandings of their teachers;
- the learning needs of a professional practitioner can best be defined by those outside practice on the basis of their expertise in propositional (factual) knowledge which is all that is of value;
- criticality, if it is valued at all, is about using theory to critique other theory, or to critique practice, never the other way round;
- there is only one basis for, and one set of headings for, designing a curriculum, whoever it is for and whatever context it is designed to serve (those headings arise from a view of the curriculum and of teaching as being about transmitting a product to the learner);
- the curriculum must contain clear criteria for immediate visible and measurable learning outcomes (without which there can have been no learning).

The erroneous fact that curriculum development is a simple matter that can be carried out by anyone who has had slight involvement in some aspect of education, *appears* to follow logically from these inaccurate and contestable ideas. Thus, it apparently seems unnecessary to take the advice of those with specific expertise in the practices of education and curriculum design and development because everyone has some knowledge of education, having been educated themselves.

However, as we will show in this book, none of these ideas is unproblematic and many are simply the result of a failure on the part of those who have become involved in curriculum planning to know about, or to go back to, first principles and to recognize the complex nature of the practice of curriculum design and development. Nor is this list exhaustive. As we shall see later, there are many more flaws in the current notion that common sense is all you need in order to design and develop a curriculum.

A better view of curriculum design and development

In fact, a curriculum is an educational programme. That is, it is *a blueprint for educational practice*. The only point of a blueprint is that it is translated into action to realize something. It is in action that a curriculum becomes a reality. A curriculum should thus be 'construed from the outset as something that has to be enacted' (Reid 1978: 15). But this does not mean that a curriculum in action is without theoretical underpinning. Indeed, such a blueprint exists tacitly even where the curriculum has not been made explicit in a written document. It underlies every attempt by every individual to engage in educational practice. Thus, all who teach are *actually* working to underlying ideas, assumptions and beliefs, about the activities of teaching, learning and assessment, *whether they know it or not*. And these ideas and beliefs are driven by the teacher's educational values, *whether they have articulated them or not*. Together these ideas, assumptions and beliefs, along with the activities they drive, make up the curriculum in practice (or 'curriculum-in-action', as it is sometimes called). The dangers, then, of failing to articulate these unstated assumptions and beliefs become very apparent.

It follows that educational practice cannot be properly developed without these matters (that is, the very educational ideas upon which teachers base their practice) being articulated and explored, and that teachers have a moral commitment to the welfare of learners to understand, express, explore and develop their curriculum, just as doctors have a moral imperative to continue to refine and develop the medical care they provide for patients. And it should be remembered that learners, like patients, are vulnerable, need specialist attention and should be worked with rather than on! (But saying that, of course, reveals some of our values as writers.) Teachers then can only properly provide for learners by making explicit the ideas to which they work, and then developing them.

A curriculum, then, which is an educational policy, finds its expression in practice and needs to be developed both *from* practice, and, as we shall see, *in* practice. This process (like the complex relationship between theory and practice itself, which it naturally reflects) engages educators iteratively in refining action (the curriculum in practice) in the light of theory (the written curriculum) and vice versa. A curriculum may be written or rewritten (i.e. *designed*) on paper, but it can only become a reality (that is, be realized and refined) in practice (i.e. *developed*). But these processes are intertwined – they develop and refine each other. The initial design will, inevitably, precede the development, but the development will, inevitably, inform the re-design, and it will do so, as we will show, through a principled and sound form of educational research called curriculum *evaluation*.

First, then, we must turn to illuminate the key elements of the practice of curriculum design.

PART 2
The bases of curriculum design for medical practice

2 The practice of curriculum design: its principles, processes, components and logic

Introduction: setting the scene

Our view, as we showed in Chapter 1, is that current curricula for postgraduate medicine, as seen in the Foundation Programme and various Royal Colleges' attempts to structure 'seamless training', lack both educational perspectives and a principled and sound curriculum base. This chapter therefore starts this entire section on curriculum design by providing an overview of what is involved in the practice of curriculum design itself. It offers support to those engaged in formal design of any curriculum for postgraduate doctors, together with all those involved in teaching and learning medicine at all levels (since they too are designers in practice in the clinical setting whether they recognize this or not).

Building on what we have said in Chapter 1, we can now characterize a curriculum as an educational policy. Such a policy can be enshrined in a document, and/or be a process enacted in practice. As a written document, it is 'an attempt to communicate the essential principles and features of an educational proposal in such a form that it is open to critical scrutiny and capable of effective translation into practice' (Stenhouse 1975: 4). It is this statement that flags up the vital importance of a full (definitive) version of the curriculum which records all the key decisions made about the design. And as we shall see, these amount to far more than simple choices about what doctors should learn and how they should learn it.

Thus a curriculum is more than a simple syllabus, and is not something which can or should be imposed on teachers by others who are not involved in that teaching. Frameworks which offer guidance at national level are, however, entirely proper as long as they are sensitive to the needs of those who are learning and teaching at the local level (developing the curriculum locally). But as a process enacted upon the ground (i.e. in practice) the curriculum requires negotiation between learners and teachers. The term 'curriculum', then, refers to all the activities, all the experiences and all the learning opportunities for which an institution or a teacher takes responsibility – *either deliberately or by default*. This includes: the formal and the informal, the overt and the covert, the recognized and the overlooked, the intentional and the unintentional (Coles 1985: 250).

Central to an understanding of the term 'curriculum' is that it is our values that drive our choices here, and we cannot easily be committed to – or act upon – ideas and processes which are in conflict with our own values. To do so inevitably leaves us dissatisfied, even though we may be unable to articulate the precise basis of, and reasons for, that dissatisfaction. That is why those engaged in teaching (for example, the educational supervisors of postgraduate doctors) and those who manage the curriculum (for example, postgraduate deaneries) must be permitted a major voice in shaping the curriculum they offer, and why teaching involves negotiating with the learner, whose values and beliefs also need to be recognized.

The curriculum, then, is determined as much by what is not offered, what is omitted, and what has been rejected, as it is by positive decisions. Further, we would wish to argue that unless those who design, or who influence the design of a curriculum, base their work on educational understanding, many learning opportunities are likely to be unrecognized and lost.

Part 2 of this book focuses on the enterprise (the practice) of *curriculum design*. For the purposes of understanding this better, we have intentionally, though somewhat unnaturally, separated it from *curriculum development*, by which we mean the activities associated with putting the new programme into practice, and evaluating and refining it, all of which we attend to in Part 3. Despite this, however, we believe with Carr (1995: 50) that, both in principle and in practice, curriculum design and curriculum development are (like the theory and practice of medicine) 'mutually constitutive and dialectically related domains'.

In focusing here on curriculum design, we have particularly in mind the design of a national curriculum framework for postgraduate medical education, which supports the design of a curriculum to be enacted in the clinical setting. But the general term 'curriculum design' refers to all that goes into the planning of any educational programme and thus its principles are equally central to design at both local and national level.

Curriculum design at any level, requires a range of expertise within the design team, demands investigative activities associated with analysing the context in which the curriculum will be taught, depends upon formulating precisely appropriate questions which are key to sound educational thought and practice, and relies crucially upon intelligent deliberation about complex moral matters, both professional and educational.

What is commonly known as 'a definitive curriculum document' is the main reference document for the curriculum. It is the repository: of the final decisions made about the curriculum; of clearly articulated rationales for these decisions; and of the recognition of their implications for educational activities on the ground, *at the time it was written*. This is because curriculum development is inevitably an endlessly ongoing enterprise, and thus even the 'definitive' document can only provide a snapshot of a frozen moment which represents its best state so far within that development.

Such a document is important because it will act as the reference source for a wide range of people and for many different purposes. Other, briefer, working documents will have fed into the development of the definitive document and the 'temporarily finalized' decisions will be published in a more portable version (a summary document) and in a handbook for learners. But the main (definitive) curriculum document is fundamentally (following Stenhouse's definition above) a basis for critique – that critique being both 'in theory' (through consultations and committee work) and 'in practice' (through pilot testing the curriculum design). Even after that, the enactment of the curriculum in practice in the various contexts in which it will be taken up will provide further opportunities for critique and development.

Thus we can see that the process of curriculum design is an iterative one in which activities on the ground and critique at all levels should feed into decision-making at policy level, and vice versa. The process, of course, can begin either with framing a policy document or (perhaps especially when designing a curriculum for practice) with educational exploration and innovation between teacher and learners in the practice setting. Ultimately it should become a cyclical process – and as we have emphasized already, a continuous one.

The design of a curriculum and its formal articulation in a definitive document arises, then, from the growth of educational understanding of the design team. But we should note that that team needs to be conceived much more widely than is usually the case – that is as comprising not only the policy formulating group, but also a team on the ground who are, as we will show later (in Chapter 10), those engaged in the evaluation of the curriculum.

This chapter introduces the principles of curriculum design (all the matters that need to be considered by any such team), and provides specific examples from the medical education context. This sets the scene for the rest of Part 2 by introducing the key issues which a design team for medical education particularly needs to investigate and deliberate about in detail, and which all teachers and learners whose work is directed by the curriculum need to understand.

The main intention of this chapter is thus to demonstrate the ways in which curriculum design is educational, is a well-developed *practice* in its own right, and is well founded on theory that has emerged from practice. It also seeks to illustrate the kind of rigour and expertise, knowledge and understanding that is required – between them – by various members of the curriculum design team, including the entire constituency that each of the team represents.

The principles and processes of curriculum design: an overview

Introduction

Curriculum designers engage in practical reasoning about an educational enterprise. The processes of curriculum design are ordered rationally (logically) and they follow general principles and are tailored to the professional context in which the curriculum will be enacted. Most importantly, at the heart of curriculum design, lie the activities of recognizing and making informed and well-argued choices between equally competing complex priorities, both professional and educational. In short, a curriculum design is never right or wrong, but rather is the result of the *choices* that the designers make (which are values-based). As such, there can never be the 'perfect' curriculum. It is always open to further debate.

In this respect, curriculum designers' deepening understanding parallels the processes of a doctor's clinical thinking, in moving iteratively from detailed context to principle and back to detailed context. For example, a hospital doctor, faced with a patient in an early outpatient consultation, attempts to formulate the patient's clinical problem, to use diagnostic processes which determine what is wrong *in principle* and which result in a *generalized* clinical solution (or solutions), but which then has to be shaped (with the patient) into an agreed treatment plan that is designed *to meet that individual patient's particular case*. The logic here thus involves starting from an appreciation of the particular patient, then developing an understanding of the relevant medical and scientific principles, and finally focusing on the specifics of the patient's individual context.

In both medicine and education, not to move from the specific case to first principles and back to the individual case is dangerous. Indeed, although expert physicians may make such decisions fast and fluently such that the thinking behind them remains tacit and appears truncated, nonetheless it respects the internal logic of diagnosis. Indeed, such logically ordered processes are disrupted or ignored at a profession's peril. Those who engage in such matters thus require some knowledge of what constitutes an appreciation of the individual situation, an understanding of the general principles involved, and the implications for meeting the needs of the individual context. This is what goes to make up medical 'practice', and we explore this further in Chapters 4 and 5.

Similarly, in curriculum design, a clear understanding of the *context* for the proposed educational programme, and a grasp of what characterizes sound educational practice must come first. These then give rise to a statement about educational *aims*, which in turn allows decisions to be made about the *means* of achieving these. Without deriving aims in this way, the first piece of the logic is missing.

Starting points: educational and professional principles and values

Thus, a curriculum designed to educate postgraduate doctors needs to begin by understanding what is involved in education including exploring and establishing its key principles and values, and then asking penetrating questions about professional values in medicine, about what is current practice and tradition in medicine and about what 'might be' or 'ought to be' its current and future values and practices. From this it will then be possible to formulate the attributes necessary in doctors who may work far into the twenty-first century. (And it should be noted that the current 'is' will be different from the future 'what might be' and 'what ought to be' since without these there will be no evolution.) We note sadly that, in the case of the definitive version of the *Curriculum for the Foundation Years in Postgraduate Education and Training* (DoH 2005b) there is little sense of such evolution!

None of these matters is simple, however. For example, the very way these questions are asked will influence the answer. We can ask: what should such doctors be able to *do* and why? But we will get a different answer if we ask what kind of person they should *be*, and why? (Thus, to ask more than one question is necessary and the competing values and priorities that will then emerge in the various responses will need to be considered – deliberated upon – very carefully.)

In designing a curriculum for postgraduate medicine, to know what questions to ask, and how to respond to them, requires a detailed knowledge of the nature of medical practice, a sound grasp of what education can and cannot achieve, and considerable well-informed debate about the priorities and views of, for example, society, government, the profession, patients, teachers and learners in respect of medical practice. What is needed too is a vision of the kind of doctors who will emerge from that curriculum and whose values, practice, expertise, knowledge and very humanity will be shaped by its design. Not to start at this point and to fail to deliberate about these matters would be to allow the values and aims to be fixed from outside the design, to be exempt from the need for justification, and thus to become accepted, and then imposed, by default. In such a case the design team would then merely supply the educational means to someone else's ends. This might provide a pragmatic quick-fix in the short term, but in the longer term it will never result in sound education in the practice setting. Rather it will lead to disillusioned teachers, uncreative approaches to teaching, and bored learners (and, in the case of postgraduate medical education, possibly unsound clinical care and even dangerous doctors). Further, there is likely to be a risk in such cases that, despite enormous expenditure on curriculum design, no change actually occurs.

Developing aims

Design team members at policy level are usually representatives of interested parties, every one of whom has a democratic right (on behalf of their constituents) to contribute to the entire design process. They first need to construct a team view about the nature of the context for which the curriculum is being designed. (This needs to be based upon practical investigations, assembling an appropriate range of evidence, and engaging in debates about values.) Their agreement about the kind of doctor their constituents wish to see emerge from such a context (itself a contentious matter), will both affect the articulation of the aims of the curriculum, and later give shape to the regulations they set up for the kind of doctor to be recruited for the educational programme. This in turn leads to a clear statement of aims, which as prior issues, will need to be expressed at the start of the main section of the curriculum document.

Such over-arching aims need to be *educational*, not just managerial, and, although they may be visionary, they need to be carefully articulated such that they express goals that are achievable by an entire educational programme, and which are neither over-ambitious, narrowly mechanistic, nor dangerously general. Since they drive the whole weight of the curriculum, aims should not bear the marks of being hastily concocted and poorly expressed.

Two examples

In the November 2004 draft of the Foundation Core Curriculum, there was no values statement, and the aims (which seemed to be about new doctors learning the management of acutely ill patients) did not overtly head up the curriculum. The February 2005 draft, republished exactly in the final document in April 2005, was slightly more explicit, as follows:

> to produce doctors who are competent and confident in selecting, requesting and interpreting reports of commonly used investigations required for the diagnosis and management of patients who present as emergencies or who are potentially acutely or critically ill.
>
> (DoH 2005b: 86)

Even so, the use of the word '*produce*' here, rather than a phrase such as 'to develop the expertise of . . .', immediately indicates a view of doctors as 'a product' of training and obscures the real educational challenge which is to develop doctors with the capacity for wise 'judgement' (since detecting and managing emergencies and the acutely or critically ill patient will, almost more than any other area of medicine, involve 'judgement'). The problem for educators and curriculum designers is that wise judgement is not something that can be 'given' to someone. Rather, it has to be cultivated *in* them.

Further, there is no rationale in this document explaining why this is regarded as the best starting point for new doctors who are learning *as doctors* for the first time in the clinical setting. (Indeed, if the principle aim is that newly-qualified doctors can detect acutely ill patients we might ask: are they the right people to be detecting acutely ill patients?) Where has this aim come from? Our understanding is that managing acutely ill patients requires a *high* level of expertise. Have the aims of the Foundation Programme really been built from first principles, and are they clear and realistic? For example, exactly how far should junior doctors be expected to go in detecting the acutely ill and making judgements about the patient's management, when 'on call' in the middle of the night?

By comparison the professional and educational values and the aims expressed in *SCP* (DoH 2005a) are explicit, clearly expressed, properly educational and apparently sensibly achievable. They lead to 'outcomes' (objectives) which are equally clear, although the heading here: 'by the end of the programme the SCP will have demonstrated', is drawn from a different design model and does not quite cohere with the spirit of the rest. Nonetheless, the following extract from the 'outcomes' (Section 3.3.2) (DoH 2005a: 13) shows a recognition that this educational enterprise is about far more than skills. It expects the SCP to emerge with (among others) the following:

- an understanding of the responsibilities of being an SCP and the values that underpin this;
- the special attributes needed to be an SCP;
- a range of theoretical and practical knowledge related to their core and specialty practice;
- the development of professional judgement;
- technical and operative skills and their ongoing development;
- an understanding of their role within the extended surgical team;
- the understanding and use of reflective practice, deliberation and other educational processes . . .

Educational aims then, once firmly in place, will properly drive all the decision-making that leads to the curriculum as a policy. But this is not quite so simple either. There are many *ways* to achieve aims that have been set, some educational, some not. Once resolved, the final agreement about what this should involve will then be set out in the main body of the curriculum document. But the discussions that lead to the final educational framework will necessarily be extensive and contentious. The benefit of this will be the increasing understanding of the educational enterprise for which the curriculum is designed to provide.

How these over-arching aims and the detail they give rise to are expressed will shape how the curriculum is translated on the ground. These are also complex matters. The language used to convey the design of a curriculum and its philosophy is crucial. For example, the term 'objectives' comes from inside an entire philosophy that sees teachers as engaging in instructional training and learners as passive recipients of this. The whole language, structure and logic of a curriculum designed for such a view does not remotely fit a curriculum where learners are to have greater control over their learning, and teaching is to become more learner-oriented. Here the term 'intentions' is more appropriate, flagging as it does the need to negotiate these between teacher and learner so that both 'own' them.

The complex nature of education

Educational matters are inevitably contentious. For example, there are many possible responses to the question: what are, and what should be, the key professional characteristics of a postgraduate doctor for the twenty-first century? Some would see skills as the only key necessity, some would see professional judgement as central. Some would see the knowledge doctors draw on as essentially textbook- and evidence-based, some would argue that many other kinds of knowledge are also important (like self-knowledge, sensory knowledge and intuition). Some would argue that medical work is and should be shaped by the ethics of professionalism, some would see it as simply 'delivering a package of care'. Some would argue that rulebooks and protocols will protect doctors from having to make difficult decisions and help them to manage risk, thus providing 'standard' care, and so avoiding the so-called postcode lottery, where some people receive better care than others depending on where they live. Some would point out that both professional judgement and trust between doctor and patient will always be and should always be defining elements in their relationship.

So how should the aims of a curriculum for postgraduate medicine be expressed? Are we, for example, seeking to develop an expert technician, or a professional artist whose expert skills are part of a more complex whole? Do we want legally indemnified, risk-protected workers (a 'workforce' whose actions are rule-bound), or wise professionals who engage in intelligent (and inevitably risky) practice? Do we have it in mind to train doctors in specific skills, making them dependent on later training when circumstances change, or should we educate them more roundly so that they can take responsibility for their own development as both their career and medicine itself evolves? Can we afford the latter? Can we afford *not to engage* in the latter? Even as we shape this question, our views and values become apparent. (These matters are pursued in detail in Chapter 3.)

Not all these choices, of course, are mutually exclusive, but certainly some do not easily cohere with others. Each choice is shaped by the agendas of those represented by design team members, and more importantly is crucially driven by their values. All educational matters are values-based (there is no one simple or 'right' answer to any educational question, the answer depends upon the values one brings to one's thinking and wishes to promote in others). Indeed, it is even the case that where such values, views and rationales are not examined and stated overtly as part of curriculum design, they will certainly nonetheless exist tacitly – but as unexamined and therefore undefended and unable to be refined influences on the educational decisions made. Traditionally the introductory section of the definitive curriculum document has made explicit the values enshrined in and to be promoted by the curriculum, together with how and why these decisions have been reached, thus offering the rationale for all that is embodied in its main sections. This is also part of the moral commitment of educators to provide a document which is open to critical scrutiny and thus to development. (How this is translated into practice and owned by those involved in the curriculum-in-action at local level is a further question!)

While it is true that with careful nurturing even a poorly drafted national curriculum framework can be developed in practice in positive directions, this will be unnecessarily slow, and will probably disadvantage those whose education is shaped in the early stages of new curriculum development. Further, it (almost inevitably) risks those on the ground taking a pragmatic approach and either rejecting wholesale or accepting uncritically the aims that policy-makers have shaped. This is dangerous. For example, it would remove the real control of the curriculum from the practitioners of the profession if they merely became agents for implementing national decisions. Policy-level decisions must take account of real practice (and the values of real practitioners), and a proper balance needs to be found between these various viewpoints. Those at local level must be given a voice in the design from the beginning of the process. Spending time on these fundamental matters is therefore not a matter of choice but of absolute necessity. In Part 3 of this book we will argue further that rather than being a 'top-down' process, curriculum design ought to be 'bottom-up'.

Curriculum design: the main principles

At all levels of curriculum design the same *kinds* of choices are always available. This is true whether the planning involves a single educational session, a whole programme for a cohort of learners, or a national framework to shape education within a profession. It is also the case whether the context planned for is the school classroom, the undergraduate lecture theatre or postgraduate education in the service setting or seminar room. The same principles and processes are used to clarify the chosen components, to choose priorities and to decide how to structure the document so that it is logical and coherent.

Planning an educational programme, like diagnosis in medicine, involves drawing upon the general principles of education, and of curriculum design, and making key choices and professional judgements in response to the individual context. This requires specialist knowledge. Indeed, curriculum design is a postgraduate specialism of education, just as paediatrics for example is a postgraduate specialism of medicine.

Professional judgements have to be made in the light of rigorous investigation and sound evidence. In the case of postgraduate medical *education*, this will mean serious enquiry into the educational needs of doctors and the context in which they work (their complex clinical setting). This means gaining a deep understanding of the human and multi-faceted demands of everyday practice, the life patterns they give rise to, and the nature of practice itself (see Chapters 4 and 5). It means: knowing about the kinds of knowledge doctors draw upon (see Chapter 6); appreciating the ways in which their medical practice is taught and learnt (see Chapter 7); and understanding how practice can be assessed in the clinical setting (see Chapter 8).

This is why no curriculum can be soundly designed by one person alone, or even by a small group. It is also why bringing in someone new (even an educationist grounded in curriculum design) *at the end* (perhaps to edit a document without detailed interaction with the design team during the design process), is antithetical to the spirit and quality of curriculum design.

Once the curriculum design team has been assembled (which is an important process in itself), there are five major areas that curriculum designers need to attend to in constructing a cohesive and coherent educational programme whose logic is sound enough to withstand critical scrutiny.

These are as follows:

- Understanding what are the key components or building blocks of any curriculum;
- understanding what turns teaching and learning activities into sound educational practice;
- knowing how to investigate the context and gain the evidence that will fuel balanced deliberations;
- recognizing and raising the key issues (which are problematic because they represent competing priorities);
- knowing how to conduct deliberations about these.

When finally the definitive or main document is written, it will need to include an indication of the exploration of these areas, the positions adopted in respect of them, the issues raised and questions asked, together with rationales for the conclusions reached, and the specific decisions they have given rise to. It will also need to highlight and defend the assumptions that underlie the design, and identify clearly the logic upon which the entire curriculum rests.

The rest of this chapter attends to key principles that should guide actions and decisions in each of these key areas in four sections as follows:

- the constitution of the design team needed to build a sound curriculum;
- the components of curriculum design;
- the main processes and key activities of curriculum design (and particularly deliberation);
- the detailed issues which need to be identified.

It illustrates these by specific examples drawn from undergraduate and post-graduate medical education. An overview of the last three of these sections is found in Table 2.1.

The constitution of the design team needed to build a sound curriculum

Who should be involved in designing a curriculum, and why? We have indicated that those who teach and learn in clinical practice at the local level will inevitably engage in developing the educational programme they are working within, and some will be more critical (able to offer a sounder critique) and innovative than others. In that sense they choose themselves. At policy level, a team has to be assembled. Each team member here must be able to contribute two areas of expertise: expertise in respect of curriculum design or matters that centrally affect it; and expertise in representing a specific constituency which has the right to contribute its voice to the deliberations about the particular curriculum under development.

In a seminal article about curriculum design, Schwab (1973) argues that (for the purpose of setting out a definitive document) only a *group* can gather together all the evidence and provide all the expertise that must fuel a sound deliberative process. He pinpoints five areas of expertise needed in building a curriculum for schools. He lists the areas that experts should represent as: school subjects; learners; relevant educational contexts; teachers; and experts on curriculum design. (In offering this list, we have changed the American terminology into English equivalents.) By this he seems to mean that representative experts (about 12 or 14 all told) should be drawn from the following areas:

- all those areas directly affected by or concerned with education in the given context;
- the knowledge-base that needs to be learnt;
- those currently involved in learning within the given context;
- those teaching in the current context;
- those with specialist knowledge of curriculum design (as contributors to the design process and/or as evaluators).

Table 2.1 An illustration of the key components, key questions and key activities of curriculum design

Components of the curriculum	Key questions to be asked	Key activities involved
A: Introductory matters		
Situational analysis	What is the nature of the context for which this curriculum is being developed?	Conducting a situational analysis and understanding its logic
Evidence of those involved	Who should be part of the deliberative core group and for what reasons?	Maintaining formal minutes of meetings and recording those present and the main arguments considered and the key decisions made
Definitions of key terms	What makes for good practice in a profession?	Clarifying definitions from educational, and professional rather than public and management discourse
Agreed principles, processes and values	What should be the criteria for sound educational practice? (What makes teaching a sound educational practice?)	Exploring and clarifying values of those involved and their proper priority for this curriculum in this context – in respect of: Professional practice
	What educational philosophy should underpin this curriculum, and what should be its underlying values?	Educational practice
	What professional philosophy ought this curriculum to cultivate, and what should be its underlying values?	
Rationale for the curriculum	What arguments, reasons, priorities have lead to the key decisions enshrined in this curriculum and how can they be justified and defended?	Recognizing (appreciating) the starting points for the learner
		Elucidating the appropriate educational paradigm to structure this curriculum in order to achieve the chosen aims

continued overleaf

B: The organization of the curriculum

General overall educational aims	What kind of person should the curriculum seek to create/cultivate? What should be the educational aims of this curriculum?	Defining sound educational aims as articulated within educational discourse
Specific intentions/objectives/agenda	What capabilities, characteristics, knowledge and capacities should be developed by this curriculum?	Choosing the right heading and clarifying the bases on which the details would be negotiated between teacher and learner
Chosen ways of seeing teaching and learning	What kinds of activities ought learners to engage in, in order to learn these things? What ought to be the role of their teachers?	Clarifying the activities of sound educational teaching learning and assessment for this context
Content/syllabus etc	Given the starting point of the learner, the overall aims and the educational rationale for this context, what should learners be required to achieve?	Listing the content/syllabus
The balance of depth and breadth The structure of the content	How deep and how wide should the content be? How should the content be organized within the curriculum? How should teachers order it in practice?	Mapping the content as a whole Indicating categories of content Considering the theory/practice relationship Considering any hierarchies
Assessment and its role	What role ought assessment to play? How will learners' achievements be recorded?	
Evaluation	How will we know that this educational development is successful? How can we evaluate both ends and means?	Making provision for sound evaluation in this context

Continued overleaf

Table 2.1 Continued

Components of the curriculum	Key questions to be asked	Key activities involved
C: Provision for the management of the curriculum		
Criteria for recruitment to programme	What kind of person ought to be recruited to this educational programme?	Setting criteria for judgements about entry to the programme
Processes for recruitment to the programme	And by what means?	Setting up workable methods of recruitment, appropriate to the context
Administrative structures	How ought the programme be best regulated (i.e. managed)?	Thinking through the learner's experience and noting implications for supporting the learner through the programme
Educational support for teachers	What will be the appropriate means of support for teachers as they engage in refining this curriculum in the practice setting?	Designing an educational programme that meets the educational and managerial needs of those teaching
Regulations for progression/failure	What rules and regulations need to be set up to ensure fairness of response to learner's achievements?	Explicating clearly the criteria for progression, principles to guide remediation and humane systems for dealing with failure
Quality control procedures	What quality assurance procedures ought to be in place in respect of this curriculum?	Making provision for sound quality assurance in this context

Another way of achieving the same ends (and which Della Fish orally advised for the curriculum designed by the **Royal College of Surgeons of England** (RCS Eng) for surgical SHOs is to set up a core group of the kind described above together with a series of specialist sub-groups which feed into the core about specific aspects of the curriculum under construction. Such sub-groups might include an assessment group, a quality assurance group and an evaluators' group (which should be there from the start of the project). The advantages of this are that it involves more people in learning about this important process, and yet keeps them in the size of group in which there is sufficient informality to foster group creativity while being able to provide for maximum interaction. The disadvantages are that without very careful coordination between the core and the specialist groups, a holistic under-standing of the process may be lost. For example, written minutes never con-vey the essence, let alone the detail, of the discussion that takes place and the developed understanding that accompanies this.

The assumptions and values that lie beneath the prioritizing of this approach are that the representatives chosen do have a clear constituency, and that time spent in exploration and deliberation is well invested, in order that 'better data lead to better decisions' (Reid 1978: 60). However, it must be admitted that the current climate of expediency is against this kind of rigour (and time commitment). Although he was writing 27 years ago (in the late 1970s), Reid's comments (1978: 60) about 'the unhealthy climate' for these activities still stand:

> The unfortunate truth is that over a long period of time, these skills have been declining. It is true in fields other than that of curriculum decision-making: in many areas of public policy expediency, pro-cedure, majority vote and authoritative pronouncements have gradually usurped the place of appreciation, deliberation and judgement.

We would add that, in the UK at least, we sense that postgraduate medical education has been too much part of the political landscape and particularly too closely linked to management timescales. We would argue strongly that this is short-term and short-sighted, that the professions in the UK need to recover their educational vision by returning to and reconstituting their curricula from first principles, that the democratic rights of those who can contribute to that vision need to be revived, and that educators (including curriculum experts) as well as the teachers and learners on the ground need to be part owners of the design of the programme within which they must work (that is, they need to be re-enfranchised by having a say in the entire design rather than just being left to find the means to enact what someone else has decided).

It should be noted, however, that none of this is to gainsay the need for a body (like the PMETB) to accredit and or validate such a curriculum. We also believe that if a curriculum is to provide for a generation of learners sound education which is well founded and will withstand scrutiny and the test of time, these processes are worth investing in, and are very likely to save resources in the longer run. In medicine in the UK we believe that they should be supported and quality assured by the PMETB, which we hope would incorporate the processes we are offering in this book in its standards for curriculum design and development.

In respect of a curriculum for the postgraduate doctor who must learn within the clinical setting then, the following areas would need to be represented (and be relevant to the general or specific context for which the curriculum was being developed – for example, Foundation Programmes, or medical specialties):

- the theoretical disciplines of medicine at the level of overview of these in respect of the ever-changing base for practising medicine;
- the practices of medicine as they currently exist at the level of overview of what constitutes practice and what practitioners need to learn in order to practise;
- the traditions, standards and regulatory requirements of medicine as represented by the Royal Colleges;
- society's needs and expectations in respect of how it views educational and professional practices (including legal requirements and policies for political correctness);
- patients and their changing needs;
- learners at the level of an overall understanding of the nature of learning in this context and of learners' needs and interests;
- teachers who have an overall understanding of the nature of teaching at higher education level within the clinical setting; of what makes education a sound practice; and of the needs and interests of teachers;
- curriculum developers and designers who have an understanding of the relevant context, who have worked in it, and who have experience of curriculum design in cognate areas.

The most important characteristics of such representatives are that they should be open-minded, and be willing and able to investigate and report on the nature of and possible developments within the area they represent. Reid (1978: 53) rightly points out that much of the work undertaken by this group will be about discovery: 'coming to know what one wants is partly decision and partly discovery'. Reid here argues that 'discovery of other people and their wants and desires leads to an amalgamation or coalescence of aims, data and judgements'. Schwab (1973) sees the processes of discovery and decision as alternating, sees their value as intrinsically educative, and as likely to conduce to sound decisions. (The deliberative processes that these representatives should engage in are discussed below, see pp. 50–51.)

The components of curriculum design

A curriculum document is created for a variety of purposes, and used by many different people. For example, in respect of education for the professions, it can:

- provide curriculum developers with the motivation to think a curriculum through clearly from first principles or to revise it from a sound basis;
- provide everyone involved with a common basis, common reference point and common language in respect of education for and within a given profession;
- provide those responsible (teachers, learners, assessors and evaluators) with a proper basis for ensuring that learners have access to their educational entitlement;
- provide teachers and learners with the means of understanding more broadly the educational activities they engage in;
- provide those who have to manage as well as those who have to enact the local-level negotiations about the curriculum-in-action with a grasp of the issues endemic to curriculum design and development (for example, postgraduate deaneries);
- provide a profession with a clearly argued explanation of the education being offered in its name;
- provide assessors and examiners with the basis for recognizing the particular purposes of assessment, and what should be assessed, and how;
- provide the public and the professional regulators with explicit parameters of professional conduct which can be currently expected of members of that profession;
- provide all relevant parties with a properly explicit basis for review, critique and development of the curriculum itself.

What then are the key areas in which information must be provided, about which discovery needs to occur and within which major decisions need to be made? In other words, what are the key components of any definitive curriculum document?

The following are arguably the key headings for designing a curriculum, whatever it is for and however it is conceived. However, since all educational matters are values-based, readers should remember that our values of preferring education to training for all but vocationally-focused school-leavers have informed these headings. (We look at this issue in detail in respect of educational practice in Chapter 3 and in respect of medical practice in Chapters 4 and 5.)

In our experience it is worth considering the components of a curriculum in three main cohering sections: an introduction (where the grounds of all decisions are set out and a foundation is laid for the design); a section on the main details of the curriculum; and a section on the management of the curriculum. The headings are listed as follows. (The Appendix shows how we used these headings in our critique of the November 2004 draft of *The Core Curriculum for the Foundation Programme*, which was offered for national consultation.)

- **Introductory matters**

  - Situational/contextual analysis
  - Evidence of who was involved in the deliberations
  - Clear and agreed definitions of key terms
  - Agreed principles, processes and values which informed the deliberations and will shape the education offered
  - Rationale for the curriculum (key choices made, on what basis and for what reason)
  - Criteria for recruitment to the programme (or place in 3rd section)
  - Processes for recruitment to the programme (or place in 3rd section)

- **The main details of the curriculum**

  - General overall educational aims
  - Specific intentions/objectives/agenda for learners
  - Chosen ways of seeing teaching and learning
  - Content/syllabus and other matters to be acquired by the learner
  - The balance of depth and breadth of what will educate the learner
  - The structure of the content and how the learner meets it (simple linear structure as indicated here; integrated structure which relates theory and practice in a number of possible ways; a spiral approach, in which the learner systematically revisits earlier learning at a higher level)
  - Assessment and its formative and summative roles
  - Regulations for progression, remediation and provision for failure
  - Evaluation rationale, principles and processes

- **Processes for the management of the curriculum**

  - Administrative and educational structures
  - Recruitment and selection regulations and criteria
  - Regulations for progression
  - Quality assurance procedures

- **Appendix**

  - Glossary of educational terms and their definitions as used within the document (this may be placed at the back or as a preliminary page at the front of the definitive document)

There is a basic logic to the order in which we have listed the headings. The first section contains introductory matters, which we believe are vital in setting the basis and context for the rest of the decisions. The second section contains the main curriculum and the final section relates to the management of the curriculum. It should be noted, however, that many of these matters are intimately interrelated and the knack of curriculum design (like that of pro-ducing a book or a thesis, or indeed any serious writing) is one of iteration – to survey continually the decisions made about each and how they affect the others, pulling them gradually into a whole, and adjusting these headings and even their order where necessary for the particular curriculum being designed and its specific context.

The main processes and key activities of curriculum design

It is tempting to believe that to design a curriculum is to work on the basis of a protocol – some simple and 'given' principles and procedures, and some standards by which it can be assessed, which can be brought in to solve all the questions that will be raised as part of curriculum design by each of the above components of the written curriculum. But it is more complex than this, because education is a values-based and moral enter-prise, and carries deep responsibilities about the way in which the next generation will be educated. As a result, much of the decision-making of curriculum designers is focused upon uncertain, complex and problematic educational questions. In short, curriculum design, like medicine, as we shall show in Chapters 4 and 5, shares the same characteristics of all professional practice.

At its heart, the design (and development) of a curriculum is a form of educational research in which rigorous educational investigation is the central thrust. Educational research (which differs significantly from scientific research and which we discuss much more fully in Chapter 10) requires both theoretical and practical investigations. But the active processes rest upon carefully defined terms, clear purposes, deep consideration of educational issues, awareness of the values base of educational practice, consideration of the fundamental purposes of education and an open-mindedness in which all ideas are welcomed, weighed and deliberated upon.

Most of the questions in curriculum design will be related to practical problems which are associated with providing sound education for this particular context. A small number will be simple and procedural (those that really can be solved by research or calculation, where finding the answer is straightforward and where known procedures can be followed). But most will be uncertain (and more contestable) questions like: what ought to be the underlying values of a curriculum for postgraduate medicine? This is more difficult. It is these about which the team needs to deliberate until a unity emerges, a consensus is achieved, or a majority view prevails, by following normal democratic processes.

Basically, then, curriculum design involves some key overall procedures as the following shows.

- Establish and formulate carefully through discussion within the curriculum design team some major questions designed to critique and understand the nature of the context for which the curriculum is being designed. For example: what would constitute the practice of newly graduated doctors entering and leaving a Foundation Programme?
- Appoint evaluators so that they are part of the design process from the start.
- Investigate (that is, research) these questions in the context in which the curriculum will be offered and for which it is a preparation. For example: engage in some form of practical enquiry such as situational analysis, utilizing educational research expertise.
- Assemble and present to the curriculum design team the evidence that best characterizes that context and which illustrate the *range* of responses to the research questions.
- Explore and clarify (appreciate) within the curriculum design team and then through consultation with a wider representation of as many of the parties involved as possible, the values that should underpin the curriculum (both the educational and the professional ones).
- Critique the evidence collected through this consultation and establish those uncertain complex issues that must be resolved.
- Establish within the design team the grounds on which the resolution of each issue will be based. For example, wherever there seems to be a conflict between the best interests of patients and the major needs of learners, on what grounds or principles will each decision be made?

- Deliberate (where necessary through wider consultation) about the available resolutions and come to a judgement in each case.
- Clarify and solve (within the curriculum design team) any simple procedural problems arising from the need to support these major judgements.
- Build a robust curriculum that is sensitive to these and is based upon firm logic and that supports the enactment of sound educational practice.
- Write a draft curriculum document and consult widely on its appropriateness.
- Set up a steering committee to support and guide the evaluators' investigations of the implementation and give advice about how to ensure their reports will be intelligible to the wider audience and whether they will be able to be implemented.
- Revise the curriculum document as a result of this consultation.
- Keep the curriculum under frequent review.

The logic of a curriculum

When it comes to building the central section of a curriculum (the organization of the curriculum), there is, as we have already said, a clear logic that should direct the subheadings. This means that there is an order in attending to activities without which the resulting curriculum will have no coherence. As we shall show in detail in Chapter 3, there are different ways of conceptualizing educational matters, each of which has its own internal logic. But in broad terms the main activities associated with building the curriculum itself are as follows (while the list is presented in the final order of appearance in the document, the numbers in brackets indicate the practical order in which these should be tackled):

- analyse the context fully (its practices, traditions and knowledge base) (1);
- recognize (appreciate) the starting points of the learner (2);
- set criteria for judgement about entry to the programme (8);
- clarify the activities of sound educational teaching, learning and assessment for this context (5);
- define sound educational aims (3);
- elucidate the appropriate educational paradigm to be used to structure the curriculum in order to achieve the chosen ends in this context (4);
- list the content/syllabus or look at ways of integrating theoretical and practical knowledge (6);
- consider an overall structure for the curriculum that is appropriate to what has to be learnt, how it has to be learnt and where it has to be learnt (7);
- explicate clearly the regulations and criteria for managing the curriculum on the ground in relation to educational provision; recruitment; progression; support for failure (9);

- make provision for sound evaluation and quality assurance within this context (10).

Clearly, these activities revolve around the following key words and ideas: 'action, judgement, deliberation, appreciation, criticism, responsibility, argument and justification' (see Reid 1978: 69). Deliberation and coming to wise judgement run through the first six, but (8) to (10) are simpler, more procedural matters and consideration of these should come last.

The importance of deliberation

Reid shows that all *central* curriculum issues are in fact moral and uncertain problems rather than procedural (or technical) in nature – there is nothing easy or self-evident in curriculum matters – and that they require deliberation (or practical reasoning) as a means of deciding the best response for the given context.

Deliberation is a process of thinking that focuses on the problematic and contestable issues endemic to practising as a professional (see Fish and Coles 1998: 68–9). Such reasoning is about deciding between competing and even conflicting moral ideals. (Sometimes all that is possible is respect for one value at the expense of another of equal weight.) In such a situation, it is impossible to resort to technical reasoning, which relies on calculations to determine what course of action to take (see de Cossart and Fish 2005: Ch. 7).

Deliberation, like the overall clinical thinking process of which it is a part, and from which this definition has been derived, has to be learnt in practice and through practice – and can only be developed and refined through experience and involvement. It should be noted that framing the problem is the first and most fundamental element of this deliberation, since it determines all future action and thought related to the problem. This thinking process is a major means of education for all those involved.

It is also worth noting that Reid argues, as we too have done (see Fish 1998; Fish and Coles 1998), that the appreciation of practice is another useful method for defining and refining complex problems and for getting facts and opinions to interact. He says, 'Appreciating is educative . . . People's minds are changed by the act of appreciation' (Reid 1978: 57), and people's practice is changed by the way that it is conceived.

The classic work on group deliberation for curriculum design comes from Schwab (1973), and in our experience no one has since bettered his portrayal of the process. He makes the point that only a group can gather together the necessary evidence and deliberate soundly about such complex matters. He also emphasizes the educational merit of the process itself. This process involves what we tend to call: research or investigation; uncovering of ideas or values; analysis, interpretation and appreciation; and creative decision-making. As we have said there is an iterative process between these. Schwab also argues for an informal atmosphere because without it people are defensive and afraid to risk assertion and to engage in contesting ideas. The ultimate aim is not a grudging consensus but a genuine 'amalgamation or coalescence' (see above, p. 44). Schwab admits that as many as ten meetings may be necessary, and implies that they should be chaired by the curriculum design specialist who, being neutral, will act as a countervailing force to personal agendas and being disinterested will be able to guide the process of mutual discovery. We were sad to note that the committee for the Core Curriculum for the Foundation Programme involved far more people and held far more meetings than is being advocated here.

In respect of deliberation, Reid makes the point that the uncertain problems identified need to be turned into carefully phrased questions that have to be answered. Uncertain problems become apparent wherever: the grounds for decisions are unsure; existing arrangements have to be taken into account but are insufficient; ready-made solutions cannot be drawn from a different context; and there are genuinely competing demands whose ends are never (and should never be treated as) fixed.

It follows that a major part of the expertise of curriculum design lies in articulating very precisely the key questions to be addressed (and in couching them as moral questions), in generating the range of possible solutions (or sub-questions) and deliberating rigorously about each until a conclusion is reached that is best for this curriculum in this context.

The following are examples of key questions which need to be asked by curriculum designers.

1 What is the nature of the context for which this curriculum is being developed and what will count as evidence for the response to this?
2 What should be the criteria for sound educational practice? (What makes teaching a sound educational practice?)
3 What educational philosophy should underpin this curriculum, and what should be its underlying values?
4 Where the context is education for a *profession*, what makes for good practice in a profession?
5 Where the context is education for a *profession*, what professional philosophy ought this curriculum to cultivate, and what should be its underlying values?
6 What kind of person should the curriculum seek to create/cultivate?
7 What should be the educational aims of this curriculum?
8 What kind of person ought to be recruited to this educational programme?
9 What capabilities, characteristics, knowledge and capacities should be developed by this curriculum?
10 What kinds of activities ought learners to engage in, in order to learn these things?

11   How should the education offered be paced and ordered? (In what breadth and depth should learners attend to various matters, and in what order should they meet them?)

12   What ought to be the role of their teachers?

13   What roles ought assessment to play?

14   How will you know that this educational development is successful (how might it be evaluated)?

15   How should the programme be best regulated and managed?

16   What quality assurance procedures ought to be in place in respect of this curriculum?

The choices we consider within a curriculum design team about each of these and our responses to them will depend on our educational values and on how we conceive of the criteria for sound educational practice in respect of teaching, learning and assessment. Clearly, these questions will give rise to many others, each of which will need serious consideration as part of the deliberative procedure. The following section explores the detailed issues that these questions will unearth.

The detailed issues that need to be addressed

In summary then, we can say that, in setting out to design a curriculum it is never the case that one starts with a blank sheet. Even where no curriculum has before been made explicit, there will always have been educational activities which have sprung from the values, theories, assumptions and beliefs of the educators involved. It may be, for example, that the unarticulated values and assumptions underpinning the existing educational programmes and activities will be very different from those of the curriculum being designed to replace them, and this will need to be acknowledged and explored appropriately as part of the introductory section of the new definitive document.

Current practice should therefore always be investigated and its underpinning foundations probed by those seeking to create a new design. It should also be considered more generally and questions should be asked about, and an analysis should be made of, the context for which the curriculum is being designed. This should include not only current provision but the needs arising for the future so far as can be predicted.

The key issues for the design of a curriculum for postgraduate medicine

The following issues are specific to the context of postgraduate medical education and will need to be investigated, and deliberated about, by the design team. We have conducted much of the necessary investigation, and raised most of the key issues in the chapters which follow (Chapters 3 to 10). Here we explore each main area in turn in more detail, provide much of the material about which the team will need to deliberate, and offer the bases for decisions about the following questions.

A: The nature of education and what makes for sound educational practice (see Chapter 3)

- What kind of enterprise is education and how does it differ from training?
- What values and principles should underpin education in any clinical setting?
- What makes the activities of teaching, learning and assessment into a cohesive and sound educational practice?
- What view of teaching, learning and assessment should the curriculum promote in order to achieve a cohesive, logical and sound educational programme?
- How are educational aims formulated?
- What aims are appropriate and worthwhile for educating postgraduate doctors?

B: Values-based issues (see Chapter 4)

- What professional values and principles currently underpin good clinical practice?
- In what kinds of ways are these usually evidenced in the practice of professionals?
- How, if at all, do practitioners currently talk about their values?
- Should traditional values be accepted, extended or replaced in future practice in medicine?
- How can values be prioritized and promoted within the curriculum?
- What values do the members of the design team bring to shaping the curriculum, and how far and in what ways are these significant and relevant to that design process?

C: The nature of professional practice in clinical settings (see Chapter 5)

- Exactly what characterizes professional expertise in medicine?
- What is the nature of medical practice in clinical settings?
- What do we mean by 'a practice' generally within the professional context?
- How can the elements of this expertise be supported and developed in postgraduate doctors?

- What traditions and practices are currently central to the context in which the programme will be offered? And what view of these should the curriculum take?
- What key medical practices should this curriculum help practitioners to develop?

D: The nature of knowledge for and in clinical settings (see Chapter 6)

- Why is an analysis of doctors' practice knowledge important?
- What forms of knowledge are currently perceived to underpin postgraduate medical *practice* and why is this so?
- What can we say about the nature of knowledge more generally (what is it to *know* in different disciplines)?
- In professional practice what sense can we make of theory and practice?
- What are the sources of knowledge for professional practice?
- What are the components of knowledge for professional practice?
- What forms of knowledge actually underpin medical practice?

E: The principles of teaching and learning in clinical settings (see Chapter 7)

- What currently characterizes the activities of teaching and learning in medical practice (in both undergraduate and postgraduate education), and how is this different from education in formal educational institutions?
- What ought to characterize these activities?
- What kinds of pedagogic understanding ought to underpin the teaching and learning of practice?
- How will the curriculum provide for these?

F: The principles and processes for assessment in clinical settings (see Chapter 8)

- How do *educators* see the nature and role of assessment?
- What currently characterizes the activities of assessment in postgraduate medicine (and in what ways is this different from assessment in formal educational institutions)?
- What ought to characterize these activities in the clinical setting?
- How can such assessment provide for the gatekeeping requirements of professional education?
- What are the implications for curriculum design for postgraduate medicine?

G: Evaluating the curriculum for and in the practice setting (see Chapter 10)

- How can and should the curriculum be kept under review and developed?
- How can rigorous and robust educational evaluation be designed as part of the curriculum?

Epilogue

Those designing a curriculum for postgraduate medical practice need to explore the above matters in great depth. The following chapters provide a key service to such designers in that they assemble, for each key area, the kind of evidence that needs to be accrued in order to deliberate wisely on these issues, and outline the resulting problematic questions which curriculum designers at all levels need to think about.

3 Clarifying curriculum aims: the practice of education, its nature and expertise

What kind of enterprise is education and how does it differ from training?
What values and principles should underpin education in any clinical setting?
What makes the activities of teaching, learning and assessment into a cohesive and sound educational practice?
What view of teaching, learning and assessment should the curriculum promote in order to achieve a cohesive, logical and sound educational programme?
How are educational aims formulated?
What aims are appropriate and worthwhile for educating postgraduate doctors?

Introduction

Contributors to curriculum design at all levels are engaged in planning an educational programme that will be enacted in practice. They thus need to have a sound grasp of both the practice of curriculum design (which we introduced in Chapter 2), and its parent enterprise, the practice of education (which we attend to in this chapter). In some ways, therefore, this chapter offers considerable educational development both to all those non-educators involved in the design of curricula for medical education and to medical educators in particular.

Like curriculum design and development, the *practice* of education is a serious enterprise in its own right. But like all practices, it is best understood by engaging in it. This is why it is so important to involve in curriculum design from the beginning of the process, practising educators who are qualified teachers, have extensive experience of teaching at postgraduate level and who have made a serious study of the practice of education. Indeed, some of the problems in **Post Graduate Medical and Dental Education** (PGMDE) arise precisely because such experts have not been engaged as part of the process. Designers then (even those who will never engage directly in educational practice), will need to strive to gain the following during their engagement in the processes of curriculum design:

- a broad overview of education as a field of study within higher education;
- an understanding of how the practice of education fits within this field;
- a grasp of the nature of educational practice as a values-based enterprise;
- a knowledge of the crucial differences between education and training;
- a recognition of what turns the activities of teaching, learning and assessment from surface behaviour into a cohesive and sound educational philosophy and practice;
- an appreciation of some key approaches to educational thinking and the curriculum models to which they give rise;
- a concern to formulate aims that are genuinely educational and worthwhile;
- a sense of what aims are appropriate for the education of postgraduate doctors.

We believe that there is a real need for people who are leading and influencing the major changes in PGMDE in the twenty-first century, and for those providing education on the ground, to know much more about education than they currently do. In order to demonstrate the depth of this necessary knowledge, therefore, we discuss in the main sections of this chapter each of these issues in turn, although of course they are interrelated.

Education as a field of study in higher education

As a field of study, at university level, education is as diverse as medicine, and like medicine it comprises both theoretical and practical elements and contains a number of postgraduate specialties. The key theoretical disciplines that feed into the practice of education are: philosophy, psychology, sociology, history, linguistics and language study, and a range of fields that lie between these like psycho-linguistics and social psychology. The practice of education is also illuminated by political studies, management studies and informatics. One of education's postgraduate fields is curriculum studies, which is a sub-specialty of education (in the same way that paediatrics is of medicine generally), and includes curriculum design, development and evaluation.

During the past 40 years (which span our professional careers as educators) we have experienced at first hand three 'waves' of development in education as a field of study in its own right. Each wave has directly or indirectly moved the study of the *practice* of education more to the centre of the stage, and cast the theoretical disciplines that underpin it into a supporting role, determined by the needs of practice, rather than determining them. Thus, rather than theory being 'applied' to practice and determining its activities, the study of the practice of education has gradually become a specialty in its own right.

The first wave of this development (of somewhat piecemeal educational change) came to its end as the 1970s began. Until then, what were ironically known as the 'four ugly sisters of education' (the pure academic subjects of philosophy, psychology, sociology and history), were considered to offer practising educators all the dimensions they needed to underpin and give credibility to their practice. Educators looking for topics that would help teachers at all levels to develop their practice plundered these pure fields of knowledge. But just as newly-qualified doctors are today steeped in, for example, biochemical pathways whose relevance to practice is doubtful, teachers often found that the theory on, say, the psychology of learning bore little relation to what happened in real classrooms.

The second wave was in full flood by the mid-1970s, when new subjects emerged in a development that brought the 'four ugly sisters' into more direct relationship with education. This was characterized by the newly entitled philosophy of education, educational psychology, educational sociology and the history of education. But although the word 'education' in the titles of these new subjects suggests that they were more directly supportive of practice, in fact these key theoretical fields were harnessed by educational practitioners in much the way the four ugly sisters had been earlier, and were still seen as providing the academic credibility for practice. They also precluded the official growth of other theoretical areas that blatantly had much to offer practising educators (like those listed in the first paragraph of this section). It was innovation without real change. Further, the context within which all this was happening saw teacher education itself moving more and more into the mainstream academic world, as teacher training colleges became colleges of education, and then merged with polytechnics which quickly became universities. Thus, academic respectability – as distinct from credibility – was the order of the day.

For this reason, close on its heels the third wave, which was beginning to emerge would but for the advent of the National Curriculum would have developed through the rest of the twentieth century. Those engaged in the practice of education (the educational activities of teaching, learning and assessment) wished that practice itself to become the focus of study, and to harness theoretical perspectives from any discipline as long as they enlightened that practice. This led to educational practice taking centre stage and to the development of a new discipline, teaching studies, for which a much wider knowledge base provided the theoretical underpinning. With this new development, the investigation and study of *educational practice* itself both led to new theoretical studies and was the determining factor in deciding which other theory would be relevant and useful to practitioners. The tide had turned in this third wave then, such that practice now gave rise to theory, rather than being shaped by theory from other disciplines. Thus teaching studies, as the new discipline, became emancipated as a study in its own right. Significantly, it also led to the development of a new postgraduate field called curriculum studies, which focused specifically on the *practice* of planning, refining and developing educational programmes which were intended to shape the practice of education. In this new field, which studied the practice of curriculum design and development, curriculum theory developed rapidly and was grounded in the realities of practice.

This particular development was concerned exclusively with curriculum projects for schools – and for teachers – and this gave rise to most of our current theoretical understandings about curriculum design and development. This phase then, had its heyday in the UK in the late 1970s. As part of all this, it was well understood at the time that there could be no curriculum development without teacher development. That decade therefore particularly saw the rise and fall of many curriculum projects led by the major names of the day like Stenhouse, Skilbeck and Reid whose work we quote in Chapter 2 because it is still relevant today. Indeed, it is striking that very little has been written since then. This is because the move to the political right that came in the early 1980s brought with it more central control, and led to a national curriculum (which sought, and achieved, an ironing-out of the educational version of the postcode lottery now seen in medical provision). But the cost of this in loss of educational creativity and of motivation of teachers is still being heavily felt in UK schools. This, to some extent, explains why there is no current tradition of curriculum development, not just for PGMDE but even for schools.

In the light of all this, it is interesting to speculate on the kinds of developments currently occurring in both undergraduate and postgraduate medicine. Are similar patterns visible historically and also emerging even now, in both areas of medical education? We believe so. Indeed, one of our intentions in writing this book is to make a contribution in this emerging field.

Clearly, for example, in undergraduate medicine, theoretical disciplines no longer totally shape how practice is understood, and, we would argue, there is a need to establish as a central theme the study of medical practice in its own right. In postgraduate medical education, too, key changes are happening. It is to be hoped, however, that the urge to control educational provision for all doctors will not result in the demotivation experienced by schoolteachers. (Indeed, there are some encouraging signs. Educationists are at last increasingly working in clinical settings to help develop doctors as educators instead of offering wisdom from outside that practice, or merely setting up courses whose intention is to take practitioners away from practice in order to learn more about what to do in practice!) Thus, too, it is worth noting that just as the term 'doctor' covers a range of specialties, so those who call themselves 'educationists' have a range of different expertise. Those calling on the expertise of educationists thus need to be sure that they have chosen someone with an appropriate specialism. Curriculum matters require the expertise of curriculum experts, not merely the importing of 'educationists'.

Education as a practice

The practice of education is an ethical activity undertaken in pursuit of educationally worthwhile ends and which seeks to realize morally worthwhile virtues. Medicine, of course, is the same in this respect at least. The practice of education, though, seeks to open minds, liberate thinking, encourage critique, explore the foundations of the good life (or in the case of education for the professions, explore the foundations of good practice) and develop creativity. These aims or goals are worthwhile because they seek to achieve a 'good', that is to provide for what are generally recognized as the virtues of an educated person. Where they are intentionally achieved, teachers may, irrespective of their educational 'know-how' or teaching skills, claim to practise in an educational way (Carr 1995: 160). Where it is not so, no amount of teaching skills and clever presentations will compensate, and no technical know-how will make the experience *educational* for learners.

These educational ends and virtues can *only* be realized through, and exist in, *virtuous actions*, and they are themselves being continuously developed. Thus 'education' can only be realized in practice. If they are to claim their practice as 'educational' then, those engaging in it need to understand what is involved in 'acting educationally' as opposed, for example, to training, counselling or providing therapy for learners (which are not 'wrong' but simply not necessarily educational).

Educational practice then, is 'morally informed and morally committed action' (Carr 1995: 64, 68), in which the educator enables the processes of growth in the learner. Education liberates individuals and facilitates their transition from passive to active learners. It is emancipatory. It cannot be morally neutral, and is always the result of deliberate choice which itself precludes other possibilities (but when educational understanding is present, the means used can be liberating even when the ends have been fixed by others). It is always directive, in that it goes beyond merely responding to and succouring learners' own wants and needs. Education is a social process and above all is the practice of freedom in which learners discover themselves and achieve their humanity.

Educators thus need to recognize fully the arguments about what they are doing 'with' and 'for' (rather than 'to') learners. Learners are not artefacts that can be 'made', or 'turned into the ideal end-product'. You cannot 'make' a doctor whose practice is intelligent, you can only seek to cultivate one (and the agricultural/botanical imagery in the word 'cultivate' is important as it emphasizes the central notion within any truly educational enterprise of 'growth' which in itself suggests 'nurturing'). This has deep implications for distinguishing between education and training.

By now it will be clear that education is itself a professional practice, distinct from medicine in some important ways as we have described above but overall sharing many of the same characteristics. As such it shares a range of important theoretical underpinnings, not least of which is the understanding necessary for clarifying and formulating aims or purposes. For education, these must be truly educational, since the activities of an educator rest upon complex ideas about what it is to educate somebody. Clearly too, education is a very different form of knowledge from science and its truths cannot be 'proved' and 'evidenced' in the same apparently objective way as those of science. That is, education is inescapably subjective and values-based and must be understood as such and investigated as such (see Chapters 3 and 10) if its practice is not to be distorted by a curriculum that prioritizes matters other than educational ones.

Education as a values-based enterprise

The importance of values

Values are those abiding and long-cherished views we all have – but do not necessarily share – about what counts as enduringly worthwhile and important. To say that a concept is values-based has implications for its definition. This is particularly important where the words used inside the specialist discourse of education are also those used by the public generally, but with less specific and accurate meaning. It means:

- that the values of the definer are necessarily embedded in the meaning given to each word;
- that this is very different from the positivistic (scientific) form of knowledge, where the definition is (apparently) pure, absolute and to be found as automatically agreed 'out there' in the world at large;
- that a once-for-all, generally agreed definition, of the kind drawn from a layman's dictionary, is apt to be unhelpful and even misleading in any complex professional critique and debate, because it both obscures each debater's personal premises, and also encourages the highly dangerous belief that complex matters are simple.

There is thus no one agreed simple definition of any educational term (except of the broadest of kinds as exemplified at the start of this chapter). In education, interpretation is central and interpretations can be in contention with each other, so that deliberation is not merely inevitable but rather is essential. Rather than being a weakness of educational thinking this is one of its supreme strengths, especially for curriculum development, where discussion that focuses on the diversity of views about educational values is a key way of arriving at a shared understanding of what ought to happen for the best and how this may be achieved.

Thus, education is essentially a matter of endless contention, of clarifying and probing ends for their morality and appropriateness, of balancing arguments and of choosing the best for the current purpose, of making difficult choices between competing ideals, and of keeping all these decisions under constant review. (This, of course, is very little different from processes involved in the clinical thinking pathway that doctors routinely use. See de Cossart and Fish 2005 and below, p. 112.) Education can never be entirely 'evidence-based' (but then neither can medicine!). This means that in order that a curriculum (or a book on curriculum design and development) can be properly opened to critique, those constructing it and those using it need to declare their values and indicate the definitions they have taken as their starting points. In short, any discussion of education involves a different kind of evidence from that commonly thought of within the scientific community. Education has its own particular kind of discourse, which is different from those of management, science and medical practice.

The discourse of education

Discourse means the vocabulary and the language structures that we use to refer to the reality we see in, or to shape the meanings we make of, our world. As McLure points out, 'notions of discourse . . . can be found "inside" almost every discipline' (2003: 20). The discourse we habitually use indicates our mindset and our particular ways of thinking about 'reality'. As Pring says: 'how we see the world depends upon the concepts through which experience is organized, objects identified as significant, descriptions applied and evaluations made' (2000: 24). He also points out that we are all immersed in a public discourse that itself is seeking to shape how we see the world, which is concerned with materialism and which is inimical to the ethical and moral thrust of the professional practices of both medicine and education.

A supreme example of this is the use in current public discourse of the term 'delivery'. Both health care and education these days are said to be 'delivered'. Our objection is that this focuses attention on the object to be delivered and the means for its delivery rather than on the role (the practice) of the person carrying out the delivery. It assumes that the deliverer is merely the instrument of the process (milkmen and postmen come to mind, neither of whom are permitted to tamper with or reshape the goods to be delivered, nor are they responsible for the quality of the product). Health care and education are not objects. They are professional practices. They cannot be 'delivered'. Professionals are people who think critically about both the ends and the means of their practice. They are concerned as much about *what is the best thing to do*, as about *how* to do it.

In much the same way the very notion of 'foundation' in the Foundation Programme comes from the construction industry, where there is an assumption that once a sound and solid base has been laid down it is possible to build a substantial structure supported by it. However, while that works for buildings it does not do so for learning, and certainly is not appropriate in the pursuit of 'learning to practise', where there is a need to revisit and revise one's earlier learning through constant reinterpretation and revision (Carr 1995: 69), which activities are the very basis of continuing professional development. This has huge implications for the structure of the curriculum in professional practice.

By contrast to the materialistic and management discourse, then, educational discourse reflects the moral dimension at its heart. Here, as Pring points out (and we recommend reading his argument in the original, see Pring 2000: 24–6) we need to be wary of 'those who, in the interests of research or political control, try to change the language of education' into the language of management which has no interest in the moral responsibilities of professionals but rather seeks to focus on matters of cost efficiency and effectiveness.

Discourse then, used in a calculated way, has the power to induce us (without either our consent or even our recognition) to begin to see things in ways *other people* want us to, for their own purposes. And ultimately it can so habituate us to these new ways of seeing that we are quite unaware of how our mindset has been changed.

Further, McLure points out, by citing terms like 'road-rage', 'date-rape' and 'The key stage one Child', how language has 'the power to create that which it seems to describe' (2003: 4). We should therefore be vigilant, for example, that the discourse of management, sometimes called 'management speak', does not blinker us to the educational and moral responsibilities of these activities. We should recognize this danger in inappropriate references to educational activities like assessment as 'a tool for appraisal' or even 'a tool of the trade'. The mindset that this induces is about employers checking on and controlling the efficiency of 'the workforce', whereas the language of education is about nurturing and emancipating the learner through morally sensitive activities. We should not be brainwashed by management discourse into losing sight of the fact that the heart of education is morally based and that all its values stem from this. The way a curriculum is designed and expressed will either support its educational thrust or distort it to non-educational ends.

For these reasons, curriculum designers need to be familiar with educational discourse and the realities of education to which they give shape and language. We therefore offer here definitions of a range of educational terms, which are values-based, and thus problematic concepts. We do so both to indicate the careful precision with which we seek to use them throughout this book, and to equip readers with a language in which to explore education and curriculum design as disciplines in their own right. Further, in doing so we illustrate the very ideas that all medical educators need to have a view upon – indeed, about which they need to come to a consensus (however temporary that may be), and which will (or should) deeply affect and shape the choices they make during their work in curriculum design.

Curriculum designers for medical education will need to be aware of the nuances of at least five kinds of discourse: that of medicine; that of education; that of training; that of management; and that of the current everyday discourse of the public in the twenty-first century (which politicians and the media have shaped or tried to shape in the mould of industrial transaction and efficiency).

The following definitions, then, offer some starting points, and a language for considering our arguments. We develop these ideas in the rest of Part 2. What we illustrate here is a flavour of those serious choices that educators have to make, which have a profound effect upon how the problems posed by the activity of curriculum design are conceptualized or 'framed', how the elements of an educational programme are highlighted and how a profession's future can be shaped. This section should be read with the following questions in mind:

- What sort of a doctor do we wish to cultivate as a result of the medical education programme?
- What aspects of professional practice in medicine should be emphasized?
- What kinds of activities should teacher and learner engage in, given the nature of clinical practice?

We have taken the following definitions as our starting points. But we have done so only after considering and critiquing a variety of definitions and value positions, and having borne in mind that the focus here is on the development either of the postgraduate doctor who is already a member of a profession and who is learning *in the service environment*, or of the undergraduate who is being prepared to enter that service, and who is working at the level of higher education but in the practical setting.

We believe that *education for practice* in a profession (that is, education which prepares professionals for practice or supports them during it) is not about topping up an essentially theoretical first degree with a few additional skills associated with practical activities. It is not, in our view, about changing or extending behaviour by means of training in which only a surface and transitory conformity to perceived requirements may be achieved. Rather, it involves gaining deep understanding of, and developing a rigorous critique of, practice in that profession as manifested by all involved – in the light of which new understandings, strategies and skills for that practice can be developed.

It follows from this that *the role of teacher* (particularly in the clinical setting) is rather more that of facilitator who enables the construction or reconstruction of understanding than that of mere 'presenter' of knowledge or demonstrator of processes and procedures. Such a 'construction of understanding' is never a one-way process. Rather it involves the 'co-construction of understanding'. Such a teacher's expertise consists of factual medical knowledge and knowledge of how to do medical processes and procedures, but also needs to extend to ways of enquiring into professional practice and to a broad range of facilitative strategies. Such a teacher understands the learner and learning as much as what is to be learnt; knows about the processes of curriculum development at least as well as about the content to be included in the curriculum; and, in particular, understands the problems posed by needing to learn practice in the clinical (service) setting.

Teaching, as Oakeshott (1967) argues, thus aims at opening up to learners their wide inheritance, and extending their (and the teacher's own) criticality, as well as the very bases for that criticality (ways of seeing the world of practice) – in every aspect of their work. The aim of teaching is to enable both learner and teacher to consider the wider implications of the procedural and propositional knowledge that they need to learn and refine. It also seeks to enable them to challenge what they take for granted, by articulating – and then considering sceptically, in the light of other ways of seeing and doing things – their own most cherished insights, ideas, procedures and uncertainties. It seeks to help them recognize and consider the costs and benefits of their professional decisions and judgements; and it encourages them to explore further and critique the very language and ideas of the relevant range of discourses that they inevitably engage in (see Carr and Hartnett 1998).

By the same token *learning*, in educational discourse, is 'a comprehensive activity in which we come to know ourselves and the world around us . . . [and whose] achievements range from merely being aware, to what may be called understanding and being able to explain' (Oakeshott 1967: 156). By this definition, learning is about conduct (behaviour enlightened by moral understanding) which is nurtured and cultivated through good teaching. This is seen as being in contrast to concern with behaviour (morally neutral surface activity) which is changed (manipulated or trained) by conditioning, in ways behavioural psychologists recommend. Given the common agreement that there is a crucial moral element in professional practice, training in behaviour is demonstrably inappropriate or insufficient. In medical education, then, learning might be described as an activity in which doctors seek to extend their understanding by constructing or reconstructing meaning for themselves, and/or by enquiring critically from a range of perspectives into events from their practice, in order to illuminate and thus improve it.

Thus, we take *professionals* to mean members of a profession 'who seek a broad understanding of their practice, paying attention not only to the development of their daily competence but also to the fundamental purposes and values that underpin their work' (see Golby 1993: 6). As we have said in Chapter 1, we fear that professionalism is being eroded, and we are not alone. As Tallis (2004) also says, there is a need to rekindle and value that vision and set it in contrast to other current priorities in which increased remuneration is currently top, and where what one has is regarded as more important than what one is.

Education as different from training

By contrast to what we have said about education above, *training* is a different enterprise with its own discourse. It is promoted by those who seek to control the professions and used as a central process for preparing and sustaining the professional 'workforce'. But training is focused exclusively upon the learning of skills, procedures and performances, without reference to the wider context in which they take place, to what lies under our actions, or to any consideration of how they should be used in the service of the public. Ironically (we would argue), training ensures that there are no critical perspectives, no sensitivity to individual cases and no consideration of ideas 'outside the box'. We see training as necessary in the learning of pure new skills like basic surgical skills as learnt in a classroom, but as insufficient to provide for the rounded education of the postgraduate doctor who needs to know why, how and when (and when not) to use them in the real clinical setting. Curriculum designers for professions should also note that another term for skills is 'competencies' (one skill is a 'competency', and so a 'competency-based curriculum' is one which provides training rather than education, which attends to skills rather than overall competence). Indeed, we would want to argue that the term 'curriculum', which implies 'education', should not be used alongside the term 'training'.

We believe, if professional practice is to be maintained as a morally based service to the public, it is necessary to resist the old-fashioned and outdated drive for competencies, seeing them as useful in further education in providing for the basic physical processes needed by school-leavers who are being prepared for relatively simple jobs, but inappropriate to higher education. We fear that this behavioural approach to complex matters is part of the current disease of the western world to give significance only to those things which can be seen and measured (see Fromm 1976; Broadfoot 1993, 2000).

It seems to us that perhaps some people in medicine are (mistakenly) using the terms 'competence' and 'competency' as interchangeable, as if they refer generally to the *practice* of medicine as opposed to its *theory*. (Though others, we believe, are talking of a 'competency-based curriculum' rather more calculatingly, in order to establish an impoverished and simplistic form of professionalism which is based only on skills.)

We see medical and educational practice as holistic (as complex rather than merely skills-based, and as involving the irreducible relationship of theory and practice throughout all professionals' activities). We therefore offer a clarification of the term 'competence', which should be used as a means of identifying the holistic nature of a person's ability. Just as we cannot talk about someone's 'gravities' but only their gravity, so the word competence has no plural form. There are no such things as 'competences'. By contrast, the term 'competencies' indicates skills ('a competency' being one skill). This term is used when a professional's practice is seen as depending exclusively on skills. We believe that professional practice consists of *more than* skills (competencies), because the professional is morally bound to use professional judgement in employing professional skills for the good of the individual patient (see Carr 1993; de Cossart and Fish 2005). We believe that these terms need to be used by everyone rather more precisely, in order not to collude with some current attempts to erode professionalism (see Broadfoot 1993, 2000; Fish and Coles 1998; O'Neill 2002; Tallis 2004). We explore these ideas in more detail in Chapter 8.

While the terms 'trainee', 'trainer', 'training' and even 'training the trainers' may have, in the past, carried with them an affectionate irony, they are used today in the context of an increasingly instrumental (management) perspective of professional practice. As a result, and in order to eliminate any misinterpretation, we see an urgent need for not just an alternative terminology but a more enlightened discourse.

What makes educational practice sound? Three approaches to educational thinking and the models of curriculum design to which they give rise

If an enterprise is to count as education, then crucially there must be a close, logical and well articulated relationship between the educational aims which shape the enterprise and the activities of teaching, learning and assessment which are the means of achieving them. And all should conduce to the same end: sound educational development (the development of *understanding*) in the learner. Here, the learner's 'conduct' (their behaviour and all that lies beneath the surface and drives that behaviour) needs to be the central focus, since this is about educating the whole person, not just about training in the performance of de-contextualized skills.

In fact there are at least three ways of conceptualizing the relationship of teaching, learning and assessment, which give rise to three models for shaping the curriculum (the product, the process and the research models). In each of these, the values and assumptions about the role of the teacher, the learner and assessment are all very different. And within these models there is a different emphasis on the significance of the context for which learners are being prepared. Their basic ways of conceptualizing education are best demonstrated in Table 3.1, which shows different roles for the teacher, the learner and assessment.

It will be clear from this table that where education is seen as a product, the aim for the learner is to come to possess something (a commodity) that the teacher has to give. Thus, the teacher transmits knowledge to a passive learner and at the end of so doing tests the learner to see whether that transaction has properly taken place. Just whose knowledge this is, where it comes from and who says it is important for the learner is not entirely clear in this view. But (as we shall see shortly) we can say that the knowledge chosen arises from outside the immediate world of both teacher and learner. Indeed, the knowledge to be gained is usually presented as de-contextualized and requires no sensitivity to context. From this, then, all else follows in support of the product view of education. The roles of teacher and learner, the motivation, the resources and the key headings for planning a curriculum all conduce to the learner gaining something visible which someone has deemed important for them to have or know irrespective of how it relates to their given context. Further, it is (or it seems) possible to describe beforehand exactly what those visible outcomes will be. This, of course, has the potential to become extremely boring to all parties! Over a period of time these so-called achievements or acquisitions by the learner can be added up into an assessment which marks the end of a long series of programmes of learning, where quantity of acquisition is taken as evidence of quality (more means better).

By contrast, where education is seen as a process and as arising from an interaction between the teacher and the learner, the aim is to help the learner to seek knowledge and make it their own (and appropriate to their own context) by working with it actively. Here the original knowledge may have been 'handed down' to the teacher by some other agent (like the government), but teacher and learner work on it together to reshape it in their understanding and for their own circumstances. Knowledge is thus no longer 'pure' coming from 'out there' and 'given', but becomes reshaped and adapted to the learner and the learner's context, while the teacher ensures that this does not distort the nature of that knowledge. Thus the roles of both are more collaborative (though the teacher is still an agent for knowledge that comes from 'above'), learning is active, and assessment during the learning helps both teacher and learner to see current achievements and also to readjust the processes of teaching and learning. Over a period of time the quality of the learning becomes apparent by charting the learner's increasing insight and understanding (and consequent conduct).

Table 3.1   Three models of teaching, learning and assessment

Education as a product	Education as a process	Education as research
Intention	*Intention*	*Intention*
Teacher transmits knowledge	Teacher promotes knowledge	Learners explore understanding
Locus of knowledge	*Locus of knowledge*	*Locus of knowledge*
Resides in teacher	Resides in teachers and learners	Resides in learner group
Student activities	*Student activities*	*Student activities*
Passive learners	Active learners	Aware of selves as active learners and negotiators
(covers material fast)	(active learning takes longer)	(this takes even longer)
Motivation via	*Motivation via*	*Motivation via*
Teacher	Own active learning	Group learning/active learning
Sees learner as	*Sees learner as*	*Sees learner as*
Receiver of knowledge	Active seeker of knowledge	Discoverer/reconstructor of own knowledge
Sees teacher as	*Sees teacher as*	*Sees teacher as*
Teller/instructor	Seeker/catalyst	Facilitator/neutral chair
Teaching activities	*Teaching activities*	*Teaching activities*
Lecturing	Facilitates learning, sets up problems, probably knows answers	Teacher is leader within group but learns alongside them
Sees assessment as	*Sees assessment as*	*Sees assessment as*
End of course tests, summative, teacher assessment	part of teaching, part of learning, formative – and summative	self-assessment, group assessment, aiding understanding
Plans by means of	*Plans by means of*	*Plans by means of*
Aims, objectives, detailed method for whole session, summative assessment	Aims, intentions, principles of procedure, list of content, assessment as part of this process	Aims, intentions, a negotiated agenda, counselling-type methods, assessment within this process

Continued overleaf

Table 3.1   Continued

Education as a product	Education as a process	Education as research
Use of resources	*Use of resources*	*Use of resources*
Chosen by teacher and brought into the learner's context from outside by the teacher, and thus may not relate to learner's context	Learner-centred and thus inevitably arising from the learner's context and relevant to it	Learner organized and thus chosen from the learner's context
View of professional	*View of professional*	*View of professional*
Teacher is a performer whose performance is significant in the quality of learner's education	Teacher is a facilitator who sets up learning for learners and whose input features less in the sessions	Teacher is a facilitator who learns alongside learners but this can only be on a highly disciplined basis

Source: after Stenhouse (1975) and adapted from Fish (2003)

Education as research sees the aim as enabling learners to explore understanding and to become emancipated from knowledge 'handed down' to them, because they both learn that knowledge and at the same time exercise their critical faculties in relating it to their current understanding and in shaping it to their own developing context. What then follows is that the roles of teacher and learner become genuinely collaborative and investigative; assessment takes its part fully in the teaching and learning process, and itself is driven collaboratively; and the context becomes central, as the place in which education takes place.

Table 3.2 shows how these different approaches give rise to very different models for designing a curriculum and that each of these models results in a very different kind of education. While each is valuable, we should note that they lead to different *kinds* of achievement for the learner, and see educational aims differently. Further, each has a different view of the importance of the context for which the learner is being prepared or developed. Each prioritizes different intentions, and each casts teachers, learners and assessment in different kinds of roles. Each has teaching, learning and assessment in a different temporal and actual relationship. The logic of each is self-contained and separate from the others. (This, for example, will determine how the curriculum is structured on paper: whether it is presented in linear fashion as shown in the first model; or sees theory and

Table 3.2   Three models of planning for curriculum design

The product model	The process model	The research model
Aims (long-term educational goals)		
These must be *educationally worthwhile,* relate to the level and starting point of the learner and be appropriate to the context in which learning will take place. Above all they must give rise to a coherent educational experience. They are likely to characterize the learner/ practitioner who will emerge from the programme with respect to professional and personal attributes, capabilities, capacities, knowledge and skills. However, having said that, each model would express these differently as indicated above.		
Objectives	*Intentions*	*Intentions*
Prescribes the specific detail of what teacher will teach/tell learners, and how learners will learn it.	A more tentative list of what learners are intended to gain in terms of new or deeper understanding, but which also recognizes that teaching and learning are not causally related	A statement about the knowledge that learners will explore, how they will explore it and what may be the results of this
Or uses behavioural objectives		
Or uses learning outcomes A prescription of what learners *will* learn and be able to demonstrate they know (totally predictable outcomes are boring)		
(Because knowledge resides in teacher who is teller and learner receives it)	(Because knowledge resides in both teachers and learners, because teacher is also demonstrably a seeker and all learners are different and seek some own goals)	(Because knowledge resides in learner group who discover or construct own knowledge for which teacher is facilitator and fellow learner)
Method	*Principles of procedure*	*The agenda*
There is usually no specific detail of teaching and learning styles to be adopted in this model, as they are normally taken as read	These indicate the ways teacher and learners will go about their respective activities – and will probably relate this to the overall educational	This usually indicates the framework within which the learning agenda will be negotiated and the parameters for this. Counselling type *Continued overleaf*

Table 3.2   Continued

The product model	The process model	The research model
A list of actions will indicate which bits the teacher does and what the learners do. Mainly it deals with content and lists of items (of appropriate length for the time available), normally derived from the agreed syllabus	rationale and aims. Note: assessment might be listed here because it is seen as a *part* of the learning process	activities will form the teacher's agenda – and share assessment too
This will lead to a linear design where what is to be learnt is listed in linear order	*Content*	*Main focus*
	This will indicate the topic to be focused on and how it relates to the agreed syllabus, but may present this as 'integrated' or as a 'spiral curriculum'	This will link the focus topic to the agreed syllabus. It may present these matters in an integrated way, or offer themes to keep returning to (as in a spiral curriculum)
Assessment	*Assessment (but see above)*	*Assessment (see above)*
End of course tests, mainly summative	Part of teaching – i.e. during unit, teacher assessment mainly formative – and summative	Self-assessment, group assessment – mainly formative, but used in a range of summative ways
Criteria for assessment	*Criteria for assessment*	*Criteria for assessment*
Stresses formal written assignments, demonstrating knowledge of: accurate content, evidence for arguments, clear structure, comprehensive coverage, basic analysis, good references	Uses a range of methods of assessment, all of which stress the understanding which underpins the surface actions or activities Expects a well-kept portfolio	Stresses creative approaches to knowledge and understanding Expects a well-kept portfolio

Regulations for progression (and for managing the failing learner)

Resources	Resources	Resources
Teacher is main resource, but any other major resources listed here	Learner-centred means heavily resource-based. These must be indicated	Learner is foremost resource but all the required main resources would be listed here

Table 3.2   Continued

The product model	The process model	The research model
Evaluation	Evaluation	Evaluation

The ways in which that which is taught is to be evaluated and developed further are indicated in this section.

Source: based on the ideas of Stenhouse (1975), adapted from Fish (2003)

practice as integrated; or as a spiral, with themes to be returned to at increasing levels of difficulty.)

Teachers and curriculum designers would be wise to understand these differences and respect the differing views of education to which they give rise and which have endemic to them a different logic. While each model may legitimately be used by a teacher with the same learners for different purposes on different occasions, it would produce a nonsense to select, in some eclectic way, an aim from one model, teaching and learning roles from another and the role of assessment from a third.

It is common across all academic institutions both in relation to undergraduate and postgraduate level, to assume that the product (transmission of knowledge) model of curriculum design is the only respectable academic mode of curriculum planning. We believe this is an error and happens because the options are rarely if ever rehearsed today, and instead all planning teams accept uncritically what they have been persuaded is the traditional approach to shaping the curriculum round 'learning outcomes'. This approach assumes that all education cashes out immediately, into visible and measurable end products (deliverables), and that without these it is impossible to engage in serious academic work. But that which is most valuable is often invisible to the eye. We should therefore be careful of pursuing only ends that are quickly visible and easily measurable. And we should be wary of assuming that we know absolutely in advance what the learner will achieve; such an approach leads to a simplified set of aims which everyone will reach and precludes the idea of anything creative happening during the learning, thus making it over-predictable and boring.

The organization of the curriculum must: be driven by carefully formulated educationally worthwhile aims; have demonstrable educational coherence; recommend appropriate teaching and learning activities; set out in terms of depth and breadth an appropriately balanced knowledge base; utilize resources aptly; and use assessment intelligently to support all these. It is the responsibility of a curriculum design team to ensure that the curriculum attends to all these.

Even the briefest glance at Table 3.2 will demonstrate that the product model is more likely to be useful in formal classrooms wherever learners seek knowledge as a commodity, and less useful for engaging learners in investigating their own practice, creating their own meaning from a range of perspectives, and using the understandings gained to help them develop and refine their professional practice. In short, the product model as the underpinning for curriculum design for professional practice is only appropriate if practice and theory, and teaching and learning, are conceived of as simple activities for transmitting knowledge. The model(s) for encouraging active engagement with education in the practice setting, such that understanding and insight develop, are clearly the process and/or research models. It will be noted here that a clear distinction is being made between 'knowing' and 'understanding'.

We also know (and designers would be wise to take account of this) that:

- the strongest motivation to acquire theoretical knowledge occurs when it is needed for immediate use in practice;
- professionals best learn both their theory and their practice in the setting in which they work;
- utilizing knowledge is the way to come to know and understand it;
- much theory that is learnt by professionals in their undergraduate courses is rarely used by them subsequently.

As indicated above, there is a further dimension to these arguments, which concerns the relationship between knowledge and power.

Knowledge and power

We have talked about the acquisition of knowledge and/or the development of understanding as the key reason for the interaction between teacher and learner, and shown that different models of curriculum make different assumptions about it. We have also indicated that where that knowledge comes from (whose it is), and why and how it is to be learnt, are also important. It might appear from this that the teacher is merely an agent, not only for knowledge, but for the entire enterprise for which the curriculum is a blueprint. But this is not so, firstly because, as we have already said, teachers must be given a full and proper role in shaping the curriculum they teach and secondly because in fact, whether or not they are given such a role, teachers are inevitably very powerful, *if they recognize and care to wield that power*. For example, in making the choices available to them both between different curriculum models and within the chosen model, they can decide: whose (and not merely what) knowledge is to be taught; how it should be construed; where they believe it is created; and to what end it is to be offered to, or facilitated in, learners. Even in deciding *not* to exercise this choice and thereby accepting that made for them by others, teachers are shaping (or rather we would say short-changing) their own and their learners' educational possibilities.

The work of Habermas mediated through Grundy (1987) and Carr (1995) identified three systems of knowledge generation and organization which might characterize a teacher's approach to these matters: the technical; the practical; and the emancipatory. The first of these, the *technical approach*, describes the interest of a teacher who seeks to improve outcomes by improving skills. But this approach, in accepting the aims and content of others and merely choosing the means by which to achieve these, allows knowledge to be controlled by someone or some group outside the teaching interaction. Those who follow it practise according to rules and use their skills to an end predetermined by someone else.

By contrast, Habermas's *practical approach* refers to the teacher whose practice is guided by choice, who seeks the 'good' of the learner, and who would break out of the framework and the rules set by others in order to achieve that. Here the teacher shows a moral consciousness, and exercises greater choice. This involves what Habermas calls 'practical judgement' which is exercised through deliberation (or reflection). Here knowledge arises directly through reflection upon practice, and is developed through bringing implicit theory to the surface, thus providing a more consciously rational basis for action.

The third or *emancipatory approach* to generating and organizing knowledge, engages students in the active creation of knowledge along with the teacher. Here educational choices are regarded as problematic, dialogue between teacher and learner is important, and theory and practice are both open to critical scrutiny and fundamental questioning. Here a curriculum is not an exhaustively detailed plan but provides for an act of enquiry in which planning, acting and evaluating are reciprocally related.

The emancipatory approach is seen as providing for more authentic ways of learning and of cultivating students who are more in control of their learning (Grundy 1987: 125). Learners construct their knowledge within a social setting, and the teacher recognizes that it is inimical to education to coerce them. Here then, the locus of control for making judgements about the quality and meaningfulness of the work lies with the participants in the learning situation, so that even accepted wisdom can and should be questioned, in order to develop a sophisticated critical consciousness and critical insight. Here theory is one resource among a number, and provides information but not direction. Here indeed, the teacher is one resource among a number! This approach transforms consciousness – and enables learners to break out of habitual ways of seeing things and of acting. There is much in all this that those who seek to design a curriculum need to attend to. Table 3.3, reproduced from de Cossart and Fish (2005: 43), shows this in detail.

Table 3.3   A summary of the arguments of Habermas

The questions	The technical approach	The practical approach	The emancipatory approach
	Teacher inculcates those skills which society needs and government has decided to require of professionals (how these have been decided may or may not have been democratic)	Teacher is a thinking agent of what those in power require of professionals, but may act partially independently for the good of learners and even the profession	Teacher is an educator who takes informed and critical responsibility for the ends and the means of the education she or he offers and who seeks to enable learners to do the same, both in education and in their own profession
What approach should teacher take?	Enact a curriculum which has been 'handed down'	Choose what will bring about learners' good	Enable learners to create knowledge along with teacher
Teacher's intention	To improve outcomes by improving skills	To develop understanding and moral consciousness	To enable learners to see that teaching and learning are problematic
Who controls the knowledge during learning?	Whoever controls the teacher's ideas about what must be taught (one group only, which is outside the teaching/ learning interaction)	The teacher chooses what is learnt during practice, but can break the rules for the good of the learner and all have equal rights within the situation	Teacher and learner learn together in dialogue. Dialogue is a vital means of learning. Knowledge is a corporate matter, created *in situ*
What is the role of educational theory in this?	Theory (from outside, which is formal, but already chosen by the 'control group') directs	A range of theory is drawn on by teacher and this guides meaning-making in a democratic	Theory (of all kinds) and practice, are questioned fundamentally. A critique is developed while

Table 3.3 Continued

The questions	The technical approach	The practical approach	The emancipatory approach
	and confirms practice	environment, and enables personal theory, belief and assumption to be to be exhumed and examined	trying to make meaning of both theory and practice
What judgements (decisions) may teachers make in practice?	They may decide only how to attain an end which has been stipulated by someone else who is not part of the teaching situation (strategic judgement)	They may engage personal judgement about the practicalities of teaching (the means to be used) through reflection, deliberation and critical thinking. They have no choice about ends (practical judgement)	They can use own judgement about ends and means by understanding the choices that can may be made and by careful deliberation about them and critique of them (professional judgement)
Teacher's role	Totally reproductive of what has been decided by others	Essentially reproductive of what has been decided by others	Emancipatory. Brings enlightenment and transforms consciousness and self-awareness

Formulating educationally worthwhile aims

An early task for curriculum designers in postgraduate medical education, then, is to have explored their own values and to have understood the educational possibilities open to them and to teachers and learners. As outlined in this chapter, a good place to start this particular element of curriculum design is for the design team to discuss what it understands by terms such as 'teaching', 'learning', 'assessment' and appraisal', as well as those terms from current discourse such as 'delivery' and 'competency'. In the light of this, they will then need to formulate sound and worthwhile educational aims from which the rest of the curriculum will be shaped.

As we have already said, the expression of these aims is always shaped by underlying values which need to be transparent and which the educator is inevitably promoting. What should these be for postgraduate medical education? We can only answer in the light of the values that characterize its present context, and our views about what future contexts ought to be like.

The *worthwhile ends, aims or goals* of education generally, traditionally include the development of the whole person and particularly the *cultivation of the mind* (because developing understanding will in turn lead to the development of practice). What, then, would be worthwhile aims for postgraduate medical education? What sort of a doctor should we seek to cultivate? This is a question readers should keep in mind as they read the following two chapters.

What aims are appropriate for the education of postgraduate doctors?

Of course it is clear that the craft skills that are important to medicine will have to be learnt and this may require some elements of training. Beyond this however, medical education could be shaped either by the notion of training or education. Those who see doctors as mainly technical experts will value and wish to argue for skills-based training which is largely concerned with learning new behaviour (processes, procedures and operations). Those who seek to cultivate a rounded physician who is aware of the importance of professional judgement and who knows when, where and how to utilize those skills in the health care setting and who does so with sensitivity and humanity, will argue for education which is concerned with changing (deepening) understanding as a basis for intelligent practice and well-considered conduct.

Doctors whose understanding has been developed will choose to change their conduct accordingly, will be responsible for, and genuinely committed to, that change, and will have the motivation and capability to continue to develop it. This would therefore constitute a major educational aim. But is it detailed enough, and will it be right for the context and the needs of society in respect of medicine? The following chapters provide evidence to fuel decisions about this.

Thus we would argue for engaging in an educational practice which is more than about 'knowing how to do educational things' (having the 'skills' of teaching). And we would make very clear distinctions between education and training. For example, although an educational method (like instructing doctors in a given skill) can be skilfully performed, it will not be an educational practice at all if it has been used to impose a process upon learners who have been required to ignore their personal perspectives including their own values, attitudes and feelings, suspend their thinking, shut down their critical faculties, abandon their moral awareness and merely parrot a performance. This would not conform to ethical educational principles of procedure concerned with cultivating the understanding which enables learners to explore and come to own a view about why, how, where and when to use that skill, which in turn commits them to develop or change their practice.

Implications for curriculum designers

The main implications for curriculum designers then are that they should:

- have or set out to gain an understanding of the professional practice of education and its key values and activities;
- be or become conversant with educational discourse;
- consult those with expertise in curriculum design and development;
- recognize that values are the driving force of professional practice (both educational and health care) and that the curriculum needs to attend to these by indicating the values upon which it is based;
- seek to understand the values that underlie the practice for which they are designing the curriculum;
- consider the values of the profession for which the curriculum is being designed and be alert to adjusting or adding to these in the light of current and likely future needs;
- recognize and explore their own values and ensure that they do not introduce these into the curriculum unless it is appropriate;
- recognize that postgraduate medical education is a higher education enterprise and that any curriculum for it needs to be at an appropriate postgraduate level and include the key characteristic of postgraduate work, which is criticality;
- ensure that the curriculum attends to the education and not simply the training of postgraduate doctors;
- ensure that the structure and discourse of the curriculum has an appropriate internal logic (for example, not using 'objectives' where more than skills are being learnt and where learners are expected to be in control of their own learning);
- formulate educational aims very carefully giving an eye to the entire educational enterprise to which they will lead;
- take careful account of the issues related to knowledge and power such that they are aware of the power relationships implied in the choices they make.

End note

Since values are the driving force of all professional practice, it is now appropriate to begin the group of chapters that provides a detailed exploration of the nature of medical practice by looking first at the actions of some individuals who work in medical practice and having access to their thinking and knowing. It is by considering these that we will begin to recognize the values that underpin their work.

4 Clarifying values: professionalism in practice – stories from the field of medicine

What professional values and principles currently underpin good clinical practice?
In what kinds of ways are these usually evidenced in the practice of professionals?
How, if at all, do practitioners currently talk about their values?
Should traditional values be accepted, extended or replaced in future practice in medicine?
How can values be prioritized and promoted within the curriculum?
What values do the members of the design team bring to shaping the curriculum, and how far and in what ways are these significant and relevant to that design process?

Introduction

In this chapter, as a means of beginning to understand the nature of expertise in medical practice – which any curriculum for postgraduate doctors must crucially support and develop – we explore the values that underlie the work of several experienced professionals and one learning practitioner. In Chapter 5, as another perspective on this, we consider the growing literature that illuminates the nature of clinical practice in medicine more generally, and draw out some further implications for the design and development of a curriculum for postgraduate medical practice.

As we have already said in relation to education, values are those abiding and long-cherished views that we all have but do not necessarily share, about what we see as enduringly worthwhile and important. For all of us who practise in a profession, values shape our view of the world at large and our professional practice specifically, and profoundly influence how we seek to conduct ourselves within both.

Values are usually tacit, often lying deep beneath the surface elements of practice. They are by definition matters of contention, since they are often not shared by others in our working environment. It is true that any health care professional will share many values with immediate colleagues, but this may not be true across professions, let alone in relation to other staff and patients. Indeed, everyone who works in health care lives at the centre of a web of complex, but subtle and largely invisible, pressures which arise from the differing values endemic to clinical practice and its management (see de Cossart and Fish 2005: 20). Indeed, because values are rarely directly discussed (so that colleagues do not recognize their differences as values-based), the pressures that arise from them are not traced to source and thus become puzzling as well as frustrating.

As we have already said, contention about values results from seriously different ways of seeing the world. It is these values which arise from, or give rise to, the different (and inimical) discourses of education and clinical practice on the one hand and management on the other. Each group here has its role, its own language, and its own place in health care. We value them all when they are working within their expertise, but in company with many others, we are aware of how, in the last two decades, the management view of the world and its associated discourse has made a major bid to impose upon medicine and education a managerial way of seeing the world. We believe that this has resulted in gross distortion of values and practice in education and health care.

Complex though values are, they are central and fundamental to the nature of professional practice and its expertise, and we therefore have to begin any attempt to understand and develop that practice by exploring them. And such an exploration is bound to begin by looking at the visible elements of what a practitioner does, and then attempting to gain access to and understand what drives these.

As we have noted, practitioners rarely talk or write directly about their values, but despite this, what they do, know and think, speaks volumes in respect of what they believe is important. Indeed, ironically, that which practitioners take for granted, and overlook (because it is so much a natural part of their practice), is often very visible to patients and other colleagues who observe them. But there is little time generally for passing observers to explore the real depth and complexity of these values. To do so, one has to approach a little closer, see in a little more detail and be made privy to more personal thoughts.

This is why we invited four practitioners (three doctors and one very senior theatre nurse) to write for us about a typical example of their medical practice and their view of this. Of course good practice is context-bound (practice that suits one context will have to be adapted for any other). Thus, we will never capture (nor wish to capture) a simple and clear recipe for 'the values' that will drive good practice under all circumstances. Neither do we expect to generalize from the specifics of the values of several professionals in order to invent some sort of worldwide 'values protocol'. The whole point is that, as professionals we are all both individuals with our own furrow to plough and our own guiding philosophies, and also members of a range of communities each of which has a particular way of seeing the world. Thus the contributors to this chapter offer us ways of making the values that underlie medical practice *intelligible*.

We have sought to increase this understanding further: by highlighting what their writing teaches us; by pointing out how their stories interconnect; by offering in the next chapter the wider literature and revealing how our contributors' stories relate to it; and (as we do now) by inviting readers to explore how the values here articulated connect with their own. And we commend this *whole process* to curriculum designers as a means of gaining access to values (including their own), offering these particular details as evidence about values of the kind that a curriculum should begin by acknowledging.

First, though, to set the context in which doctors have to practise, we examine the expectations that many members of society currently have of doctors, and the values that underlie these.

Society's expectations

Society's expectations have changed, and this has changed medical practice. As Tallis (2004: 243) observes, society (in many countries) has become 'consumerist':

> The patient as client or customer in the shopping mall of medical care will see the doctor as a vendor rather than as a professional. There will be an increasing emphasis on the accoutrements that make the first experience, or the first encounter, customer-friendly. The key to the doctor-as-salesman will be the emphasis on those aspects of customer care that give the patient a feeling of 'empowerment'.

In the deliberately striking metaphors used here, we see a critique of the values endemic to the growing view that medicine is, in the discourse of today's world, to be bought and sold. These values lurk tacitly beneath society's prevailing demands of medicine as illustrated in the following. Interestingly, however, we suspect that faced explicitly with their attitudes and values, many might still wish to reject the longer-term implications and likely results of reshaping medicine in consumerist terms. These may be characterized as follows.

- *People want to be seen* – they do not expect to have to wait, they want prompt attention, at whatever time of the day or night. There should be no waiting times – especially for them! And where necessary they expect to be attended to and operated upon by the most senior and most highly competent doctor available to them. They want that doctor to perform effectively and efficiently, and for any treatment to be not just correct but the best there is. They have the notion that there is 'right action' that has been predetermined by someone, somewhere, who has decided what should happen in each and every circumstance such as the one they find themselves in. However, 'consumerism in patients who see the doctor as addressing their customer rights . . . will push the profession from a calling to a business' (Tallis 2004: 248).
- *Members of society expect doctors to be experts in their field*. Indeed, they believe that professional practice is all about expertise, which they see as unshakeable knowledge and an utterly dependable technical base that is driven by sound scientific evidence. And this expertise would, they conclude, naturally be enshrined in clear guidelines (protocols for action) for doctors and others to follow.
- *And people want it all*. Throughout the latter part of the twentieth century and into the twenty-first, they have come to believe that there is a 'cure for all ills', that there are 'magic bullets', that there are constant new discoveries, new treatments, new technologies, new advances, and they want these. But although ironically the enormous explosion of technological advance in medical care seems to threaten the very nature of professional practice and challenge the doctor's autonomy, this is not the case. It is true that technology is no individual practitioner's intellectual property, and that the public now thinks it owns all medical knowledge. But doctors' expertise is vital in interpreting such technology in ways lay persons cannot even comprehend.
- *Patients do not expect anything to go wrong*. How could it if doctors and other health care staff are experts and are doing the right thing? So, if anything does go wrong it must be because someone 'wasn't doing it right', wasn't following the protocol, wasn't adhering to the guidelines. Error then, is always someone's fault; someone must be to blame. How could this have been allowed to happen? Why couldn't it have been anticipated? Why wasn't it prevented? Who is in charge of this? What did they do wrong? And even today's bland (and unhelpful) riposte that much error is 'systems failure' fails to pacify those critics who demand a review of the system in question. If someone is at fault, then there must be an inquiry, and if an inquiry, then there will (of course) be litigation (those who have

done wrong must be found guilty), and compensation (someone must pay). There's money to be had when things go wrong.

- *People don't want to pay, or rather they don't want to pay too much, for this.* In the UK there is a (notionally) free NHS – free that is at the point of access (but not free in any other terms, as the cost is met from taxation). In some countries there are other methods of funding health provision, most commonly either through private payment or through some form of health insurance. Nevertheless, whatever the funding method, health care costs are rising rapidly throughout the world as the nature of health care provision becomes more expensive, technically more sophisticated, and in any case more available. Everywhere there is concern about cost – and patients (society) must, in the end, bear the brunt of this. The pressure is on the politicians to limit costs while maintaining public support.

So people's expectations in a consumerist world are driven by self-interest. They value only what they see as immediately affecting them. This view often goes unchallenged because it resonates with general societal values. But is this realistic, and does it take account of the real nature of medical practice and the values that actually drive it?

The stories of four practitioners

To help us characterize the realities of professional practice, we asked four clinicians to narrate an experience from their daily practice. The brief we gave them was this:

Please help us to characterize the nature of professional practice. In no more than about 800 words please write for us as follows:

1   In no more than 200 words describe as richly as possible a small piece of your clinical practice which either typifies or is starkly in contrast to your experience of working day by day in the clinical setting. (It is up to *you* to choose the size here. It could be an event that lasted little time or you could offer a diary of a selected day. We are not looking for dramatic 'clinical events/incidents' which led to an investigation, but rather something that *typifies* your professional life. Tell it as it is.)

2   In no more than 600 words use the example you have given as the basis from which to characterize life as you experience it daily in the clinical setting. Here you can use bullet points within a framework of flowing prose.

3   We shall then write a tail piece which picks out the key characteristics and particularly the values that emerge from everyone's contributions, together with any interesting differences. (So if you know someone else who is doing this, please don't talk about the details of yours.)

4   We shall then draw out the implications of this for all those who educate postgraduate doctors in the clinical setting.

Note
We acknowledge that while our comments in the commentaries that follow the stories are based firmly on the texts they provided, it is possible that our personal knowledge of these individuals has also flavoured our appreciation of their work.

Linda's story: cancelling a patient's operation on the day of surgery

It takes more than just knowing about the condition and being able to do *the operation.*
   Linda de Cossart, Consultant Vascular and General Surgeon, March 2004

The case
It was a Tuesday morning at 8 a.m. and I arrived to review the patients on my all-day operating list. The previous Friday I had reviewed the list and it showed a patient with an abdominal aortic aneurysm from my vascular waiting list and two patients from the common waiting list for thyroid surgery. On the Monday I had been working away from the Trust. Late on the previous Friday, one of the patients listed for thyroid surgery had phoned to cancel their operation because of a concurrent medical problem. In order not to miss the operating space a patient requiring recurrent incisional hernia surgery was included to fill the space left by the cancellation. This new patient was admitted to the ward on the Monday and consented by the trainees ready for theatre on the Tuesday. I enquired why another thyroid case had not been added and was told that this patient was next on the list. I visited the patient for the hernia repair on the ward. His case notes were very thick and were being read very carefully by the consultant anaesthetist. I observed that the patient walked with a stick and he told me that he was very disabled with joint problems. After a short conversation with him it seemed to me that both he and I were less informed than we should be about his surgical problem. This was my first knowledge of him. His understanding of the possible postoperative events that might complicate his recovery was very limited. I made the decision to postpone his case and arranged to see him again the following Friday in my outpatient clinic. There was a feeling abroad that I was over-reacting.

At the outpatients clinic the patient and I had a long conversation and I added to the information he already knew about the consequences of such surgery. He was booked for the following week, was admitted and had an uneventful operation. Postoperatively he was cared for on the high dependency unit. Thirty-six hours post surgery he suffered a respiratory collapse and **Computerized Tomography** (CT) scan confirmed multiple pulmonary emboli. He was anticoagulant. Forty-eight hours later he had a bleed into his abdominal wall, which required his emergency return to theatre and a postoperative period on the intensive care unit. He subsequently made a satisfactory recovery and was discharged home. His comments about his care were that he had had a very scary time but he had felt that at all times the doctors and nurses had kept him informed and that we had had his best interests at heart. The Trust nevertheless earned a black mark for an operation cancelled on the day.

Being a surgeon daily involves far more than following protocols, doing surgery, and ensuring that targets are met. In this event I exercised a level of professional judgement which was greater than that based on a clinical decision-making strategy. Such a strategy provides a diagnosis and a plan of action to treat based on history taking, examination and investigation. This locks the patient into a care pathway designed to result in timely and efficient treatment. This patient was inside such a process. But it was not personalized to him. It took no account of the fact that he was a high-risk patient with an uncommon and complex problem. I was perfectly capable of doing an appropriate operation, but I was not convinced it was appropriate for him.

My professional judgement resulting in my action on the day was informed by:

- my factual knowledge about the patient's condition extended by my wider exploration of it on the day (he was disabled and 'unfit' and therefore a higher risk than many, and crucially more than the thyroid case that he had replaced on the list);
- my personal knowledge of the procedural reasons why he had been added to the list at short notice and the potential mistakes that can be made through trying to 'be efficient' rather than concentrating on the specific needs of the patient;
- my professional responsibility as consultant and therefore the most senior clinician managing the case, to be sure that the things that had gone on before my intervention surgically were as sound as they could be – and if they were not, to do something about it;
- my previous experience in recognizing that if I felt uncomfortable about a case (even if I could not entirely explain why) I should take very careful stock of things before inflicting more injury (the operation and its subsequent consequences) on the patient;

- my personal knowledge of my trainee staff, who lacked my experience and intuitive feel, who were responding to the need to fill the list, and who I felt may not have appreciated all the potential consequences of proceeding unprepared;
- my ability to be able to 'break the rules' and be able to justify why;
- my recognition that my responsibility was first to the patient;
- my knowledge that I am morally accountable and will be held professionally answerable for the process of care of this patient;
- my belief that where such a duty of care is in conflict with Trust targets, the patient's welfare must come first;
- the courage to conduct myself professionally in the face of pressures to conform.

Commentary

This story demonstrates, in Linda's actions and the thinking that underlay these, her commitment to (valuing of) the best interest of the patient above those of the Trust and her own self-interest. This is a key value which almost all professionals would aspire to. In maintaining this priority she has to resist the demands of targets and the associated pressures from the management systems, stand firm in the face of her sense that her peers were critical of her, and even allow it to be thought that she has let down those whose education she is responsible for (and to whom she will have to explain) because they had unwisely consented the patient and she could not help but draw attention to this. These pressures are considerable. The timing of the cancellation has severe consequences for the hospital, which will lose revenue and increase its waiting lists, both of which are politically very sensitive areas in today's NHS. Her language (earning 'a black mark' and 'over-reacting') shows the strength of these pressures on her.

The story also shows how she is caught between conflicting values (the patient, the Trust, her peers and her colleagues) and how important it is in the face of these that she can think clearly, and be sure which principles and values she will hold to *on this occasion*. These are not easy choices, and professionals have to consider them in respect of every case, because the context will change the arguments, though the *principles* (of commitment to patient care as the priority) will apply in all cases.

Linda clearly values the partnership in which a multi-professional team cares for a patient, but on this occasion, she values even more the importance of 'going out on a limb' about the patient whose entire well-being as an individual overrides the importance of supporting the decisions of her colleagues. Her discussion with the patient also shows her valuing of empathetic communication between doctor and patient.

Doctors have to be able to explain their actions (as Linda does), but even then they rarely talk directly about values (any more than she does). Curriculum designers need to consider whether a curriculum for medical practice should help learners to be alert to the implications of their own values and those of the profession they belong to, and if so, how they might do so.

Linda's subsequent thoughts about all this are further revealing. They illustrate her valuing of professional judgement as opposed to 'following protocols'. She highlights how her judgement went well beyond what she calls the 'clinical decision-making strategy', which sets out protocols for the generality of cases. She sees such protocols as locking 'the patient into a care pathway designed to result in timely and efficient treatment', but sees that this takes no account of the fact that he was a high-risk patient with an uncommon and complex problem. She notes the importance of the relationship of trust between patient and doctor (and of the role in this of clear and precise communication between staff and patients). She is concerned to treat the whole patient. But she also recognizes and values the wide-ranging accountability to which she is subject. And she is sensitive to its moral thrust.

Interestingly, she also values, and indeed listens carefully to, her intuition, recognizing that 'feeling uncomfortable' about a case is an important indicator of some underlying (and potentially serious) factors; and being aware that other staff (who perhaps lacked her 'experience and intuitive feel') may not have appreciated all the potential consequences of proceeding unprepared. Finally, in recognizing that she needed to exercise it, she acknowledges her own (moral) courage.

It is true that the word 'values' does not appear anywhere in Linda's story. But nonetheless it is values that drive her actions and thoughts.

Rosie's story: an elderly lady in acute distress

Rosie Lusznat, Consultant in Old Age Psychiatry, April 2004

The case
An elderly lady (aged 77) was referred urgently to me for psychiatric opinion by the medical team at the local general hospital because she was (in their words):

- 'completely non-responsive, even to mild pain';
- 'not eating or drinking';
- 'wanting to be left to die'.

She had been admitted with hypothermia following a collapse at home ten days earlier. Investigations so far (including CT scan and neurological assessment) had revealed no abnormality.

When I visited the lady, she was in bed but responsive, talkative, friendly and cooperative. She gave me a rather rambling account of the circumstances leading up to her admission. There was a strong paranoid flavour to her account, and slight disorientation for place and time. Her mood was variable and she was preoccupied with death. She wanted to return home as quickly as possible.

After my interview, she became aggressive towards the nursing staff and demanded to see me again. I saw her as being agitated and frightened. She insisted on me taking her away under police escort and revealed that she had just heard a voice saying 'next time you'd better use a revolver'. I immediately arranged transfer to my own psychiatric assessment ward located at another hospital.

Reflection

This case is not unusual as it illustrates a number of features common to everyday practice in Old Age Psychiatry:

- the complex nature of many presentations including both psychiatric and physical aspects;
- the unpredictable nature of many psychiatric conditions (and my working life in general!);
- the need for risk-taking (and risk management);
- the crucial role of communication with a wide range of people – the patient, carers and other health care professionals.

More particularly, my judgements illustrate the need to make (and frequently review) decisions at different stages, often based on little evidence. My thinking was as follows.

1   Although the information in the initial referral was scanty there were 'pointers' which made me decide that this needed urgent attention. These were:

- the patient was described by the acute ward staff as 'non-responsive' suggesting either an organic or a severe depressive episode;
- the potentially unsuitable nature of the environment provided by an acute ward and (based on previous experience) the inability of the medical staff there to deal appropriately with a patient such as this;
- the potential danger to the patient of dehydration/starvation/suicide.

2   Since 48 hours had elapsed before my visit, and in view of the limited information available to me, I decided to review the medical notes and speak to the nursing staff and the referring doctor on my arrival at the ward. This revealed vital further information regarding events prior to admission (blindness, failed eye operations, treatment for depression/insomnia). When I saw the patient she was no longer unresponsive, was taking adequate food and fluids but had become agitated, confused, aggressive and psychotic.

3   The patient initially questioned my reason for seeing her but when I explained my role and intentions she appeared reassured and talked freely about her recollection of events, as well as her concerns, fears and hearing voices. She clearly trusted me, which became even more apparent when, following the interview, she refused to cooperate with the nursing staff and insisted on me taking her with me.

4   During my interview with the patient I had formulated an initial management plan, including further investigations, antidepressant treatment and discharge home with active follow-up by my own community team. I wanted to avoid transfer to a psychiatric ward and further unsettling the patient who had already been moved three times within the general hospital. However, interviewing her made me review my plan very quickly! There was no doubt in my mind that she required care that was not available within the acute hospital.

5   I spent the next hour reassuring the patient, finding a bed, negotiating with nursing staff at my own hospital and one of my consultant colleagues, communicating the decision to the medical staff both verbally and in writing, and liaising with the patient's daughter. Inevitably I had to cancel my next appointment!

The outcome

This lady spent the first day in the psychiatric ward resting and sleeping. She made an excellent recovery and was discharged home a month later with a package of care including attendance at our day hospital and bereavement counselling. I saw her a week after discharge. She appeared well, happy to be home, and extremely grateful. We are currently awaiting the results of a repeat brain scan to exclude (or confirm) a possible stroke as causing her initial collapse.

Commentary

Rosie is a consultant in Old Age Psychiatry – on the face of it at the very opposite extreme of medical practice from a surgeon, yet her story is very similar to Linda's. She comments that this case is not unusual, with many features common to her practice more widely. She notes that the case was complicated in having both psychiatric and physical elements. It was unpredictable – it was difficult, if not impossible, to say precisely what course the condition might take. She was aware of the need to take risks – risks to the patient who could, if left, have committed suicide, as well as risks to the service, with the costs of transfer and admission for a month to a psychiatric hospital possibly being unwarranted if the patient's conditions turned out to be physical.

Like Linda, Rosie had to call upon (and clearly values the importance of) professional judgement. Her story points up the complexity of the judgements that doctors have to make on the one hand, and the flimsiness of both the signals that call for such judgements and the evidence which supports them. As Rosie puts it 'my judgements illustrate the need to make (and to review frequently) decisions at different stages, often based on little evidence'. She notes that there were what she calls 'pointers' that she says 'made me decide that this needed urgent attention'.

Rosie, like Linda, values highly good communication, and particularly listening to the patient. The significant feature of the judgement that Rosie made occurred with a review of the notes (revealing elements of the case which had not been thought by the acute staff as important to communicate) and the long conversation she had with the patient (which revealed the extent of the patient's concerns and fears, and that she was hearing voices).

A key feature of Rosie's story is the recognition of the frequent need to review judgements made. She clearly values highly what might be called 'seeking to get these as right as possible' in a volatile situation, and sees this as more important than claiming to be, or being seen to be, 'right'. This meant that the initial clinical decision that Rosie had formulated when originally speaking with the ward staff and on first meeting the patient, not to transfer her to the psychiatric hospital, was later able to be recognized as inappropriate. Her later judgement was that rapid transfer was in fact indicated. And she shows the conflicting values web in which she is caught when she describes her decision as constrained by the costs involved, the necessity of finding a bed, 'negotiating with nursing staff at my own hospital and one of my consultant colleagues, communicating the decision to the medical staff both verbally and in writing, and liaising with the patient's daughter'. And of course the time pressures (also apparent in Linda's story) merely compound the complexities of all this.

Patrizia's story: 'Just do it!'

Patrizia Capozzi, SHO in Surgery, April 2004

The case

I am a surgical senior house officer on a Basic Surgical Training scheme. I am currently in my first six months of general surgery and have previously completed six months Accident and Emergency and six months in Orthopaedics.

I was on call on a Friday evening. I got bleeped from Theatre 2 for an emergency Laparotomy on a 68-year-old man with small bowel obstruction. Because I had been busy since taking over from the day on-call I didn't know what needed to be done in theatre. I contacted the house officer on call to make sure all was OK and to let them know where we would be if there was a problem.

I went to the ward to see the patient to ensure all was ready and that he had been consented. There I met the patient and his wife for the first time. I very briefly introduced myself and ensured the patient knew what was going to happen. Almost immediately the theatre staff then arrived for him. At the same time I bleeped the registrar to tell him that the patient would be ready imminently.

I quickly changed into scrubs and went to Theatre 2. The patient was already anaesthetized and the theatre was ready. I scrubbed, gowned and gloved in preparation. But there was no sign of the registrar. The scrub nurse and I prepped the patient for the laparotomy. This involved the correct preparation and appropriate draping.

The registrar appeared. He was drinking coffee and seemed in no hurry to get scrubbed. I said, 'Come on John, we're waiting for you,' but he replied, 'You go ahead and start.' Quite taken aback by his command I explained that I had never made the first incision for a laparotomy and suggested that perhaps he would rather I wait until he was scrubbed and present?

Although I didn't want him to take over because this was the opportunity I wanted, I was hesitant to do anything without him being at the table as a clinical supervisor. I sought reassurance about the position of the incision. He said, 'Come on, you've been involved in plenty of these, just do it, you know you can.' Two other members of the theatre team (the scrub nurse and anaesthetist) also actively encouraged me.

I cautiously moved around the operating table from the patient's left side to the right – the operating surgeon's side. It felt new and odd being on this side when everything had been so familiar to me when on the left side as the assistant. I hadn't been aware that I had become so used to being in a certain place, but I obviously had. I looked up at the scrub nurse, who was now standing across from me, took the scalpel he offered and checked that the anaesthetist was happy for me to begin.

So I started, feeling positive, having belief in myself, but somewhat hesitantly.

The unexpected nature of this event helped me take a large step in my surgical progress.

Reflection

My clinical job is diverse and differs on a daily basis. Although some aspects are constant (ward rounds, daily duties on the ward, clinics and theatre sessions) the content varies widely and each day is unique because each patient is different. It is emotional, busy, practical, fascinating, exciting, stimulating, challenging work. It is endlessly unpredictable.

My job is physically and mentally demanding. It is unusual to have a moment to collect your thoughts before another bleep or question. My surgical training involves me in both elective and emergency operations. On-call duties will often require a visit to emergency theatre to assist in an operation when you might not have necessarily seen the patient or know the history. This is routine practice. The elective theatre lists are an opportunity for the surgical team to work together and develop, over time, practical skills and knowledge.

As part of this I take considerable responsibility for patients and junior members of the team. My clinical work involves interaction with a huge number of professionals, and we interact in a variety of ways (verbal interaction, written referrals and reviews, multi-discipline meetings, informal conversations in the corridor). Each relationship is unique and requires different skills.

The relationships I have with patients are again entirely different. There is a degree of intimacy due to the nature of the job, a need for absolute confidentiality, respect and trust. Meetings may be only a few minutes in length or relationships develop over months of care. Often you are meeting a person at a time when their need is so great, they are frightened, vulnerable and need help.

In developing as a surgeon, there is far more to learn than just the operating procedures.

Commentary

Patrizia's story offers a case of the values of a learner in clinical practice. Indeed, we see her here when she is learning to operate, and finding her skills, knowledge and thinking being put on the line. But what also comes through this story, as it has through the previous two, is that whenever a doctor's expertise is 'on the line' (as it almost always is), then the kind of person you are also plays a central role. And the kind of person you are is very much about the matters that you value. (Cultivating a learner is about nurturing the whole person, and recognizing the significance in this of their values. This has huge implications for curriculum designers.)

Patrizia's narrative begins when she is on call on a Friday evening – a notoriously busy time (not least because doctors in the community tend to admit potentially urgent cases that then might become acute and more demanding for them over the weekend).

Her careful documenting of the lead-up to the emergency operation shows attention to and concern for the patient. What comes through here (though it is not said, but rather is demonstrated in her actions) are empathy and compassion for the patient, fuelled by imagination, but not over-identification.

Once properly scrubbed and ready in theatre, she is 'quite taken aback' at being told by the registrar to go ahead with the operation, never having made the first incision for a laparotomy before. She is in two minds. This is a rare opportunity to gain vital experience, but she feels bound to remind her supervisor (in case he had forgotten) that this is new territory for her. She is torn between seizing a special chance for herself, getting it right for the patient and being honest with her supervisor. But (as the registrar clearly knows) you can only learn by doing, and he almost surprises her into it, knowing perhaps that she needed to get the feel not only of the new side of the table but also of 'feeling confident, having belief in myself'.

Reflection on the event teaches her that its unexpected nature 'helped me take a large step in my surgical progress'. She had been given real, authentic experience, but only because she was prepared to rise to the unexpected, to be flexible, to stay open-minded – even to value the diverse and unpredictable. She values too the idea that each day is unique because each patient is different. Her breathless and enthusiastic list of adjectives ('emotional, busy, practical, fascinating, exciting, stimulating, challenging') shows how she relishes it all.

She also values the 'interaction with a huge number of professionals . . . in a variety of ways', and implicitly recognizes the wide range of communicative abilities that this calls upon. Indeed, she is alert to just how much there is to learn beyond operating procedures.

Cath's story: the essence of my job

Cath Fazey, Theatre Sister, April 2004

The case
I am a Theatre Sister with more years of experience than I care to admit. Since November 2003 I have been working as Emergency Surgery Co-ordinator. The essence of my job means that I have to anticipate and manage the flow of emergency operations. The order of cases can change several times during the day depending on priority; major emergencies can arrive in theatre at very short notice. This is work I usually enjoy and find satisfying.

One day a few weeks ago I arrived to start my day at 8.00 a.m. and soon realized it would be a different and challenging day. There were two patients in the department both critically ill, being cared for in the theatre suite as there were no intensive care beds available [in the North West Region]. One patient was being cared for by the recovery staff, the second was in his bed *in* my operating theatre! This meant we would not be able to carry out any surgery until the patient in theatre was found an **Intensive Treatment Unit** (ITU) bed, and the emergency anaesthetist and my team would be needed to care for him. If a dire emergency occurred an elective list would have to be stopped.

Once we had assessed the situation my flexible team quickly adopted the roles best suited to their abilities: the anaesthetic support worker used his skill in caring for the patient in theatre, and assisted the anaesthetist; our very capable support worker became a 'go for'; and I became the general organizer and liaison between the two groups, while also taking care of the relatives belonging to both patients.

Although this was different from the norm it still called upon personal characteristics and ways of working that are typical of my professional role. These are:

- communicator;
- organizer;
- teacher;
- supervisor;
- team worker.

In no particular order the list covers most of my professional/clinical work. The amount of time given to each varies with each day, as do the workload, time frame, and the complexity and variety of the cases on the emergency list.

A significant part of my working day is spent trying to be certain everyone involved in emergency surgery is aware of what is happening in the theatre, so that surgeons know when they are needed, and the ward staff know to have the patients ready for theatre. On a good day this should ensure minimum delay between cases and best use of available operating time. I speak directly to medical and theatre staff in the department; and to the wards, X-ray and medical staff on the telephone and via the bleep system.

On this day I used my wider experience of the hospital in general, when locating and talking to people I do not normally deal with. I was a little surprised to find that when I called the chaplain my own parish priest arrived (he was standing in for the hospital chaplain who was on holiday). This made my dealing with that patient's relatives a little easier. I also worked with the transplant coordinator as the other patient had died and was to become an organ donor. I was with his family when this was discussed and together with the coordinator helped to arrange the best time for the transplant team to come.

Reflection
Organization of people, skills, equipment and time is a capability I need in order to manage the flow of work through the emergency theatre. It is like fitting the pieces of a jigsaw together. Some days it only requires a basic ability, but on other days, despite my own and the team's best efforts, the pieces fail to fit. I often get involved with things unrelated to my own theatre. I have worked in theatre for a long time and am a useful resource. If I do not know the answer to a question, I usually know someone who does.

My team normally includes an inexperienced member of staff and often students. Teaching is an ongoing process. Sometimes it is formal, but more commonly involves practical experience, demonstration and explanation, scrubbing up, or circulating to give support with unfamiliar or complex cases. It is rewarding to see someone I have taught working with skill and confidence.

Another aspect of my role is supervising, and monitoring the team. We all work to standards and policies, and need to be aware of health and safety, clinical risk and accountability. I try to do this in a supportive way.

The emergency team is small and we have a busy and varied workload, so working together is important. When I scrub up alone, it can be the least stressful part of my day!

Commentary

Cath's story develops much that is introduced by the other three about clinical work involving liaising (and being concerned with relating in different ways) with a wide variety of people. The situation she describes happened when she arrived at work one morning to find that two critically ill patients were being cared for in the theatre suite (one of them in the theatre itself) because intensive care beds were not available. This has potentially far-reaching consequences similar to those that Linda describes in her story.

Cath's practice involves a large number of people from a wide range of backgrounds in many different departments within (and outside) the hospital, as well as work with patients and relatives. She characterizes this as 'fitting the pieces of a jigsaw together' but admits that 'some days . . . the pieces fail to fit'. As do the previous three writers, Cath values the human and unpredictable. She does not look for perfection where it cannot be found, although she clearly strives to enact her values and ideals to the very best of her abilities even in extreme circumstances.

In addition, she explicitly recognizes that, because the team includes inexperienced staff, 'teaching is an ongoing process, sometimes formal but more commonly practical demonstration and explanation, scrubbing up or circulating to give support with unfamiliar or complex cases'. This recognition reminds us that all practitioners are also teachers all the time, whether they realize it or not.

Acting, knowing, thinking and the values that drive these in practice

Running through these stories are several threads that begin to reveal the true nature of practice. The brief we gave our colleagues was deliberately open. We asked them to write about a small piece of their practice, yet one that typified their day-by-day working experience. They wrote independently of one another. They represent a range of professions, of grades within a profession and contrasting clinical specialties. Yet they have much in common.

These four stories suggest four interlocked facets of practice: the actions of practitioners; the knowledge they have and use; the thinking (including their learning) that enables them to act in the way they do; and beneath all these the values, principles and ideals that drive the whole of their practice. Although they are indivisible in practice, we shall look at each in turn.

Acting in practice

Each of our colleagues shows, from the stories they relate, that their practice involved acting in certain ways. These include the following (which we explore further in Chapter 5).

- *Complexity, unpredictability, paradox and uncertainty.* While there is much that is routine about the practice of these practitioners, all four are acutely aware that this is not their ultimate *raison d'être*. Rather, they are there precisely for those situations they describe, and these are characterized by complexity, unpredictability, paradox and uncertainty. They need to be prepared to expect the unexpected – to be 'surprised' (Schön 1987a). Each situation they face can become 'hedged around with competing alternatives' (Coles *et al.* 2003). Rather than following predetermined formulae or instruction, they do their thoughtful best.
- *Improvisation.* As each of these practitioners tells their story, they reveal that their practice is centrally concerned with responding to the particular needs of the people involved, be they patients, relatives or other staff. While each situation they describe has a technical element, each practitioner utilizes their expertise flexibly. They are adaptable in their actions.
- *Not acting.* A central feature of practice may be non-action, may involve not saying or doing something in a particular situation as compared with what they might have done in another similar one. Sometimes, the correct way of acting may be to do and say precisely nothing.
- *Community action.* Each of our colleagues recounts the importance of acting in concert with others, in a community of action. They describe a strong sense of community, and not just one that involves their immediate colleagues but a wider sense of belonging, both with others with whom they must relate in their immediate setting but also with those outside it, as well as others who have formed part of the tradition of their practice.
- *Acting as being.* The actions of these practitioners go beyond thinking about specifics and carrying out particular activities. They represent a way of being and of treating others as whole persons. This is because as caring practitioners they value and prioritize wise ways of knowing, being and thinking.

Knowing in practice

Our colleagues also demonstrate a range of forms of knowing in their practice (and we elaborate further on this in Chapter 6).

- *Formal knowing.* Each has a clear and sound base of formal knowledge, including technical aspects of their practice. They are well versed in the textbook knowledge of their specialty and their profession to the point where it is tacit. But actually this forms a smaller part of the whole knowledge they draw on than is realized.
- *Procedural knowing.* Similarly, these stories demonstrate that each practitioner has, literally in some instances at his or her fingertips, certain procedural skills and abilities. Yet, like their formal knowledge, these appear to form a kind of backdrop to their practice. They are the 'given' of what they do and say.
- *Intuition and hunch.* A crucial element of the knowing in practice comprises what might be called 'intuition' or 'hunch'. Each story contains an element where the practitioners sensed what was happening, or had some kind of 'gut feeling' about what was needed.
- *Knowledge of people.* Each, too, reveals a knowledge of people (both patients and colleagues), and of the human and humane situations that they find themselves in. This involves not just recognition but understanding, empathy and compassion.
- *Organizational knowledge.* In addition to a knowledge of people, they clearly possess an organizational knowledge, which goes beyond merely knowing *about* the organization. They know how their particular organization operates, and how this affects those within it.
- *Managerial knowing.* Similarly, on occasions, practice for these people involved knowing the managerial systems within which they work and *how* and *when* to question or cut across what might be considered to be 'the official management line'. Thus the risks they had to take were not merely 'clinical'.

Thinking in practice

This third element of practice was clearly evident. Each of our colleagues was actively engaged in complex thinking (see also Chapter 5).

- *Mindful practice.* For these practitioners, their practice is mindful. It is thoughtful, sensible and principled – they do things with clear reason. It is justified practice. They do not blindly follow the protocol or rulebook. Indeed they find they cannot. The situations they faced necessitated thinking it through, often changing their mind, possibly going against what others might consider 'right'.

- *Asking uncomfortable questions.* On occasions, our colleagues had to ask uncomfortable questions (of themselves and of others) and sometimes were *faced* with uncomfortable questions. This was routine, and something they had learned to cope with.
- *Decision-making.* Each had to make decisions in the situations they found themselves in. These decisions could be at two levels: clinical and professional decisions about what was the best thing to do; and managerial and humane decisions about what was actually feasible. The values basis of these decisions was not lost on them. They recognized the importance and complexity of the judgements they made.
- *Teaching and learning.* These accounts demonstrate that a clear thread about teaching and learning runs through all clinical practice. On occasions it is unclear who the teacher is and who is the learner. These roles appear to rotate, to flow back and forth. For example in Patrizia's story, a registrar's decision to delay entering the operating theatre was probably a strategic one, to allow her the opportunity to move forward in her development as a surgeon – to 'go for it'.

The values endemic to medical practice

Our four contributors have helpfully illustrated the visible or explicit actions that are central to their practice, which can be seen both within their stories and which, by implication, are visible in their practice more generally. They have illuminated this further by telling us about the knowledge, the thinking processes and the feelings that lay invisible and implicit under the surface of their actions.

None of them, however, refers directly to the values that drive these. They are tacit (so deep beneath practice and so much a part of their very being that they are no longer consciously in touch with them). And yet these are the very drivers of their practice, which is why our commentary on each story seeks to begin to uncover them. It is also why curriculum designers need to understand and provide for the needs of learners in respect of values.

Broadly the values which we could see beneath our contributors' practice fall into the following categories. They value:

- working with and treating patients holistically;
- being a partner with patients and colleagues in providing the best possible care;
- being trustworthy and respecting the moral and ethical nature of the patient/doctor relationship;
- attending carefully to honest and clear communications with patients;
- striving for excellence even in the face of the impossible;

- recognizing the importance of accountability in maintaining standards in practice;
- continuing to learn and to develop and refine practice;
- the ability to call upon a wide range of ways of knowing;
- professional judgement as crucial to decision-making;
- the exercise of practical wisdom in all circumstances.

Interestingly, these are very similar to the values made explicit in *The Curriculum Framework for the SCP* (DoH 2005a: 8), which in turn are modelled upon the RCS Eng's draft curriculum for surgical SHOs, which the college developed between 2002 and 2004, but never published as a formal document.

Previously, in Fish and Coles (1998), we proposed a metaphor for practice – that of an iceberg. Our observations now reinforce the view that this is a helpful way of depicting medical practice, and we offer this in Figure 4.1. What

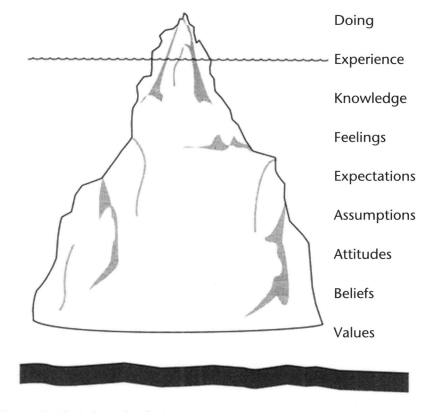

Doing

Experience

Knowledge

Feelings

Expectations

Assumptions

Attitudes

Beliefs

Values

Figure 4.1   The iceberg of professional practice.

others observe of someone's practice is that small part of the iceberg that lies above the surface. This depicts what a doctor says and does. However, as with an iceberg, what lies above the surface is 'buoyed up' by what lies beneath. In our view, there is a huge and complex body of support for one's professional practice. And at the base of this, colouring it all, are values.

Implications for curriculum designers

The four stories we have recounted in this chapter show that society's expect-ations of practice in health care situations are not just unrealistic; they are seriously misinformed. They fail to appreciate the nature of practice. They see it as scientific. Designers of a curriculum for practice must beware of falling into such a trap, of undervaluing values, and of ignoring the need to foster them. The curriculum must find ways of acknowledging their importance and offering ways in which they can be recognized and cultivated in learners. Designers must decide in respect of the future practice of medicine whether the curriculum should do no more than accept traditional values, or encourage the extension of some and replacement of others. This is a profound responsi-bility, shaping as it will, what will drive the conduct of a whole profession. We recommend the following as a starting point:

- devise ways of unearthing and exploring the values endemic to practice so that practitioners not only recognize and acknowledge their values but perceive them as an essential basis for their practice;
- declare in the definitive document the values of the curriculum and the profession;
- recognize explicitly, where relevant in the definitive document, the values of those in the design team;
- offer a language in which teacher and learner might discuss their profes-sion's values and their own, and consider the similarities and differences between these;
- promote reflective practice as a means of teaching, learning and assess-ment (since reflection is after all what our four contributors have engaged in at our request specifically here, and which we have drawn out further, perhaps also drawing on our own knowledge of them);
- use this chapter and the following one, together with other relevant litera-ture (Tallis 2004: Ch. 9; de Cossart and Fish 2005: Chs 2 and 5) to foster further explorations of values.

End note

Our colleagues know that medicine is not an exact science. They have shown that in their practice they face complex and unpredictable situations where there is considerable uncertainty not just as to the actions they need to take but also in the very nature of the problems themselves. Above all they know that they must take risks – that their judgement is central to their practice – and that for this they can never be fully prepared. The definition of 'medical practice' implicit in the public's view is almost the opposite of what is really the case. Medical practice actually happens when the guidelines and protocols that practitioners have at their fingertips for dealing with the generalities of practice no longer apply in the particular situation that they are faced with. This is why they are there – to deal with these kinds of uncertainties, and to take these kinds of risks. It is why they undertake a lengthy undergraduate and postgraduate education.

In the next chapter we explore these matters further by referring to the literature. We look to see whether the conclusions we have reached with just four of our colleagues resonate more widely, not just in medicine but in the practice of other caring professionals. For the moment we merely reiterate our aim in these two chapters, which is to consider the nature of professional practice. This will then enable readers to consider: what kind of curricular framework will support practitioners as they learn to practise in these ways and in this context; and how such a curriculum framework can ensure that current practice will develop further in the future.

5 Analysing the context: the nature of practice in medicine – a survey of the field

Exactly what characterizes professional expertise in medicine?
What is the nature of medical practice in clinical settings?
What do we mean by 'a practice' generally within the professional context?
How can the elements of this expertise be supported and developed in postgraduate doctors?
What traditions and practices are currently central to the context in which the programme will be offered? And what view of these should the curriculum take?
What key medical practices should this curriculum help practitioners to develop?

Introduction

Without an understanding and appreciation of the nature of the practice in question and its underlying values, a curriculum for that practice can never be soundly based. In the previous chapter we presented accounts of incidents that four of our colleagues had experienced which typified their practice, and drew out from these the values base. But one concern that might be felt by readers about this is that what we have presented might be atypical or have been fashioned for us to help us make some narrowly partisan point. However, as this chapter shows, our colleagues' stories of and comments upon practice are well supported in the published literature.

What characterizes professional expertise in medicine?

In order to explore the expertise of doctors, we have drawn on various literary sources to show what doctors have to cope with in practice and how they do so. We have treated these matters under the following headings:

- complexity, unpredictability, paradox and uncertainty;
- professional judgement and its centrality to professional practice;
- complications (fallibility and error).

Complexity, unpredictability, paradox and uncertainty

The following case history vividly reveals as key components the complexity and unpredictability that are inherent in medical practice.

In October 1994, Michael Foulkes, a schizophrenic patient, known to be violent and with a history of psychiatric illness stretching back eight years, was seen by a consultant psychiatrist at an outpatient clinic in London and that night murdered a young woman, Susan Miller. In the UK, while there are estimated to be about 2700 such patients detained in hospital, it is estimated that 1200 are 'conditionally discharged ... under active supervision in the community' (Astal *et al.* 1998). Michael Foulkes was one such patient.

The report of the Mental Health Inquiry that followed these tragic events stated: 'We take into account that Michael Foulkes's case was one amongst many difficult cases and that the pressures inherent in the management of this case were not isolated but should be seen against the backcloth of the clinicians' stressful caseload' (Astal *et al.* 1998: 1).

While recognizing the dangers of judging such a case with the benefit of hindsight, the Inquiry panel said that in approaching the writing of their report they:

> Summarised the beginning of Michael Folkes's mental illness and the psychiatric interventions before 1986 ... [examined] the whole sequence of [his] care both as an in-patient and an outpatient ... Have chosen to examine in greater depth issues such as Michael's housing, his aftercare and his occupations. Lastly ... what we felt to be areas deserving of special attention [were] the Probation Service, Forensic Community Psychiatric Nursing, the role of Social Services, the Police's relationship with the mentally disordered offender, and the subject of bereavement. We have devoted considerable time and attention to the chapter on the Mental Health Act as the interpretation of its provision, and the impact which it has upon the clinical

management of patients, permeated virtually all of the major issues with which we were concerned.

(Astal *et al.* 1998: 1–2)

They add that:

During this Inquiry some major issues have surfaced. Amongst the most important have been the continuing need for appropriate housing for vulnerable mentally disordered offenders, the importance and use of [appropriate medication], the need for effective multi-agency working and the efficient flow of information and communication within the Aftercare team.

(Astal *et al.* 1998: 2)

The report notes in particular that the nature of the patient's housing was, in their view, a crucial component of the community care that the patient received, as it 'affected the number of opportunities the Aftercare team had to observe him, and influenced the quality of information upon which the team members based their assessments of his mental state' (Astal *et al.* 1998: 2). Against this background the Inquiry makes a very important observation that is central to our discussion in this chapter of the nature of clinical practice, important because it applies not just to the rather specialized field of forensic psychiatry but to professional practice generally:

Each decision made in the care and treatment of a mentally disordered person involves risk ... There are no simple answers. The complexity and the difficulty of the balancing exercise which clinicians have to make daily as the guardians of the patient's health and the public safety, should not be underestimated ... Clinicians are often placed in an invidious position forced to choose between options which are not ideal.

(Astal *et al.* 1998: 2)

This case first points out (and thus points to) the significance of complexity in medical practice. The kinds of situations that doctors and other health professionals are called upon to work in are complex and unpredictable. Schön (1983) characterized professional practice as 'the swampy lowlands', which aptly captures its basic nature. He added that the problems professional people face are seldom straightforward and more often than not 'indeterminate': not only is the solution to the problem unclear but the very nature of the problem itself is often difficult to determine. Practice is 'messy'.

However, patients' problems are not the only complexity. As was shown by the Mental Health Inquiry just outlined above, there are often huge numbers of people from many different services involved that clinicians must take into account. The context in which an individual patient's case may be embedded can sometimes be enormously complicated.

As well as being complex at the outset, sometimes more complex than practitioners are aware of (or have time to notice because of competing pressures from patients or political imperatives to conform or 'deliver'), practice is at the same time unpredictable. A practitioner cannot be certain that what is happening at one moment will be the same the next. Not only might the patient's condition change suddenly but other information may come to light (from another health professional, from the patient's notes, from a relative, from the patient, or from practitioners' observations of the setting in which they find themselves) that could change the whole nature of the problem and quite possibly the course of action that needs to be taken.

The complexity of the social setting of health care must not be overlooked. We have shown in all the cases cited above the numbers of people involved and the various backgrounds they come from. Doctors don't talk just to other doctors. They talk with many other people. And each person has his or her own particular background and way of approaching the situation at hand, which potentially makes their responses unpredictable. Sometimes this variety can be illuminating in managing the problem and of great assistance in dealing with it, with the benefit of the many perspectives being provided. Other differences can be highly constraining to the resolution of the problem. For example, people bring what is in common parlance called 'baggage' to situations – personal beliefs, assumptions, expectations and values – and this needs to be articulated and understood ('unpacked') in the course of dealing with the problem.

As a result, all practitioners face uncertainty (Hunter 1996). In medicine it is the core predicament – its 'ground state' (Gawande 2002: 229). It follows naturally from the complexity and the unpredictability of the problems facing professional practitioners. When a patient enters a consulting room, when one is admitted to the emergency department, when a doctor visits a patient at home, there will always be uncertainty – not just of what to expect, or what will unfold, but about what to do: 'We look for medicine to be an orderly field of knowledge and procedure. But it is not. It is . . . an enterprise of constantly changing knowledge, uncertain information, fallible individuals, and at the same time lives on the line' (Gawande 2002: 7).

Health professionals practise with 'an abiding confidence' (Gawande 2002: 4). They have to, not simply because the public expect this of them but because they know that the margins between 'right' and 'wrong' are tantalizingly narrow. Quite probably their confidence is learned early on – often during their initial training (Sinclair 1997). It is to do partly with the characterization of medicine as 'science' with its aura of 'fact' and 'certainty', but it is also because, certainly at the present time, society has 'an unrealistic hankering for a world in which safety and compliance are total, and breaches of trust are totally eliminated' (O'Neill 2002: 19). In reality, medicine is 'an imperfect science' (Gawande 2002: 7).

An abiding confidence can, at times, appear to the outsider – the patient or another health professional, perhaps their manager or a politician – as arrogance. But this, to a large extent, is most likely a covering up for the uncertainty that all practitioners face in their practice. Admitting that you don't know is hard. Paradoxically, although patients might not like it, they prefer to hear it.

In an important series of articles written for the *British Medical Journal* in 2001, Greenhalgh and her colleagues characterize medicine as what they call 'complexity science', where 'unpredictability and paradox are ever present, and some things will remain unknowable'. They note that: 'In mechanical systems boundaries are fixed and well defined . . . Complex systems typically have fuzzy boundaries . . . This can complicate problem solving and lead to unexpected actions' (Plsek and Greenhalgh 2001: 625).

Human beings, the series suggests, 'can be viewed as composed of and operating within multiple interacting and self adjusting systems (including biochemical, cellular, physiological, psychological, and social systems)' and that 'illness arises from dynamic interaction within and between these systems, not from failure of a single component'. This means that 'health can only be maintained (or re-established) through a holistic approach that accepts unpredictability, and builds on subtle emergent forces within the overall system' (Wilson and Holt 2001: 685).

There is, these writers claim, a relationship between 'uncertainty' (because of the complexity of health care practice) and 'agreement' (among practitioners). Simple problems are associated with high levels of both certainty and agreement, and what they call 'chaotic' problems with low levels. However, they point out that most clinical situations involve 'an irreducible element of factual uncertainty and [rely] to a greater or lesser extent on intuition and the interpretation of the wider history of the illness' (Wilson and Holt 2001: 687). We in fact believe that this is true of *all* situations within a professional's practice because of the necessity to anticipate uncertainty and paradox, and to be prepared for the unexpected. Only very rarely are the problems faced in practice totally and completely either simple *or* chaotic.

An important point emerges from this: practice involves interpretation. Human beings are not machines. Health professionals interpret what they see and hear. We perceive things – and we mis-perceive them. Practice can appear illusory.

For all these reasons, we believe that it is necessary to understand that practice is a dynamic and ever-changing matter. We agree with Greenhalgh when she says that she is 'forced to reject the notion of pure objectivity, for the very existence of interpretive possibilities implies subjectivity, ambiguity and room for disagreement' (1998: 257).

Likewise, even physical events only follow 'rules' under very limited circumstances. Most of the world that we experience is a 'dappled' one – 'a world rich in different things, with different natures, behaving in different ways. The laws that describe this world are a patchwork, not a pyramid' (Cartwright 1999: 1). This is the world of practice, or rather of professional practice.

Professional judgement and its centrality to professional practice

We are arguing that the design and development of a curriculum for practice should be based on a deep understanding of the nature of that practice, which we have referred to as 'professional'. We use the term 'professional' here to mean the practice of members of a profession. We see this form of practice as distinct from the practices of other workers and other members of society (although we do not want to imply that professionals are better than other workers, merely different), and we see professional judgement as the central characteristic of such practice. What then do we mean by this?

What makes practice professional?

The crudest distinction that can be made is between the professional and the amateur. However, it is interesting to observe that today the term 'professional' is accorded to anyone whose behaviour or presentational skills show efficient expertise, but who do not necessarily have some moral dimension to their practice (as in the term 'professional killer'). By contrast, we would wish to limit the use of the term 'behaving professionally' to interactions that are efficient, well managed and which demonstrate the standards and virtues (values and morals) that we believe members of a profession aspire to.

It is interesting to note that this term, which is used so freely (and we believe indiscriminately) in broad approbation of any well completed job, is borrowed in fact from the very group – the members of professions – that society most complains about and who, as we have previously argued, are under siege from endless critical scrutiny and even inappropriate litigation (see Fish and Coles 1998). It is the work of these people we are referring to when we write about professional practice. Their professional membership is conferred under certain conditions that distinguish the member of a profession from the person who is simply 'doing a good job' in any other context. Since a curriculum for practice is intended to cultivate a professional practitioner, it is important for designers of such a curriculum to recognize what these distinguishing characteristics are. See box opposite.

Membership of a profession

A profession is an occupation. It is *specialized* work by which a living is gained.

But it is more than an occupation. It is *work for some good in society* (education, health, justice).

A member of a profession *exercises a 'good' in the service of another*, and engages in *specific activities which are appropriate to the aims of the service*.

The service that a member of a profession renders a client *cannot entirely be measured by the remuneration given*.

Members of a profession have a *theoretical basis* to their practice and draw upon a *researched body of knowledge*.

Work by a member of a profession is: *esoteric, complex, discretionary* requiring *theoretical knowledge, skill and professional judgement that ordinary people do not possess, may not wholly comprehend and cannot readily evaluate*.

Professionals have an *ethical basis* to their work. This is about much more than having a code of conduct to follow. It is about having to make on-the-spot judgements and engage in actions which are *immediate responses to complex human events*, as they are experienced. (That is, professionals create meaning *on the spot in response to a complex situation*.)

This brings with it the *moral duty* for the professional to be aware of the values (personal and professional) *that drive his/her judgements and actions* and the duty to *recognize and take account of them as part of their on-the-spot responses*.

Being aware of one's *personal and professional values is therefore vital*.

It also brings with it the need for *some autonomy of action*. This needs to be *circumscribed by the traditions within which professionals are licensed to practise*.

The capacity to perform this service depends upon retaining a *fiduciary relationship with clients* ('fiduciary' means that it is necessary for the client to put some trust in the judgement of the professional).

In the public interest, professionals also need to have a *commitment to life-long education*.

This raises important questions about the nature of professional knowledge and about how to enable someone to learn professional practice.

With acknowledgement to Freidson (1994).

If these are the key descriptions of members of a profession and how they conduct themselves, it follows that when we use the term 'professional judgement', we mean both those complex and major judgements made by members of a profession who are licensed to serve the public in this way, and also the capacity which has been cultivated in professionals to distinguish between complex and competing demands and moral ends. The nature of such judgement also needs to be centrally recognized and nurtured within a curriculum for practice.

The nature of professional judgement and its centrality to practice

By drawing on the work of de Cossart and Fish (2005), which has developed further the earlier work of Fish and Coles (1998), we offer in Figure 5.1 a way of understanding professional judgement within the broader processes of clinical thinking. de Cossart and Fish see clinical thinking as the overall process that the clinician engages in. They map three pathways of clinical thinking: from diagnosis to agreed treatment plan; within treatment; or in respect of wider clinical issues. But all pathways have as their core the components outlined in Figure 5.1.

This entire process they see as imbued at all stages with the personal professional judgement of the practitioner, which enables adjudication between competing demands of all kinds. At the start of the clinical thinking process, a complex clinical problem is construed or formulated by the doctor (whose understanding is shaped by personal and professional values, knowledge and experience). This problem triggers the need for clinical reasoning, which involves clinical and scientific investigation, and results in clinical decisions/ options. Since this is not contextualized in detail to the patient, there then follows a process of deliberation which weighs, prioritizes and responds to the context-specific demands and pressures. These emanate from: the patient's needs; the clinician's views, vision, abilities and knowledge; and the requirements and possibilities of the particular Trust. Practical wisdom (or what Aristotle calls *phronesis*) then helps the practitioner to focus on and understand the particular ethical dimensions and moral situation of this individual patient. This thinking process leads to a professional judgement, which is a decision about the best action to be taken in this particular patient's case. It is the end result of the whole process of clinical thinking. Where practical wisdom has been harnessed to consider the moral and ethical issues, the resulting activity can be referred to as wise action or what Aristotle calls *praxis* (see Carr 1995: 71). Complications can arise at any point within this process and so 'each stage, together with its associated decision-making must of course be kept under frequent review' (de Cossart and Fish 2005: 136).

de Cossart and Fish make it clear that their basic pathway (here offered in Figure 5.1), presents a simplified version of the components of a thinking process which begins with a clinical problem and ends with a plan for wise action. They emphasize the need, at all points along this pathway, to identify and weigh the salient features involved, to recognize the significance of various elements, to interpret the meaning of even the most scientific of evidence, and to continue to respond to developments and to refine or reconsider their conclusions.

The need for such endless adjudication and adjustment to decisions in the

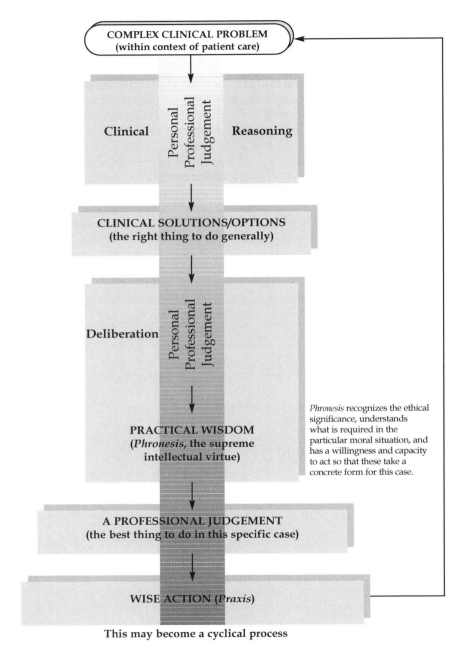

Figure 5.1 Clinical thinking: the key elements and their basic relationship (with acknowledgement to de Cossart and Fish 2005: 137).

light of complexity, ambiguity and competing demands, is what requires of the professional the capacity to exercise personal professional judgement. This de Cossart and Fish depict as the core of the whole process (that is, the core of medical practice).

They thus accord the term 'professional judgement' both to this personal capacity through which a professional processes all aspects of decisions to be made, and also to the final major product of this, the public decision itself, which is the result of practical wisdom and which leads to wise action.

These ideas (which are developed more fully in de Cossart and Fish 2005), certainly indicate the need for a curriculum for practice to recognize the significance of clinical thinking and professional judgement.

Complications

Thus far we have shown that our practice as professionals is complex, unpredictable and uncertain. Paradox is ever present. Crucially, this requires engaging in interpretation and decision-making. This makes judgement central to professional practice. However, this leaves us with some further difficulties to be faced that complicate matters. In particular, because practitioners are constrained to exercise discretion in situations of considerable uncertainty (Eraut 1994), they commit errors. But how inevitable is this?

Error and fallibility

A surgical registrar (Anwar 2004) writes that 'complications determine a clinician's performance and confidence limits. They are unfortunate events but, when they happen, they often change our lives'. His story concerns what on the face of it is a routine hip replacement operation, 'a procedure in which I was very experienced. I knew I could never go wrong'. However, halfway through the operation, he lost control of the power-saw he was using 'cutting almost twice the amount of bone I wanted to cut'. He recalls asking himself: 'That's a disaster. How could you be so careless?' He says that 'adrenaline bombarded my body. My hands trembled, and I felt fatigued and helpless. Continuing the operation became difficult'. At that moment 'a colleague rushed in to help and the problem was soon dealt with'. He said: 'Don't worry, such things happen in life. They are important and are meant to make you wiser'.

The experience left the trainee wracked with self-doubt, questioning his decision to choose a surgical career. 'Was it the right move? Perhaps it was another of those hasty decisions I often take in my life'. He recounts that the incident 'brought me face-to-face with the realities of the clinical world. Iatrogenic complications play a very important role in medicine'. He concludes by observing 'Anyway, why am I talking about my own complications when no one else does?'

Well not quite everyone! Atul Gawande has written what we consider to be a very important book with the very title *Complications* (to which he adds as an equally important subtitle *A Surgeon's Notes on an Imperfect Science*). This book is important for two reasons. First it sets out, through graphic case studies from his own clinical experience, a clear description of the nature of professional practice. The book is divided into three sections: fallibility, mystery and complexity. Second, it brings all of this to the public's attention. In our view, doctors have for too long shied away from sharing with their patients in particular and the general public at large, and not least with the media and politicians, the truth not just that their practice is far from uncomplicated but that error is inevitable. Gawande writes:

> Medicine is, I have found, a strange and in many ways disturbing business. The stakes are high, the liberties taken tremendous . . . What you find when you get in close, however – close enough to see the furrowed brows, the doubts and missteps, the failures as well as the successes – is how messy, uncertain, and also surprising medicine turns out to be.
>
> (2002: 4)

Very significantly, he adds:

> These are the moments when medicine actually happens . . . [Medicine] is an imperfect science, an enterprise of constantly changing knowledge, uncertain information, fallible individuals and at the same time lives on the line. There is science in what we do . . . but also habit, intuition, and sometimes plain old guessing. The gap between what we know and what we aim for persists. And this gap complicates everything that we do . . . As pervasive as medicine has become in modern life, it remains mostly hidden and often misunderstood. We have taken it to be both more perfect than it is and less extraordinary than it can be.
>
> (2002: 7–8)

Medical errors, or as they are termed in the UK 'adverse events' (Aylin *et al.* 2004), and which Gawande calls 'fallibility', are very common. Sometimes known as 'iatrogenic injuries', these errors have been defined as: 'An unintended act (either of omission or commission) or one that does not achieve its intended outcome' (Leape 1994: 1851).

In the UK the current definition is: 'An unintended injury caused by medical management rather than a disease process, resulting in death, life threatening illness, disability at the time of discharge, admission to hospital or prolongation of hospital stay' (Aylin *et al.* 2004: 368).

In both definitions the emphasis is on the error being 'unintended', to distinguish these events from intended harm, yet understandably they are of great concern to members of the public, and thus to national governments. In the UK a series of widely reported incidents of this kind led to a report from the DoH (1999a: 6–7) that said:

> When poor outcomes of care or mistreatment of patients occur . . . they can cause a great deal of public concern . . . In such circumstances, the public and the wider medical profession are entitled to ask: Why wasn't the problem identified earlier? Why wasn't something done about it? Why were people unwilling to raise it with the powers that be? How could such a situation have been allowed to prevail?

In the UK this report led to the establishment of the National Patient Safety Agency, which has reported that 'about 850,000 medical errors occur in NHS hospitals every year, resulting in 40,000 deaths' (Aylin *et al.* 2004: 369). Similar findings were reported ten years earlier in the USA suggesting that '180,000 people die each year partly as a result of iatrogenic injury, the equivalent of three jumbo-jet crashes every 2 days' (Leape 1994: 1851).

Gawande cites studies that show that up to 40 per cent of autopsies indicate major misdiagnoses in the cause of death, and that 'in about a third of [these] the patients would have been expected to live if proper treatment had been administered', adding that these rates 'have not improved since at least 1938' (2002: 197). For him, it is important 'to learn from knowing when our simple certainties are wrong'.

In his seminal article on error in medicine, Leape discusses the reasons why this level of 'iatrogenic injury' is not more widely reported than it is. He suggests this is partly because these are single incidents occurring across thousands of sites (unlike jumbo jet crashes) but also because there are often not well developed reporting procedures. He adds, however, that the culture of health care professions is to strive for error-free practice, with 'a powerful emphasis on perfection':

> In everyday hospital practice, the message is . . . clear: mistakes are unacceptable. Physicians are expected to function without error, an expectation that physicians translate into the need to be infallible. One result is that physicians . . . come to view an error as a failure of character – you weren't careful enough, you didn't try hard enough.
>
> (Leape 1994: 1851)

This was precisely the reaction we saw with the incident reported by Anwar which we discussed above.

*Error reduction through standardized, evidence-based and
protocol-driven practice*

Gawande discusses at some length some apparent solutions to the problem of fallibility. One, which resembles the first level of error reduction is to restrict doctors' practice to a limited number of procedures. He shows, for example, that even with the relatively straightforward procedure of hernia repair, in 10 to 15 per cent of cases the operation eventually fails. But when surgeons are specifically trained and carry out only this operation, this error rate drops to 1 per cent (Gawande 2002: 38). Thus, where the medical problem is relatively straightforward to diagnose and to treat, and where the surgeon and other members of the surgical team repeatedly carry out the same procedure, error rates can be dramatically reduced (at least in the short term).

The principle here is that medical interventions should be standardized (carried out uniformly) and based on the best available evidence. Evidence-based medicine is 'the conscious, judicious and explicit use of current best evidence in making decisions about the care of individual patients' (Sackett *et al.* 1997). In respect of this, Greenhalgh (1998: 247) notes that:

> the notion of 'evidence' in this context is generally taken to mean evidence about risk and probability derived from research studies on population samples. It relates especially (but not exclusively) to the results of randomised controlled trials and large cohort studies, which are promoted as more valid and reliable than anecdotal reports.

Greenhalgh's response to this is to take Karl Popper's view that science is concerned with the formulation and possible falsification of hypotheses 'using reproducible methods that allow the construction of generalizable statements about how the universe behaves'. She further notes that:

> Conventional medical training teaches students to view medicine as a science and the doctor as an impartial investigator who builds differential diagnoses like scientific theories and excludes competing possibilities in a manner akin to the falsification of hypotheses. Such an approach assumes the *positivist* paradigm – that there exists an external reality separate from the observer and mode of observation whose properties can be determined through measurement and experimentation (*empiricism*), and whose behaviour can subsequently be predicted from laws thus derived.
>
> (1998: 248)

She goes on to say, however, that:

those of us who practise medicine in a clinical setting . . . know all too well that clinical judgements are usually a far cry from the objective analysis of a set of eminently measurable 'facts' . . . Doctors do not simply assess symptoms and physical signs objectively; they *interpret* them by integrating the formal diagnostic criteria of the suspected disease(s) . . . and their own accumulated professional case expertise.

(1998: 250)

This more liberal view of evidence-based medicine is also taken by Sackett *et al.* who make it very clear that they see the professional's *judgement* as the defining factor as to whether the evidence is useful in a particular case. They argue that external evidence 'can inform, but never replace, individual clinical expertise and it is this expertise that decides whether external evidence applies to the individual patient at all, and if so, how it should be integrated into a clinical decision' (1997: 4).

Gawande cites the, work of the British psychologist James Reason in his book *Human Error*, who argues that: 'Our propensity for certain types of error is the price we pay for the brain's remarkable ability to think and act intuitively – to sift quickly through the sensory information that constantly bombards us without wasting time trying to work through every situation anew' (Reason 1992: 63).

However, the danger in merely relying on this quick sifting of sensory information is very evident in the case of the 'Three Mile Island' incident. In a lecture given in 1987, Schön analyses a near disaster that occurred at a nuclear reactor in New Jersey in the mid-1970s. Operators were alerted to a problem by one alarm ringing. In fact multiple errors had occurred. Complicating this, a light designed to indicate a malfunction was covered by a maintenance tag, and nobody saw it. The actions that had been taken to deal with what had been thought to be an isolated problem had, in fact, made the overall situation much worse. Observers reported that, suddenly, the whole control panel was a 'Christmas tree' of alarm lights. None had experienced anything like this before. There was no guidance in their book of procedures that could help.

Schön's observation was that the operators were not prepared for what he called 'surprises'; indeed, that the management of the reactor had attempted 'to avoid surprise, employing for this purpose a full panoply of measures, systems of control, targets and systems of reward and punishment to reinforce measures' (1987b: 227).

He locates the failure of the operators to respond appropriately to the complex problems they faced in what he calls 'proceduralization and control'. He notes that 'surprises' will occur and are not eliminated by having carefully written procedures, because those protocols were drawn up to cope with previous problems rather than completely new ones. He comments that one consequence of proceduralization is that 'people get to be very good . . . at not noticing surprise' and systematically avoid attending to information – which he calls 'weird' or 'junk' data – that would cause uncertainty.

A further problem of proceduralization, according to Schön, is the development of multiple systems of control. As he says: 'When things go wrong in spite of the fact that we multiply procedures to keep them from happening, the response is to increase and improve procedures. So after Three Mile Island, investigators proposed to expand the book of procedures.' However, he comments:

> when we adopt such remedies we drive out wisdom, artistry and 'feel for phenomena', all of which depend on judgement. We produce a world of increased routinization and control and dubious achievement with respect to the disasters we wish to avoid . . . For practitioners, the cumulative effect of such remedies is [that] artistry, wisdom, judgement, feel for materials, all of which depend upon discretionary freedom, get progressively squeezed out of practice as control and procedures are multiplied in order to avoid unpleasant surprises.
>
> (1987b: 228)

He notes on the same page that 'managers try to control subordinates by imposing measures of performance on them; and subordinates find ways to meet the letter of the measures without meeting their spirit'. He suggests that, as a result, 'the system of the organisation becomes undiscussable . . . Moreover, undiscussability turns readily to indescribability. Without discussion, we do not practise describing what goes on; and since we cannot describe it, we would not be very good at discussing it even if we were willing to do so' (Schön 1987b: 228).

This contrasts with Carr's view (1995: 69) of how the traditions of professional practice ought, in principle, to develop:

> The practical knowledge made available through tradition . . . is constantly being reinterpreted and revised through dialogue and discussion . . . It is precisely because it embodies this process of critical reconstruction that a tradition evolves and changes rather than remains static or fixed. When the ethical aims of a practice are officially deemed to be either uncontentious or impervious to rational discussion, the notions of practical knowledge and tradition will tend to be used in a wholly negative way.

Dealing with error through self-regulation

Gawande describes in some detail, through recounting an incident from his own practice in which he committed an error, a common feature of the medical community's approach to error reduction – the **Morbidity and Mortality** (M&M) conference. In his hospital this takes place once a week, and is where doctors 'can gather behind closed doors to review the mistakes, untoward events, and deaths that occurred on their watch, determine responsibility, and figure out what to do differently next time' (Gawande 2002: 57–8).

Critics would argue that this is 'sweeping things under the carpet', a matter of 'closing ranks', or as Gawande says: 'a rather shabby approach to analysing error and improving performance in medicine' (2002: 64). Is this the mark of a profession that is too self-serving? Gawande is more optimistic. His experience is that the M&M does in fact deal with these important issues, both in the meetings themselves through close cross-questioning by peers but also informally, as when his attending surgeon colleague talked with him privately:

> The day after the disaster [my colleague] had caught me in the hall and taken me aside. His voice was more wounded than angry as he went through my specific failures . . . I offered no excuses. I promised to be better prepared for such cases and to be quicker to ask for help.
>
> (2002: 61)

This incident, and the learning that came from it, underlines one reality of practice, which is that (as we will see in Chapter 6) the knowledge that underpins practice and how it is acquired (see Chapter 7) are themselves complex.

The social nature of error and its containment is shown in an enquiry into huge differences in mortality across different intensive care units in medical centres in the USA. It was found, for example, that:

> The differences . . . were related more to the interaction and coordination of each hospital's intensive care unit staff than to the unit's administrative structure, amount of specialised treatment used, or the hospital's teaching status. [The] findings support the hypothesis that the degree of coordination of intensive care significantly influences its effectiveness.
>
> (Knaus *et al.* 1986: 410)

This is echoed by the report of the Mental Health Inquiry we cited earlier. The authors write:

> Even the most eminent can be tested to the utmost of their skill, and occasionally fail . . . [This Inquiry] has brought into sharp focus the importance of clinicians not being so overburdened that they do not have time for mature reflection or to foster appropriately strong links with their teams.
>
> (Astal *et al.* 1998: 2–3)

Gawande concludes optimistically:

> Whatever the limits of the M & M, its fierce ethic of personal responsibility for errors is a formidable virtue. No matter what measures are taken, doctors will sometimes falter, and it isn't reasonable to ask that we achieve perfection. What is reasonable is to ask that we never cease to aim for it.
>
> (2002: 74)

Tallis similarly argues:

> the right to self-regulation is one of the distinguishing features of a profession and is of the greatest significance because it reflects the trust invested in it by society at large. Individual practitioners can be trusted with unsupervised responsibility because they have a well-developed sense of internal accountability . . . At the heart of a profession . . . is a justifiable autonomy expressed in self-regulation and in having a say in the mode of delivery of care. This is the compliment that society pays to the professions it trusts and values . . . If this goes, much else will go along with it and the world for sick people will be a much colder and less safe place.
>
> (2004: 241)

What are the implications for curriculum designers?

In this final part of the chapter we bring together the themes running through the stories presented by our colleagues in the previous chapter and our discussion of the nature of practice in this, and we point to some of the educational implications for designing a curriculum for practice.

First, though, it is worth observing that not only is the literature that we have presented above supportive of the stories of our four colleagues, it is also substantial. The evidence we have presented (not in the form of data from randomized trials but perfectly valid nevertheless) is, certainly for us, compelling, not least because of the variety of sources from which it emanates. But another observation is that this literature is burgeoning – more and more of it is emerging. Why?

One reason is because medicine – indeed all professional practice – is currently under threat. Professionals are under siege (Fish and Coles 1998: 3). The writers we have cited are all attempting, in their own way, to rekindle the notion of professionalism.

Tallis argues that the current 'deprofessionalizing' of the professions is occurring because of a clash of values. Professionals have, until recently at least, been driven by a sense of vocation:

> . . . an accountability to conscience that goes beyond strict legal liability and the duty of care defined by one's job description [and which] cannot be captured in the number of reimbursable or remunerable activities one engages in [and] goes beyond 'accountantability' (*sic*).
>
> (2004: 240)

He contrasts this sense of calling with the values now endemic within a society of 'consumerism':

> In a consumer-led society, with a high level of distrust in the professions and a hostility to authority, I can testify to the power of the opprobium of a patient's relatives to force one down a track that is at odds with one's sense of the right thing to do. This will become more common if doctors, too, are consumers and import consumerist values into their work.
>
> (2004: 244)

The danger as Tallis sees it is that doctors grow up in, are drawn from, and must practise within, just such a consumerist society. It is almost inevitable that medical practice will reflect this. His writing, together with the main thrust of our argument in this and the previous chapter, attempts to provide a counterweight to that dark prospect. One hope is that the education of doctors will make a difference and that is a matter for curriculum designers.

We wish, at this point, then, to reiterate what we said at the outset: unless we have a clear understanding of the nature of practice we cannot with any assurance embark on developing a curriculum that enables others to learn what practice is and what it means to practise, nor perhaps more importantly how to practise effectively and appropriately. What then does this and the previous chapter teach us about what is meant by 'a practice'?

What we mean by 'a practice'

The word 'practice' changes its meaning in different contexts. For a **General Practitioner** (GP) (or perhaps a doctor working in a suite of offices), it could be the physical location, the building, the rooms and the facilities – *the* practice. More usually we think of 'practice' as the actions of an individual person – *my* practice. It can also be thought of as the collective actions of several practitioners – *our* practice is to do such-and-such, or 'it is the practice of my profession to do X'.

'Practice exists whenever a more or less settled body of activities is carried out to some distinctive end . . . [it describes] particular things people do to [serve] some overall social purpose' (Golby and Parrott 1999: 3). It is 'the range of activities which cannot be seen in isolation but which are intelligible . . . because they encapsulate not only what should be [done] but also *how* . . . [It is] a transaction between [people] within a framework of agreed purposes and underlying procedural values' (Pring 2000: 27–8).

Practice is more than mere expertise. It goes beyond 'performance' to what lies beneath the surface. In respect of this, we prefer to use the word 'conduct' here rather than performance:

> to signal that we are interested in not only the professional's visible behaviour, but also the motivations that drive it. These we see as shaped by the practitioner's underlying humanity and self-knowledge, and underpinned by moral and ethical sensitivity to the individual patient and particular context.
>
> (de Cossart and Fish 2005: 132)

'To practise . . . is always to act within a tradition, and it is only by submitting to its authority that practitioners can begin to acquire the practical knowledge and standards of excellence by means of which their own practical competence can be judged' (Carr 1995: 68–9). Practice, then, is a social phenomenon. It is not simply the actions of an individual. This has led some writers to speak of 'communities of practice' (Lave and Wenger 1991).

This makes professional practice (as well as the learning of that practice) a social and collaborative enterprise. Within such social settings, professionals:

> endlessly create, negotiate and develop meanings; have to be appropriately flexible about some things and (temporarily) inflexible about others; engage all the time with multiple activities, factors, and perspectives; ceaselessly formulate problems and solutions; and learn to live with the insoluble, the ephemeral, the tentative, and the incomplete.
>
> (de Cossart and Fish 2005: 100)

In medicine, as the cases and incidents we have reported here have shown, the corporate nature of practice is particularly important. What is also clear is the wide range of people involved. It includes those within one's own clinical specialty, others within one's own profession, others from related health care fields, and yet others outside health care itself, such as managers, social workers, housing officers and the police. The range extends, too, of course to patients and relatives, as well as to the public at large, and not least to people from the media, and politicians.

Each of these groups requires a different approach because each has its own discourse, values and forms of practice. Indeed, we find it useful to consider practice as something that is context-specific. Even within a doctor's own clinical specialty there will be a range of practices. For example, the practice of a newly-qualified doctor will, in some significant ways, be different from someone with further experience undertaking, say, basic or higher specialty training. And this will be different again from the practice of a medical consultant. Similarly, the practice of a medical student will be different from that of a qualified doctor. A student's practice is related more to the formal study of medicine rather than its practical manifestation.

The implications of these distinctions

Understanding these differences between practices is an important consideration in the design of a curriculum for practice, since 'practice' is not a static or unitary entity. There is no such thing then as 'medical practice', only 'the practice of medicine' at any particular point in a doctor's emerging career.

Quite fundamentally we have seen in this chapter that the practice of medicine is characterized by complexity, unpredictability and uncertainty, with paradox ever present. Judgement lies at its heart. The curricular challenge is to provide a framework to enable doctors to learn to 'exercise discretion in situations of considerable uncertainty' (Eraut 1994) and to cultivate a learner who can rise to the complex realities of the whole range of practice. The practice of medicine is 'what happens when the simplicities of science come up against the complexities of individual lives' (Gawande 2002: 8).

Professional judgement is a special form of judgement. It underpins a doctor's capacity to practise. It is far more complex than a clinical decision (which, as we have shown, is the logical end result of clinical and scientific reasoning). We have seen that it is the core (and humanistic) capacity to decide between competing and complex moral demands during the whole of the clinical thinking process, and also that it best describes the final decision within the deliberative element of that thinking. Teaching professional judgement to postgraduate doctors requires a curriculum that highlights its importance, offers language in which to discuss it, and empowers teacher and learner to explore these sensitive matters more openly.

Acting professionally, then, is more than being highly skilled and knowledgeable, or even performing with expertise. It is a matter of 'being professional' and is concerned with developing 'a capacity for autonomous professional self-development through systematic self-study, through the study of the work of [others] and through the testing of ideas [through researching one's practice]' (Stenhouse 1975: 144). Above all, and crucially, being a member of a profession is to be engaged in a moral endeavour, with consideration for others – not just patients and their relatives but colleagues as well – being paramount, together with the requirement to act with discretion at all times. A curriculum for practice needs to be focused on professional conduct, not merely on encouraging surface behaviour.

Practice is more than performance, more than mere action. It is concerned with what lies behind performance – the beliefs, assumptions, expectations, and above all values that the individual holds. It is defined by what one is, not simply by what one does. Medical practice requires considerable knowledge and high-level procedural skills. However, successful practice requires the doctor to use that knowledge and to exercise those skills *appropriately*. Harvey Cushing, in a letter to a colleague in 1911, wrote 'I would like to see the day when somebody would be appointed surgeon somewhere who had no hands, for the operative part is the least part of the work' (***British Medical Journal BMJ*** 2004: 34).

When the best thing to do in practice is to do or say nothing, students and less experienced doctors are sometimes surprised and confused on observing such practice. The age-old surgical aphorism has some truth to it. A good surgeon knows how to operate. A better surgeon knows when to operate. The best surgeon knows when *not* to operate! This means that teachers have a duty to make explicit that which underlies their actions and non-actions.

On occasions, practice means deciding what is 'best' in a particular situation rather than what is 'right' in some absolute sense. As Carr puts it, such an action 'is not "right" action in the sense that it has been proved to be correct. It is "right" action because it is *reasoned* action that can be defended discursively in argument and justified as morally appropriate to the particular circumstances in which it was taken' (1995: 71).

Practice is certainly not entirely 'evidence-based', and the public is not well served by it being characterized as such. That is not to say that doctors ignore evidence or that evidence may not influence clinical decisions. But most practice is a mixture of intuition, professional on-the-spot experimentation, hunch, risk-taking and second-guessing, all of it informed by an understanding of the need for accountability, but much of it inevitably having to be trusted by the public. Practice involves trust. It relies on a fiduciary relationship between doctor and patient. This must not be jeopardized even in the interests of engaging in education in the practice setting.

Errors in practice are normal. However unfortunate and distressing they may be, they are inevitable. Naturally, every step must be taken to reduce error but it can never be eliminated. To err is human, and medical practice is a human activity. Attempts to eradicate error through technical means (e.g. computer diagnostics), by restricting the range of doctors' practice to a small number of procedures, or through setting protocols for action, have only limited effects. Even when all these measures have been taken, the unexpected can always occur, and does more frequently than is realized by those who, seeing medical practice as a technical matter, attempt to turn doctors into machines (see Gawande 2002: 38).

A curriculum designed for practice

Curriculum designers need to recognize, value and take account of these complexities and subtleties, these taken-for-granted elements of everyday practice (many of which lie beneath the surface of a doctor's overt actions and which may not even be recognized by the doctor as being part of his or her practice), in order to prepare doctors for them. The education of doctors needs to enable them to investigate and develop critical perspectives on what they do in their community of practice, and how this relates to the wider world of medicine. It also needs to enable them to reconsider and even redesign their practice and ultimately that of their profession.

In part, too, a curriculum for practice must address the wider question of how to enable doctors to respond in some appropriate manner to society's unrealistic expectations of them and their practice as we outlined at the beginning of the previous chapter.

Quite fundamentally though, a curriculum for practice must take 'practice' as its starting point, and this means basing such a curriculum on and in actual practice – the lived experience of practitioners – and not some simulation or approximation of it. This requires curriculum designers to have first-hand experience of practice, and this means having actual practitioners as part of their design teams. It may also mean undertaking research into the nature of practice in different specialties of different practitioners at various stages of their professional development.

It also means understanding the nature of the forms of knowledge that underpin practice and how these are acquired. These matters are addressed in the next two chapters.

6 Clarifying the content: the nature of professional knowledge in medicine

Why is an analysis of doctors' practice knowledge important?
What forms of knowledge are currently perceived to underpin postgraduate medical *practice* and why is this so?
What can we say about the nature of knowledge more generally (what is it to 'know' in different disciplines)?
In professional practice what sense can we make of theory and practice?
What are the sources of knowledge for professional practice?
What are the components of knowledge for professional practice?
What forms of knowledge actually underpin medical practice?

Introduction

We have already provided evidence of, and explored the *nature of practice* in postgraduate medicine and the professional values upon which it is based, in Chapters 4 and 5. That is, we have conducted an *ontological analysis* to fuel the deliberations of curriculum designers. This is a major part of the situational analysis of the professional practice of medicine. We showed in Chapter 2 that this is the necessary starting point for developing a sound curriculum for practice which will both reflect the current and forthcoming needs of, and be workable within, medical practice itself.

In this chapter, we attend to a further part of that situational analysis – that is, we probe the *nature of knowledge* (conduct an *epistemological analysis*) of the knowledge used in professional practice generally and postgraduate medical practice in particular. This will provide the proper basis of understanding for the deliberations about how the curriculum should select and structure what it is that postgraduate doctors should be learning (which is often referred to as 'the content of the curriculum').

In medicine generally, epistemological analyses have often been conducted *within* the bio-medical field in order to consider the components of the formal theoretical knowledge necessary for medical students to learn (as it is understood from within that field). But the focus of our analysis is different. It is on the nature of knowledge as needed *in medical practice*. Much of the health care literature (which is well developed in this area) refers to this as *practice epistemology* (see Higgs *et al.* 2004). There has been very little formal exploration of practice epistemology within medicine. The most detailed attempt seems to have been by de Cossart and Fish (2005), and we are grateful to the publisher and co-author for permission to draw extensively on that work in this chapter. In doing so we also refer to our colleagues' writing in Chapter 4 above, to the literature across health care and to the (much smaller) literature from postgraduate medicine.

Why is an analysis of doctors' practice knowledge important?

There are at least five reasons why the knowledge that doctors use in practice needs close attention from curriculum designers, learning doctors and their teachers.

1   Unchallenged beliefs and assumptions about the nature of knowledge to be acquired by doctors can mask ill-founded and false ideas that may misinform our expectations of what should be learnt and can misdirect the focus of assessment, thus inadvertently distorting the curriculum.
2   Much of the knowledge doctors call upon is tacit and is not readily made visible to learners, and so is easily overlooked, and much underplayed as a key component of the medical curriculum.
3   Failure to recognize the existence of other than factual and simple procedural knowledge will mean that those who teach doctors in the practice setting will continue to know more than they can ever attempt to articulate, and so will short-change those for whom they have an educational responsibility.
4   Doctors do not currently have a language in which to characterize the various kinds of knowledge they use, and thus are not able to refer accurately to them, let alone teach them explicitly or develop their own understanding of them.
5   Wherever doctors and especially surgeons refer to themselves as 'mere doers', they erroneously call into question the quality of their practice by

denigrating their knowledge base and denying the intelligence of their actions.

By the very way in which any curriculum sets out 'what must be learnt', it inevitably takes a view of the nature of the knowledge it is promoting, and a view of the order and way in which that knowledge should be learnt. In order to be sure that it is being rigorously acquired, teachers and learners need to focus consciously on and make explicit the importance of a much wider range of knowledge, both in their own practice and in that of the learner.

A serious medical curriculum needs to offer a clearly set out view of and sound grasp of the nature of 'practice knowledge', its sources, categories and components, and of the principles that might inform the choices of the knowledge needed to underpin doctors' practice in order to provide the best possible care for patients.

Discussion of these matters has until recently been less available to medical educators than to those in other health care professions, where the nature of knowledge has been more fully explored (see for example the collection edited by Higgs *et al.* 2004). In medical practice the work of White and Stancombe (2003) offers some discussion of epistemology, and de Cossart and Fish (2005) provide a chapter which explores these matters in detail in relation to surgeons (but which is also highly relevant to physicians).

What forms of knowledge are perceived to underpin medical practice and why is this so?

Beyond our own work, all of which is based on *researching medical practice* (de Cossart and Fish 2002, 2005; Coles *et al.* 2003; Fish 2003, 2004, 2005), there is a distinct absence of published work that analyses the knowledge to be learnt as the basis for the *practice of medicine*.

This is probably because it is not seen as a problematic area, it being assumed that there would be little disagreement about what the term 'medical knowledge' should include. Indeed, the field of knowledge broadly believed to be the basis for medicine is that of the bio-medical sciences, which are assumed to provide 'the' evidence base (facts) for treating patients. This form of knowledge is factual and theoretical (known generally as 'propositional knowledge') and (even in the postmodern world of the twenty-first century) is still widely assumed to consist of absolute facts which are regarded as the only real key to sound medical practice.

On three counts this is emphatically not the case. Firstly, bio-medical knowledge is not absolute, it develops and changes, and being theoretical it offers only the best evidence known or found at the time (and there is much medical practice for which there is no evidence). Secondly, science deals in general principles and laws, but the doctor deals with the particularities of the individual patient and must therefore have some other knowledge about how to adapt this theory to practice. Thirdly, such propositional knowledge may constitute a major component of practice epistemology, but it is by no means the only one, since for example, the ability to carry out skills, processes and procedures rests in knowledge of procedures (known as procedural knowledge).

It is a convenient myth that 'medical knowledge' consists specifically and *only* of the propositional knowledge of the bio-medical sciences. Since the base knowledge for medicine is scientific and apparently consists of clear-cut right and wrong answers, this myth enables doctors to be easily labelled as 'correct or not', and, since no doctor can be 'right' all the time, it thus provides managers, governments and the public with an easy stick with which to beat them (see Cunningham and Wilson 2003). It also provides an apparently easy basis for assessing doctors and organizing their careers. But though very important, its *exclusive* importance is more apparent than real.

These unchallenged ideas are ubiquitous and distorting. For example, as de Cossart and Fish (2005) noted in respect of 'medical knowledge', until recently there has been a strong assumption that a medical degree together with the membership examinations will provide the main motivation for the acquisition of, and will take care of the assessment of, all the knowledge that doctors and surgeons need in professional practice. Indeed, they point out that surgeons seem to believe '(without perhaps having examined this belief in detail), that excellence in medical factual knowledge is the key foundation of good surgical practice' (de Cossart and Fish 2005: 187). This idea in turn implies that the role of the doctor educator in the clinical setting is to provide help with examination revision (providing learners with the knowledge they will need in order to pass the college exams), and to provide coaching about the ways of caring for patients. Often both teachers and learners see only the first of these as an *educational* activity, while the second is seen as part of service in which the senior needs merely to tell learners what to do and how to do it in respect of patient care.

The basis of this myth is certainly also nurtured within universities. For example, whenever undergraduate medical degrees are newly planned or redesigned, the knowledge to be taught has tended to be shaped from within the theoretical fields taught in the institution. That is (rather than starting with the needs of medical practice), universities generally focus on what the university can actually offer in terms of university disciplines and learning processes, and only then consider what the practice placements can do to supplement this.

At postgraduate level too, the only published interest in epistemology tends to be part of a wider thesis and not directed to uncovering what should be taught in the postgraduate years. See, for example, Cunningham and Wilson (2003) who investigated attitudes to practice knowledge as part of an interest in how the medical practitioner can be made to feel guilt and shame; and Little (1995) who looks more broadly at what constitutes humane medicine.

It should be noted that one exception to this narrow view of knowledge is the report for **Cancer Research-UK** (CR-UK), in which educational consultants, working outside university employment, offer an in-depth analysis of the practice of cancer care and deduce from this what medical and other health care professions' curricula should incorporate at first degree level and immediate postgraduate level (see Coles *et al.* 2003). Their research showed the complexity of practice and the needs of practitioners in terms of their knowledge base to be very different from what was currently being taught. But this is an exception to the rest of the published literature.

The myth of the sole knowledge base in medicine being the bio-medical sciences has also been fuelled by all the recent examples of medico-legal problems which appear to be about doctors getting their propositional knowledge wrong, while in fact their errors are often in many of the other areas of knowledge. Thus the case for the acquisition of propositional knowledge as the only armoury for the doctor is more apparent than real (though of course we would not wish to undervalue the importance of such knowledge). This attitude seems also to have deeply affected the new medical curricula for postgraduate medicine that are currently emerging.

For example, while the *Curriculum for the Foundation Years* (DoH 2005b) pinpoints a number of processes and procedures that need to be assessed, when it comes to 'content' it provides a syllabus based only upon knowledge skills and attitudes, which assumes that 'knowledge' consists solely of medical and scientific facts. Further, both this document and the Joint Committee for Higher Surgical Training website list 'the' knowledge to be learnt by doctors, without reference to the underlying decisions about how and on what basis it has been categorized, and apparently without any recognition that this is complex and problematic. This nurtures the false notion that knowledge is a commodity out there in the universe waiting to be acquired, captured or discovered.

Sadly, for so long as postgraduate medical curricula are required to be structured on the subheadings of the National Curriculum for schoolchildren (which are 'knowledge', 'skills' and 'attitudes'), there is little hope of a clear understanding by doctors or their educators of the real scope of knowledge used in practice and which therefore needs to be learnt by new doctors. Indeed, there is not even a widespread recognition that skills are themselves a form of knowledge. In the absence of all this, there will be little hope of developing and refining such knowledge. Further, doctors will fare badly in multi-professional teams where other professions have been looking at far wider 'ways of knowing' within their own profession for almost 30 years (see, for example, Carper 1978 in nursing).

Thus, we would argue that while medical factual knowledge is clearly important, there is much more that needs attention if doctors are to conduct themselves appropriately in the practice setting. We would further point out that in the practice setting some propositional knowledge that has been assimilated to pass exams is actually irrelevant, or inappropriate for direct use (being generalized theory, and laws, which need to be adapted rather than simply 'applied' in the face of particular patient needs).

Before we turn back to the details of practice epistemology for medicine, we need to understand the nature of knowledge more generally.

What can we say about the nature of knowledge more generally?

In this section we look at the nature of knowledge in different disciplines and this leads into a consideration of ways of knowing in professional practice generally, its sources of knowledge and the components of practice knowledge which underlie practice in all professions.

What is it to 'know' in different disciplines?

Those who study the nature of knowledge generally (epistemologists) show us that it is possible to divide up knowledge in a number of different ways (see, for example, Phenix 1964 and Carper 1978). We call these different divisions 'subjects', 'disciplines' or 'fields of study'. And different disciplines use 'proof' and 'truth' differently, and see the world from different angles. Indeed, each of us needs to be aware of our own position with respect to this, since our own education will have emphasized one way of conceiving of knowledge, which we may never have challenged:

> Education within a discipline stamps us with particular views about the origins of knowledge, ways of seeing truth, what counts as evidence (ways of handling proof), views about theory and practice, and views about appropriate means of achieving rigour. Even the very meaning of rigour itself is disciplinarily-determined. It is easy when one is steeped in a particular way of seeing knowledge, to apply that approach unthinkingly to other kinds of knowledge (such as knowledge of another field) where it may not be appropriate or applicable.
> (Higgs *et al.* 2004: 64)

For example, although science and art are by no means mutually exclusive, since it is possible to find deep aesthetic meanings in things studied scientifically, and to find scientific truth in aesthetic experiences, nonetheless, a key difference between them is in the *kinds* of understanding gained within each and the contrasting views of the world to which they give rise.

Scientists use the methods of observation and experimentation to come to know empirical truth, which is then generalized in general laws and theories, which are connected with observable particulars by way of prediction and verification. Science strives for objective certainties and often downplays the theoretical nature of its discoveries. Scientists see these certainties as new truths and expect others to apply them to practice. While this is how science works, it is not how knowledge is created, verified and given significance in other fields. For example, the arts are concerned with the particular. Aesthetic understanding is not contained in propositions but in particular and presented objects (like poems, pictures, plays, novels, symphonies). And although such objects may contain general truths (as do Shakespeare's sonnets in respect of love, for example), nonetheless the value and quality of them is not based upon this general truth alone, but on how their form and content are organized into a patterned whole to become an organic unity *whose form underpins its content*, and how form and content are each equally part of the language and expression of those truths. Indeed, each sonnet is a perfectly wrought (and wittily presented) object with a clear logic of its own. But the truths that such poems offer about the human condition, and the beauty that they possess, are validated not by scientific means but by the *frisson of recognition* created in the audience. Thus, truth and proof, and validity and reliability, exist in different forms within different ways of knowing.

Professional practice itself (where knowledge is eternally incomplete and insufficient and which has elements of artistry about it) has its own ways of knowing, which need to be studied by teachers and learners so that they do not harbour unrealistic expectations or assumptions in respect of it. For example, it should not be assumed that objective knowledge of all aspects of practice is out there waiting to be discovered, or that perfect ways of curriculum design or assessment processes exist somewhere in the universe waiting to be stumbled upon.

In professional practice, what sense can we make of the relationship between theory and practice?

For the professional practitioner too, there are particular ways of understanding and construing knowledge, which will open up new ways of seeing and thinking about practice. In particular, the working professional has to make sense of the relationship between theory and practice. An understanding of the complexities inherent in this is therefore vital to the sound design and to the structure of a curriculum for *any* professional practice.

What is the relationship between theory and practice?

All statements about the nature of the world and the nature of knowledge are fiercely contested, as Golby and Parrott (1999) and White and Stancombe (2003) demonstrate. Indeed, among the habitual and inaccurate assumptions about knowledge, few are as prevalent and serious as those related to the relationship between theory and practice. Indeed, it has long been traditional to think of knowledge as divided, fairly simply, between theory and practice (or 'knowing that' and 'knowing how'; or 'knowing' and 'doing'); to see theory as 'coming first'; and to see it as needing to be learnt in order to *apply it* to practice. Questioning this therefore comes as a shock.

Yet, when we grapple seriously with structuring education for the professions (or within professional practice), we quickly see the following.

1   The division between theory and practice is not watertight (we learn the facts in order that they inform our doing; our doing is rarely mindless; and our intelligent action is one thing (acting intelligently) and not two (being intelligent on the one hand and acting on the other).
2   Each enlightens the other. For example, placements in degree courses leading to professional practice and masters courses leading to qualifications as 'advanced practitioners' are now interspersed with classroom-based theory such that theory and practice can illuminate each other.
3   Thus, in professional practice, the role of theory is not applicatory. Rather we use and adapt (even reinterpret and re-create) theoretical knowledge to meet the specific context and needs of individual and particular clients or patients. We do not use our professional factual knowledge as a simple template to impose upon the practice we meet, nor do we use theoretical knowledge as a simple lens through which we observe and understand practice. Rather we are sceptical of how we see and how we interpret that seeing, and we question the relevance of facts to individual cases.
4   There is more to professional practice than knowing textbook facts on the one hand and knowing how to do something medical on the other. For example, practitioners develop a repertoire of experiential knowledge, which they probably draw on most frequently of all and they improvise, develop insight, and gain and develop knowledge through their senses (looking, touching, hearing and smelling).
5   Further, theory does not always come first. Indeed, there are actually arguments for the 'primacy of practice' (literally seeing or thinking about practice before recourse to theory, or recognizing that theories emerge

from practice or are created to explain, explore or extend practice). The primacy of practice encapsulates the belief that in the development of new knowledge (and professional knowledge particularly), practice comes first, and theory is developed from it.

6   Understanding the nature of knowledge involves adopting a position about how knowledge is created. The idea that knowledge is a 'given', objective, impersonal truth, discovered by research and handed down to practitioners to act upon, is not proven. It is a belief that springs from an entire world view (positivism), as defined by western science or technology. This positivistic view of the world emphasizes measurement, and belittles that which cannot be measured (see Broadfoot 1993). Others however, argue that this wrongly accentuates objective versions of reality and of knowledge, at the expense of much that is highly valuable though not so visible or measurable. They tend to see knowledge as socially constructed and created by practitioners *in practice*.

Clearly there are different views of knowledge in different disciplines and its nature is context bound. On what basis, then, do we argue for the primacy of practice?

Practice, theory and the primacy of practice

For any practitioner the relationship between theory and practice is a highly significant matter. Many in the wider health care field recognize that in professional practice there is no hierarchical order between theory and practice, and that they are intimately related. Higgs and Titchen (2001) talk about a dialectical relationship which confronts the differences between knowing and doing and reconciles them by producing a higher-order process of doing-knowing which encompasses them both. And we would argue that the combined power of knowing and doing is often invaluable in dealing with the contradictions, uncertainties and complexities of practice.

Gilbert Ryle has called our attention to the arguments for the primacy of practice (the idea that in developing knowledge, practice often comes before theory). And we would argue that this is certainly true in relation to some of the knowledge created by practitioners in practice. In arguing for the primacy of practice, Ryle challenged the traditional relationship of theory and practice. In his seminal book *The Concept of Mind* he declared that often:

> efficient practice precedes the theory of it . . . It is . . . possible for people intelligently to perform some sorts of operations when they are not yet able to consider any propositions enjoining how they should be performed. [He also added] Some intelligent performances

are not controlled by any interior acknowledgments of the principles applied to them.

(Ryle 1949: 31)

Later he says: 'we learn *how* by practice, schooled indeed by criticism and example, but often quite unaided by any lessons in the theory (1949: 41). This is why we argue in the introduction that curriculum design and development are practices that are best learnt by engaging in them. But we do also make the point that we have to engage in them on the basis of a range of knowledge and understanding!

Ryle argued that we should not imagine that behind intelligent action is the ghost of intelligent thought. Instead, he argued: 'When I do something intelligently, i.e. thinking what I am doing, I am doing one thing and not two. My performance has a special procedure or manner, not special antecedents' (1949: 32). He also made the point that theorizing is a practice itself, and offered us the useful term 'intelligent practice', saying: 'intelligent practice is not a step-child of theory. On the contrary, theorising is one practice amongst others and is itself intelligently or stupidly conducted' (1949: 27).

The relationship between theory and practice, then, is complex and 'integrated' or 'dialectical' and involves 'knowledgeable-doing'. This has profound implications for how a curriculum for practice is set out and structured and for the order in which that knowledge is offered to learners. This is why a curriculum may need to be integrated so that factual knowledge is not taught separately from knowledge about procedures. This issue also relates to where we think knowledge comes from.

What are the sources of knowledge for professional practice?

Knowledge is often assumed to be 'a given', to be 'theoretical', or to have been proved by research and thus to be acceptable as absolutely true. Traditionally the key sources of knowledge for doctors have been consultants, textbooks and research. But behind these there lie deeper sources. For example, the knowledge of practitioners can be seen as socially constructed, emerging from practice, and as the product of how we see the world.

We have argued (Fish and Coles 1998), as do de Cossart and Fish (2005), that both the conduct of professional practice and the evolution of professional knowledge involves *creating knowledge in practice* and that knowledge that is generated in practice, during practice, is in fact a major component of practice knowledge.

This also means that *practitioners* are the source of practice knowledge.

Practice knowledge is the outcome of reflection by individuals and professional groups on their knowledge and practice. (Whereas *formal* practice knowledge is practitioners' practice knowledge which has been further critiqued and sharpened by publication and public debate.)

As a reminder to teacher and learner alike, de Cossart and Fish list the wider sources of practice knowledge for surgeons (2005: 200). Their list applies equally to all doctors. It values medical practice coupled with reflection as a major source of knowledge, and the importance of the multi-professional (or disciplinary) team in theatre, ward and clinic, and of the learner interacting with colleagues in order to clarify understanding. They also acknowledge the importance of narrative, both of immediate events and the history of other relevant cases, by means of which the consultant can extend the passive knowledge of the learner.

What then can we now say about the map of knowledge for those engaged in professional practice?

What are the components of practice knowledge in the professions generally?

There is very little that is 'absolute' about knowledge, then. How we see it will be determined by our particular world view, which will result in our emphasizing particular components, perhaps at the expense of others. Four relevant formal views of the components of practice knowledge are already available in the literature from Ryle (1949), Eraut (2000), Higgs and Titchen (2001) and de Cossart and Fish (2005). These show the ideas as becoming increasingly sophisticated and also increasingly holistic in nature, thus pulling theory and practice back into one whole.

The most fundamental division of knowledge, then, is into theory (propositional knowledge) and practice (procedural knowledge) (see Ryle 1949). Higgs and Titchen (2001) offer three main divisions, in effect recognizing one component for propositional knowledge and two for procedural knowledge (one of which also contains propositional knowledge). These are: knowledge derived from research and formal theory; knowledge derived from professional experience (theory and practice); and knowledge derived from personal experience. Eraut (2000) uses 'formal' and 'personal knowledge' as his main categories. Within 'formal' he extends the meaning of propositional knowledge by offering 'codified knowledge' as a better term for what he sees as 'knowledge that includes propositions (including propositions about skills)', and which also includes the 'public knowledge controlled by editors, peer review, and debate and given status by being incorporated into educational programmes'. Within personal knowledge, he includes 'the cognitive resource which a person brings to a situation that enables them to think and perform'.

He argues that this incorporates codified knowledge in a personalized form, together with procedural knowledge (including skills) and process knowledge (although he does not explain this further), experiential knowledge and impressions in 'episodic memory' (Eraut 2000: 114). de Cossart and Fish (2005) explored their own and colleagues' medical practice and found 14 elements or components of knowledge, many of which span both procedural and propositional knowledge. Of these they say:

> we would want to see all this knowledge coming together ultimately in the fluent and holistic practice of an expert practitioner, but we believe that better knowledge of the components provides a vocabulary in which to discuss the details, and a means of diagnosing problems or particular expertise in any of them.
>
> (2005: 195)

Their key components are: knowledge of facts of all kinds (*propositional knowledge*); knowledge of up-to-date medical thought and research (*evidence-based knowledge*); knowing how to act and how to get things done (*procedural knowledge*); knowing how to organize and adapt propositional knowledge to the context (*propositional adaptation knowledge*); knowing how to improvise procedural knowledge to suit the given case; (*procedural improvisation knowledge*); knowledge of the traditions of the profession and conduct of its members (*professional knowledge*); knowledge gained through the sense of touch, sound, smell and sight (*sensory knowledge*); knowledge of ethical and moral principles of practice which guides safe adaptation and improvisation (*ethical knowledge*); knowledge gained as a result of previous experience and reflection upon it (*experiential knowledge*); knowledge created during practice (*practice-generated knowledge*); knowledge of the higher levels of thought that shape the creation, adaptation and development of practice knowledge, and the overall processes of clinical thinking (*meta-cognitive knowledge*); knowledge for which there is no immediate explanation (*intuitive knowledge*); knowledge which comes suddenly as a fully-fledged vision, without the underlying reasoning being apparent (*insight/imagination*); knowledge of one's own strengths, weaknesses and limitations (*self-knowledge*).

They indicate that some of these forms of knowledge are *tacit* (this describes knowledge that practitioners do not even recognize they have, and which it is difficult and in some cases impossible for them to surface). Others, they say, are *implicit* (they are forms of knowledge that lie just under the surface of practice or within procedures, processes and organizations and which can, with effort, be surfaced). Interestingly, relatively few are explicit, publicly documented and structured, or as Eraut calls it, 'codified' (see de Cossart and Fish 2005: 194). Of all this they say:

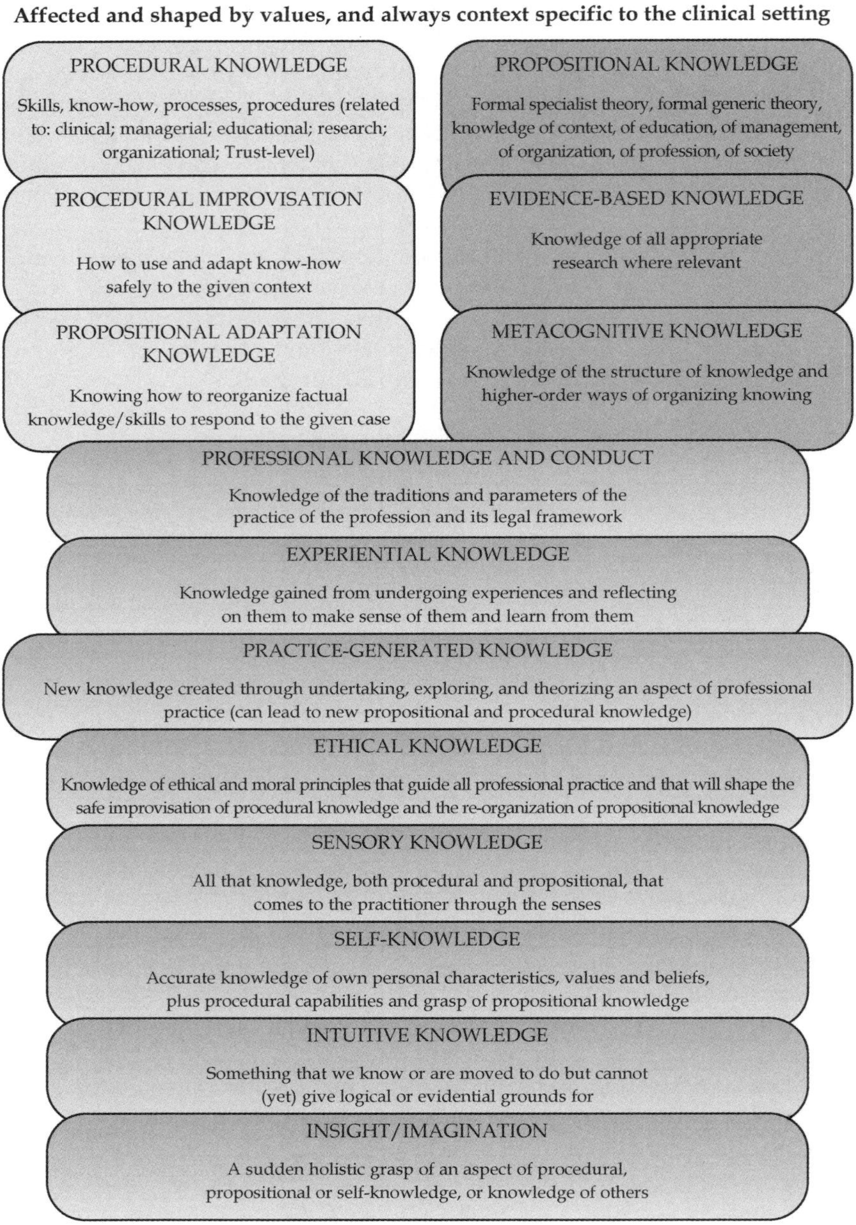

Affected and shaped by values, and always context specific to the clinical setting

PROCEDURAL KNOWLEDGE

Skills, know-how, processes, procedures (related to: clinical; managerial; educational; research; organizational; Trust-level)

PROPOSITIONAL KNOWLEDGE

Formal specialist theory, formal generic theory, knowledge of context, of education, of management, of organization, of profession, of society

PROCEDURAL IMPROVISATION KNOWLEDGE

How to use and adapt know-how safely to the given context

EVIDENCE-BASED KNOWLEDGE

Knowledge of all appropriate research where relevant

PROPOSITIONAL ADAPTATION KNOWLEDGE

Knowing how to reorganize factual knowledge/skills to respond to the given case

METACOGNITIVE KNOWLEDGE

Knowledge of the structure of knowledge and higher-order ways of organizing knowing

PROFESSIONAL KNOWLEDGE AND CONDUCT

Knowledge of the traditions and parameters of the practice of the profession and its legal framework

EXPERIENTIAL KNOWLEDGE

Knowledge gained from undergoing experiences and reflecting on them to make sense of them and learn from them

PRACTICE-GENERATED KNOWLEDGE

New knowledge created through undertaking, exploring, and theorizing an aspect of professional practice (can lead to new propositional and procedural knowledge)

ETHICAL KNOWLEDGE

Knowledge of ethical and moral principles that guide all professional practice and that will shape the safe improvisation of procedural knowledge and the re-organization of propositional knowledge

SENSORY KNOWLEDGE

All that knowledge, both procedural and propositional, that comes to the practitioner through the senses

SELF-KNOWLEDGE

Accurate knowledge of own personal characteristics, values and beliefs, plus procedural capabilities and grasp of propositional knowledge

INTUITIVE KNOWLEDGE

Something that we know or are moved to do but cannot (yet) give logical or evidential grounds for

INSIGHT/IMAGINATION

A sudden holistic grasp of an aspect of procedural, propositional or self-knowledge, or knowledge of others

Figure 6.1 A map of practice knowledge for professionals generally (with acknowledgement to de Cossart and Fish 2005).

We believe that making as much as possible explicit would seriously improve the rigour of teaching professional processes and procedures. Careful reflection on practice and enquiry into it will yield the secret of much of its underlying knowledge, and working with this to turn it into understanding will show us new ways to develop our practice.

(de Cossart and Fish 2005: 196)

We offer in Figure 6.1 their map of knowledge for professionals generally (see also de Cossart and Fish 2005: 198). This includes more detail within each of these areas named above, in terms of both the content of components and their interrelationship. For example, they have used shading to indicate the jointly propositional and procedural nature of many of their components and have 'honoured the primacy of practice by placing procedural knowledge first' (2005: 199). The small print in each component box gives examples. And they have used a standard size for all boxes except that for knowledge generated in practice, because that is the component they believe to be most significant, while not wishing to imply comparisons between any of the rest.

On this analysis, practice knowledge for any health care professional (which of course includes doctors) consists of a wide range of important elements, many of which are difficult to disentangle from each other, but which the curriculum designer and the teacher need to have a grasp of if they are not to short-change the learning professional. While there is no evidence that this list is 'correct', nor that it is comprehensive, it would certainly behove designers of any curriculum for postgraduate practice to consider critically these suggested components and their implications for curriculum design.

We can now say a number of things about the nature of knowledge endemic to medical practice.

What is the nature of the knowledge endemic to medical practice?

We seek here, by drawing on our contributors to Chapter 4 and on the literature already available in medicine, to demonstrate the *nature* of practice knowledge used by doctors, its complexity; its composition; the importance of knowledge creation and improvisation in practice; and the different uses of propositional knowledge at different stages in learning medicine.

How complex is knowledge in practice?

As our contributors to Chapter 4 demonstrate, and as White and Stancombe (2003) imply, Tallis (2004) indicates and de Cossart and Fish (2005) show, the nature of knowledge drawn upon and generated within any professional practice setting is complex. This is perhaps best summed up as follows:

- it is always incomplete;
- it evolves *during* the collaborative relationship with colleagues and clients;
- it works *with* not *on* clients;
- it involves professional judgement which opens professionals up to taking risks and thus to risk being wrong;
- it is characterized by mystery at its heart;
- it is based more upon uncertainty than upon total expertise;
- it involves a spiritual dimension;
- it opens professionals up to moral answerability;
- it involves theorizing about practice *during* practice;
- it is about creating new understandings *during* practice;
- it espouses a moral and ethical approach to practice and demands from practitioners an endless critical examination of their beliefs;
- it is more dependent on artistry than on science (de Cossart and Fish 2005: 186).

However, as we have also seen in the demands the lay public makes as characterized on pp. 83–85, it is clear that they assume that professional practice is about expert, unshakeable knowledge, and an utterly dependable technical-rational base (although they do recognize the need sometimes to seek a second, and therefore potentially different, opinion). Their false expectations spring from and are consonant with western thought generally where 'doing' is often split off from and is assumed to be more lowly than 'knowing facts', and where society recognizes and rewards experts in factual knowledge, and tends to refer to those whose expertise involves extensive practical activity as 'artisans' and 'blue-collar workers'.

Doctors need to be clear about the nature of their knowledge in order to defend their practice against these false assumptions. This means having the language to discuss the components of medical practice. We believe with de Cossart and Fish (2005) that doctors certainly know about medical facts, know them, and know ways of learning about them (that is, they become expert in 'knowing that', or in propositional knowledge). They also consciously acquire during their clinical work the knowledge of how to respond to the needs of patients, to enact processes and even to perform procedures (they become experts in 'knowing how' or procedural knowledge). But many are unaware that these two main components of knowledge (theory, or propositional knowledge; and practice, or procedural knowledge) have a more complex relationship than the simple one of theory as something which should simply be 'applied' to practice. Neither have they recognized, nor do they know about, the need to consider any other ways of seeing knowledge.

What are the components of knowledge that underpin medical practice?

Both a few moments thought and quite a short period of exploring medical practice itself will reveal that the rich range of knowledge that doctors call upon as they work with and for patients has been well captured in Figure 6.1. This includes not only knowledge of the procedures and processes involved in caring for, treating and managing patients both generally and in a particular specialty; know-how and knack of various kinds; knowledge of and ability to enact or utilize a range of Trust-level procedures and processes, protocols and guidelines (and knowledge of when to use professional judgement instead); knowledge of clinical thinking processes; knowledge of managerial procedures and educational processes but also self-knowledge; intuition; sensory knowledge; insight; common sense; 'plain old guessing' (Gawande 2002: 7); and metcognitive knowledge (knowledge about knowledge).

de Cossart and Fish (2005) provide a version of Figure 6.1 in which they characterize the knowledge components (or forms of knowledge) specifically in terms of surgical practice. It would be equally possible to do this for medical practice. Indeed, such an activity or exercise would be necessary in respect of the specific medical context for which the curriculum for postgraduate medicine was being designed. It might also be a useful way of bringing the design team together and exploring what understanding they actually share about the realities of medical practice in general and the specific context for which the curriculum is being designed in particular. We therefore offer in Figure 6.2 the main headings from Figure 6.1, and invite design teams for medical curricula to critique, reshape if necessary and adapt it for their particular purposes. It should be noted that in saying this we are recognizing the ever-changing nature of knowledge.

The importance of knowledge creation and improvisation in practice

The nature and detail of these kinds of knowledge for medical practice can really only be learnt in practice as part of that practice, and much of it springs from the need to improvise during practice. Indeed, as our colleagues have shown in Chapter 4, the knowledge that medical practitioners call upon most extensively in their practice is that which becomes apparent or is created during practice (see pp. 98–99). de Cossart and Fish (2002) also make a similar point as a result of analysing an incident from de Cossart's practice, in relation to breaking bad news, where it became clear that while factual medical knowledge was drawn upon (briefly) to identify the significance of test results and thus to precipitate the rest of the incident, it in fact then gave way to (much greater time spent on) common sense and human values, sensitivity and imagination. They concluded: 'How well such bad news is broken depends more on the person you are, and your own beliefs and values and how you can

Affected and shaped by values, and always context specific to the clinical setting

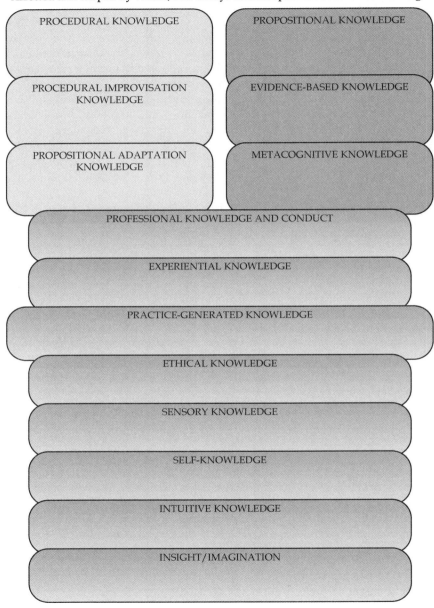

Figure 6.2   The key components of knowledge for medical practice (with acknowledgement to de Cossart and Fish 2005).

harness them to help other people, than on the learnt skills [and medical knowledge] of breaking bad news' (2002: 2).

Just how such knowledge is and can be acquired in the practice setting is the subject of the following chapter. But we do need to note here that, until the Foundation Core Curriculum was published, new doctors' education in the practice setting was without a proper structure, and that the activities of SHOs without a formal curriculum in surgery were characterized as 'magpie-like' and without rigour and structure (Brigley *et al.* 2003).

Using propositional knowledge differently at different stages

We should also note that there is substantial evidence that doctors use propositional knowledge differently at different learning stages in their postgraduate careers. For example, the knowledge that novices call upon is largely scientific in nature and has been structured for them in textbooks and lectures which, being largely theoretical, highlight the intrinsic structure of the *academic* discipline from which they have come. Few teachers in medical school invite learners to restructure this for themselves (make it their own). By contrast, postgraduate doctors gradually have to discover how to repackage their knowledge to enable it to be drawn on quickly and appropriately in their everyday clinical practice. Schmidt and Boshuinzen (1993) set out a model for considering the difference between novices and experts in their use of knowledge.

They say that being an expert is not necessarily knowing more than novices but having learnt to organize knowledge differently, combining it with increasing experience of cases, until the cases become more significant than the scientific knowledge. Eraut and du Boulay (2000), referencing Chang *et al.* (1998), point out that as the postgraduate becomes more experienced, there is evolution of both knowledge *structure* and diagnostic skill. Further, they seem to suggest that in postgraduate medical practice, new ways of structuring the knowledge already possessed become more important than accruing large amounts of new propositional knowledge. For example, increase in *knowledge* of patho-physiology is small compared with the reorganization of what is already known in order to make it more readily and rapidly available (see Eraut and du Boulay 2000: 1.1). They also remind us that every practitioner's knowledge base is highly individual and will have evolved from their previous personal clinical experience. But it is Cox who puts all this in perspective when he says: 'it should be remembered that expertise lies not in the knowledge *per se*, but in the judgement of what's pertinent and important' (1999: 277).

Practical wisdom (*phronesis*): the synthesis of all these forms of knowledge

Although this chapter has perforce focused on the kinds of knowledge that practitioners draw upon in practice, we would not wish to leave the reader either with the impression that gaining such forms of knowledge is a simple matter, or that such ownership would constitute a practitioner's total expertise. Having knowledge (of all kinds) is one thing, but it can mistakenly become a goal in its own right. Indeed, we see this as a particular danger in the current consumerist world, where we are deluged with information and data in the guise of 'equipping us with knowledge', but where much of such knowledge is irrelevant to our individual needs, and where acquisitions are not, in fact, the measure of the person. Indeed, we are reminded of T.S Eliot's words:

> Where is the Life we have lost in living?
> Where is the wisdom we have lost in knowledge?
> Where is the knowledge we have lost in information?
> (T.S. Eliot, 'Choruses from "The Rock" ': 1, 1965)

And we might add:

> Where is the information we have lost in data?

Knowing how, when and where to use the knowledge and understanding they have, in the best service of an individual in a given situation, is the mark of wise practitioners. And this is a far cry from simply 'having' the knowledge. It is being able to use it wisely. Here (as we said in Chapter 5), doctors need to be able to exercise the ability to deliberate by harnessing best general medical knowledge to the ethical and moral needs of the individual. Indeed, Aristotle argued that good deliberation is entirely dependent on the possession of *phronesis* (or practical wisdom), which is the virtue of knowing which general ethical principles apply for the best in a particular situation, and being willing and able to act to achieve this. For him this was the supreme intellectual virtue (Carr 1995: 71). This, then, is the real challenge for designers of a curriculum for practice: that they shape a framework that places emphasis not on the acquisition, but on the wise use, of these forms of knowledge.

Implications for curriculum designers

How then do these ideas about knowledge impact on the practice of curriculum design for postgraduate medicine? In other words: how should knowledge be conceived, organized and prioritized within the postgraduate medical curriculum and how should it be developed in postgraduate doctors? We offer the following thoughts.

- Designers need to be sure that the aims they set, the content they prescribe, the way and the order in which they present knowledge to be acquired, and the assessment processes they set in train, are all sensitive to the nature of medical knowledge as used by postgraduate doctors in the practice setting.
- They need to introduce teachers and learners to the precise language in which these matters are best discussed. That is, they need to attend to the meta-cognitive level of knowledge and to the meta-language in which it is expressed (and certainly they need to introduce 'the epistemology of practice' as a key term and a key area of study).
- The key characteristics of the knowledge that they need to attend to are: its complexity; uncertainty; its artistic as well as its scientific elements; the interrelationship of theory and practice; the collaborative nature of learning in a community of practice (the co-construction of knowledge); and the different use of propositional knowledge at different stages of learning.
- The curriculum needs to draw teachers' and learners' attention to this range of forms of knowledge and ways of knowing, and provide ways of ensuring that their relevance to practice is discussed and understood by teachers and learners.
- Designers need to ensure that they provide incentives to teachers and learners to unearth their tacit and implicit knowledge in order to do justice to the important invisible elements. This might best be done by investigating that practice (which is where the Stenhouse 'research model' of the curriculum, or at least the process model, would be useful).
- They also need to find ways to recognize the importance of the theory that learners can generate *within their practice*, by engaging in practice and reflecting upon it.
- The curriculum should also provide a rationale for the kinds of knowledge it attends to and for the ways it chooses to do this.
- It should disabuse teachers and learners of the idea that knowledge is merely a matter of facts (theory) and know-how (practice)
- It should provide a carefully reasoned approach to the educational validity and reliability of its assessment process (which relates to the nature of knowledge more generally).

Finally, curriculum design teams for postgraduate medical practice should especially remember that much of the knowledge that underpins practice is not 'out there' waiting to be discovered, but *implicit in the way we see things* (embedded in how we see and construe our world), and endemic to the way doctors interact with their colleagues.

The challenge for curriculum designers is to develop a curriculum framework that supports teachers' and learners' exploration of their practice in these terms.

7 Selecting appropriate educational strategies: how doctors learn to practise

What currently characterizes the activities of teaching and learning in medical practice (in both undergraduate and postgraduate education), and how is this different from education in formal educational institutions?
What ought to characterize these activities?
What kinds of pedagogic understanding ought to underpin the teaching and learning of practice?
How will the curriculum provide for these?

Introduction

The challenge of this book is to devise a curriculum through which doctors can acquire and develop their practice. To this end, curriculum designers need to: understand how in reality doctors learn to practise and learn their practice (review the traditions of educational practice which the new curriculum will extend or challenge); and consider and select the educational strategies that might best achieve their curricular purposes within the current and future contexts of postgraduate medicine.

In this chapter therefore, we seek to address the questions at its head by examining first how doctors have conventionally been learning and being taught in undergraduate and postgraduate education, and then looking at recent reforms that have addressed the problems that have emerged. We follow this by offering a critique of these reforms and considering alternative strategies. We then consider the ways in which both teaching and learning are themselves educational practices (within the more general practice of education). Finally we pinpoint useful principles to guide the selection of educational strategies for the practice setting.

The traditional teaching and learning of medical practice

Introduction

In Chapter 3 we suggested that there were at least three ways of conceiving of an educational activity (as delivering a product, as engaging in a process, and as a research enterprise) and that whether consciously adopted or assumed, these concepts influence the teaching and learning that occur.

Where education is seen as delivering a product, the teacher is the major resource, whose function is to transmit knowledge efficiently to passive learners. Here, the emphasis is on teaching *methods*, and teachers are themselves 'instructed' (trained even) in how to teach.

In the process view of education, there is more interaction between teacher and learner. Here, the emphasis is on *principles of procedure* (the ideas that will shape how teachers and learners engage). The teacher is still likely to be the initiator of these processes but becomes a facilitator. The learner is much more active and may learn more than either party imagined at the outset.

As a research enterprise, education brings teachers and learners into a more equal, learning partnership. Teaching methods, and even principles of procedure, give way to *an agenda*, which both can determine so that a genuinely collaborative and investigative approach evolves.

We shall now use these ideas to help us understand the history and traditions of teaching and learning in postgraduate medicine.

Earlier times: similar problems

Concerns about teaching and learning in medical education are not new. In the second half of the nineteenth century, shortly after the GMC had been formed in the UK, all was not well even then, since:

> [There was an] . . . overloading of the curriculum of education . . . followed by results injurious to the student (GMC 1863). Whoever will consider the great extent of the sciences which lie at the foundation of Medicine and Surgery . . . will see that some limit must be assigned to the amount of knowledge which can be fitly exacted (GMC 1869). The burden we place on the medical student is far too heavy, and it takes some doing to keep from breaking his intellectual back. A system of medical education that is actually calculated to

obstruct the acquisition of sound knowledge and to heavily favour the crammer and the grinder is a disgrace.

(Thomas Huxley 1876 in GMC 1993: 5)

Rather than reducing the load, since that time the undergraduate medical course in the UK has been shortened from six years to five (and currently is becoming four years for graduate entry students), and the amount of information available vastly increased.

If the medical curriculum was overloaded in 1863, what can be said of it today? In fact, precisely the same observations as were made by the GMC 140 years ago are still being made today (GMC 2001), despite many decades of curriculum development. Medical students are overloaded with content, fail to see the relevance of much of what they are learning, and quickly forget what they have learnt, such that when they begin to practise medicine they are ill-equipped for what is expected of them. Once qualified, they find they must begin again to learn what is needed to practise effectively, and that to pass postgraduate medical examinations, on which their progress depends, they must absent themselves from their clinical practice and engage in more textbook revision. Why is this, and what has caused the failure of the various interventions that have been introduced in an attempt to ameliorate the situation?

We look first at undergraduate teaching and learning because we believe that many of the problems and issues facing postgraduate medical education (not just in the UK) stem from this. In particular we focus on how both undergraduates and postgraduates learn *to practise* medicine, though we recognize that this too is influenced by what happens in the education they receive within classrooms as well as in the practical setting.

Undergraduate teaching and learning

Traditionally, the undergraduate medical curriculum has been divided into two distinct phases: pre-clinical and clinical. The pre-clinical phase, often lasting up to two years, presented students with largely bio-medical information, almost all of it from the laboratory-based scientific disciplines of anatomy, physiology and biochemistry. Other subjects were added through the years, including pharmacology, embryology, genetics and pathology, together with the so-called behavioural sciences of psychology, sociology and epidemiology.

Very typically, these subjects would be taught through formal programmes of lectures and seminars, largely within a 'product' conceptualization of education. A student's daily timetable would be almost entirely filled with teaching activities. Private study would be undertaken in a library or in a students' residence, in a student's own time. 'Spoon-feeding' and 'pot-filling' are metaphors often used to characterize this experience.

When students passed through to the clinical phase of the undergraduate curriculum (usually successfully undergoing an examination of their knowledge of the pre-clinical subjects they had been taught), their ways of learning (and the forms of teaching that accompanied these) changed dramatically. Students now found themselves 'on the wards' (Sinclair 1997), undertaking attachments with various clinical disciplines, chiefly in medicine and surgery, with other mostly hospital-based disciplines such as obstetrics and gynaecology, paediatrics, geriatrics and psychiatry. Increasingly over the years, students also attended attachments in primary medical care.

In the clinical phase students would typically receive at most very informal teaching (but often little or no teaching at all). They would be allocated patients to see and to 'clerk' (meaning to find out from patients what their clinical problem was, what treatment they were receiving and what progress was being made), and would from time to time 'present' their patients to a senior doctor (often the consultant or a senior trainee), which would be accompanied by some form of 'interrogation' by their teacher concerning their knowledge of the condition being described. This knowledge would typically have been acquired by them through private study or more rarely through programmed seminar teaching by doctors in their clinical units. Most of the formal teaching would relate largely to clinical management of patients, including discussion of pathophysiology, and increasing over the years with the addition of clinical genetics and molecular biochemistry. The intellectual level of the teaching (and corresponding learning) was dependent on the quality of the unit to which they were attached, whether it was an 'academic' one in a teaching hospital or was located in a district general hospital.

The teaching and learning that occurs in the clinical years could be characterized as a 'process' view of education, on the grounds that very little 'formal' education occurs. However, it is better described as *laissez faire*, where students are largely left to their own devices. Indeed, some of the teaching could well be characterized as within the 'product' view of education, that is, where the teachers indicate the 'right' way to go about clinical practice, and indeed (quite legitimately) where there is a clinical procedure to be mastered. Whether or not there are 'principles of procedure' (consistent with the process approach) that govern and perhaps determine the education of students, might be a function of the design of the curriculum. But these principles may not have been made explicit, and are likely to have been the enlightened whim of an individual clinical teacher. In reality, the more insightful students will construct a curriculum for themselves – engaging teachers (which might include other students in informal learning groups) in conversations to deal with questions, uncertainties and confusions. Some learners even adopt a 'research' approach, going beyond seeing their teachers as 'facilitators of their learning' to using them as 'supervisors' of their developing understanding. However, where students engage more particularly in traditional research activities, this can appear to be more of a 'product' approach than a genuinely 'research' one if they have merely been set a research project to undertake (Coles 1985).

The general feature of the undergraduate curriculum, then, was a clear separation of theory (often called basic science) from practice (or clinical medicine). Various calls were made (in the UK by the GMC and in North America by several reports) to integrate the two, and we will look at this in more detail shortly. For the moment we note that traditional teaching and learning reflected this separation, with the pre-clinical phase being taught largely by academic scientists and the clinical phase by clinicians who usually neither knew nor engaged with each other.

Postgraduate teaching and learning

Traditionally, postgraduate teaching and learning (known as training) has followed a pattern that has been described as an apprenticeship – 'learning to be the professional by practising the profession under conditions of supervision and careful selection of appropriate levels of independent responsibility and experience' (The Open University 2001: 15).

Postgraduate training typically lasted five to ten years in the UK, with the length depending on the specialty (shorter for psychiatry, longer for surgery). Trainees would be attached for between six months and a year to a 'firm' (clinical unit) with its strictly hierarchical nature – consultants at the top, senior registrars and registrars below them, and house officers at the bottom. Trainees worked their way up through this structure, gaining experience and by taking examinations run by the Royal College of their specialty. Assessment of their practice was to say the least perfunctory – 'signing people up' at the end of an attachment, largely to show that they had attended.

The first year of postgraduate training has been known as the pre-registration year, precisely because at the end of this time trainees became fully registered with the GMC (and could then legally carry out certain clinical actions and procedures such as independently prescribing certain medications).

Until the 1990s trainees' time was unregulated, and it was not uncommon for them to work 100 hours per week. The pressures on them clinically, however, were by no means as great as they are today. Patients were in hospital for longer periods, their clinical management was less aggressive, the medications used were considerably less toxic, and there was much less pressure on the utilization of resources (chiefly bed occupancy). Many of the more junior trainees 'lived in', being accommodated on the hospital site. Typically, there was a 'juniors' mess' where trainees congregated when not actually with patients. There was a much greater sense of community about being a trainee than perhaps there is today.

Trainees' work during the day typically involved 'clerking' patients, checking on patients' progress, ordering clinical tests, requesting test results and carrying out clinical procedures appropriate to the level (though in reality often above their level) of expertise. Much of this work was unsupervised clinically and educationally. It was not uncommon for them to undertake procedures that they were not fully trained to carry out, despite the GMC's exhortations that this should not occur (GMC 1997). They would attend ward rounds led by senior trainees or consultants, where patients were reviewed, which often led to trainees requesting further laboratory tests or changes to the clinical management plan. Typically, trainees were not involved at all (or at least to a very small extent) in outpatient clinics, which were held by senior trainees and consultants.

Most of the 'out of hours' work was carried out by junior trainees, with more senior trainees and consultants being 'on call' from their homes. When juniors faced a clinical problem that they felt unable to deal with themselves they would telephone the senior on call for advice, perhaps leading to the senior coming into the hospital to manage the situation.

Reductions in junior doctors' hours (especially with the introduction of the **European Working Time Directive**) (EWTD) led in 2004 to a 56-hour week. This has meant that their exposure to clinical situations has similarly been reduced – they gain less experience than before. Related to this lessening of experience, patients now demand to be treated (and where possible seen) by the most senior doctor available – ideally the consultant. This has meant that a trainee's actual 'hands on' clinical experience has been further reduced.

At the same time, and largely because of these changes, clinical work previously carried out by junior doctors is now undertaken by other staff, such as nurses, phlebotomists and clerical staff.

Trainees learnt to practise, then, through experience, that is by undertaking clinical work with a greater or lesser degree of supervision depending on the availability (and willingness) of more senior doctors to teach them. Some teaching occurred on ward rounds and through junior trainees being shown how to conduct a clinical procedure by more senior trainees (and occasionally by consultants). As we saw in the traditional undergraduate clinical curriculum, the teaching and learning in the postgraduate years is often similarly *laissez faire*, and whether it follows a 'product', 'process' or 'research' approach is largely determined by the (often unstated) educational values of the teacher and/or the learner.

In recent years, 'core teaching' was introduced, often consisting of a weekly formal teaching session where topics thought to be relevant to the trainees' work were presented (often in lecture format or through seminar discussion). Trainees on occasions would be asked to present a topic themselves, which they would 'work up' from textbooks and formally present to their colleagues. This appears to be very much a 'product' view of education.

The examinations that trainees prepared for were typically held entirely outside the clinical environment (often at a national examination centre), and comprised formal assessments such as multiple choice, short answer, and essay question papers. Trainees would prepare for these by taking 'study leave' to revise the propositional knowledge in current textbooks for their specialty. A growing market has developed in recent years for taught courses aimed at trainees' examination preparation.

Developments in the teaching and learning of medical practice

Undergraduate medical education

Perhaps the major concern regarding undergraduate medical education during the twentieth century was 'overload'. As we saw earlier, this had been identified over 150 years ago, yet despite attempts on the part of the GMC to reduce the amount being taught and learnt (most notably through the GMC's recommendations in 1957), little change had occurred.

Our focus in this book, however, is the education of doctors in the practice of medicine, and here we look at how this is currently taught and learnt in the undergraduate years.

A number of developments have occurred, which in reality took two courses: the linking of the subjects that were being taught contemporaneously; and a blurring of the traditional division of the curriculum into pre-clinical and clinical phases. We will refer to these as 'horizontal' and 'vertical' integration respectively.

Horizontal integration

Traditionally, as we have shown, medical students were taught what were considered to be the sciences on which medicine was based as separate subjects, reflecting the distinctive identity of the academic departments that undertook the teaching. In the 1950s curricular developments in the USA (chiefly at Case Western Reserve Medical School, see Williams 1980) created what were termed 'systems' courses. These courses brought together the basic sciences into topic-based courses such as 'the respiratory system', 'the cardiovascular system' and 'the renal system'. The intention was to show how each of the traditional disciplines combined together (integrated) in particular bodily systems. The hope was that this would give greater 'relevance' to the teaching, and hence aid medical students' learning.

However, horizontally integrated curricula typically retained the traditional 'lecture system' – timetabled lectures which presented the content, followed by self-study where students learnt the material (often to pass an examination which tested their knowledge of that content). However, this system failed to make curricular links to the teaching and learning of medical practice and to challenge the more fundamental division of the curriculum into pre-clinical and clinical phases (Coles 1985). In short, horizontal integration still focused on teaching and learning in the classroom rather than in practice. A 'product' model of education was thereby maintained.

Vertical integration

A more significant attempt to reform undergraduate medical education directly addressed the relationship of the pre-clinical and clinical phases of the curriculum. One approach was for undergraduates to experience clinical medicine early on in the curriculum, and although this appears to reflect something of a 'process' view of education, the results were to say the least of variable success (Coles and Mountford 1978), probably because of the dominance of the overall educational model, which at that point in the students' lives was largely a 'product' one. As one put it: 'Seeing patients might be relevant to being a doctor but it's not relevant to being a student!'

A more radical approach to vertical integration was developed which attempted to link what have loosely been referred to as 'theory' and 'practice'. This became known as '**Problem-Based Learning**' or PBL.

PBL in undergraduate medical education was first introduced on a curriculum-wide basis at McMaster Medical School in Canada in the mid-1960s, and has since spread to many other sites. Typically, PBL students worked in small groups, facilitated by a faculty member trained in this role. They studied what became called 'paper cases' – written descriptions of actual clinical situations, comprising background data, clinical findings, laboratory test results, referral correspondence, etc. – as a basis for understanding the basic sciences.

While this small group work was intended to give vertical integration to the curriculum, in most PBL medical schools it formed the basis for learning the basic sciences in the early years. This was then followed by a clinical phase not unlike the traditional curriculum described above, though with a greater emphasis on the 'application' of the previously acquired understanding, but now in a clinical setting.

During the initial phase of PBL, the facilitator would encourage the group to discuss the paper cases presented to them so as to identify what they needed to know in order to understand the clinical scenario. The facilitator most probably would prompt the students towards certain sources of information (for example texts, journal articles, anatomy specimens). Much of the students' time would then be spent in seeking out this information and preparing résumés to present to their colleagues. Contact time with the facilitator was at a bare minimum, comprising perhaps two or three programmed sessions each week, each lasting an hour or so. This appears to reflect more of a 'process' view of education than a 'product' one.

A considerable amount of interest and attention has been devoted to evaluating the contribution of PBL to undergraduate medical education, and it is not our intention to rehearse this here to any great extent; suffice it to say that the findings are equivocal. Students generally (though not universally) appear to enjoy this form of teaching and learning, and it has been shown that they develop approaches to studying that are considered to be beneficial (Coles 1985). However, some concern has been expressed as to the efficacy of the knowledge acquired in this way for clinical practice.

One critic, Margetson, comments that 'traditional' PBL focuses students' learning on the mechanisms of clinical problems (that is on the so-called basic sciences) rather than on solutions to those problems. So, ironically, just like the conventional curriculum it sought to improve, PBL has been found to separate understanding from action. He says, 'traditional curricula and some problem-based curricula are structurally similar, both following a knowledge first, application second view'. The problems that form the basis of PBL are, he suggests, in danger of being no more than 'convenient pegs on which to hang the coat of basic science knowledge which students need to acquire'. This 'convenient peg' concept, he argues, 'perpetuates an atomistic view of medical education in at least three ways':

- the pre-clinical and clinical phases of the curriculum are held structurally distinct from one another through the notion of the 'application' of knowledge;
- the two phases are quite separate in nature, the one being seen as 'theoretical' the other 'practical';
- the pre-clinical phase is seen as 'an absolutely secure foundation on which clinical practice rests' (Margetson 1999: 362–3).

For Margetson, then, the weakness of much PBL (that is, where it separates understanding from action) is that it fails to recognize that 'human action . . . makes no sense apart from understanding; rather, action raises questions of the *extent* of understanding and its soundness' (1999: 361). For him, the alternative is a 'rigorously problem-based' curriculum that requires 'the thorough integration of understanding (in the widest sense), knowledge and skill' (Margetson 1999: 363–4). This view is echoed by researchers in Holland who suggest that 'asking students . . . to evaluate paper cases . . . involves a significantly different process from that involved in diagnosing and managing real patients' (Rikers *et al.* 2004: 1041).

What these critics appear to be suggesting is that while the conventional approach to PBL might reflect a 'process' view of education, what is required *for the students to begin to understand medical practice*, is a more 'research' orientated view.

In this connection, one innovation in undergraduate medical education, which deserves a mention here, concerns not problem-based learning *per se* but the timing of the 'basic science' examination. Traditionally, a student's pre-clinical knowledge is examined at the end of the pre-clinical phase. At the University of Southampton medical school it is held one year later – after students have had 12 months of clinical experience. Studies have shown (for example, Coles 1985) that the timing of this examination crucially affects students' understanding of the basic sciences. Many (though by no means all) students find that revising their pre-clinical notes *having now had some experience of first hand clinical medicine* leads to an enhanced understanding of what they are learning, so that 'things begin to fit together' (Coles 1985). This may well reflect what the Dutch researchers cited above call 'encapsulated knowledge' (Rikers *et al.* 2004: 1035). Even though the early part of the Southampton curriculum is 'traditional' (in Margetson's sense of separating understanding from action) and despite its attempts at curricular reform through 'horizontal' integration (Coles 1985), the timing of this important pre-clinical examination could be thought to provide a basis for 'rigorous problem-based' learning (Coles 1990). Put another way, in the very act of revising for an examination of what might be termed 'factual' knowledge, they were in reality 're-searching' their own clinical practice, because by now they had experienced it for themselves.

Postgraduate medical education

As we saw above, traditionally postgraduate medical education (like much of the clinical phase of undergraduate curricula) is largely informal (*laissez faire*) and based on acquiring experience, with trainees receiving more or less practical teaching and clinical supervision depending on their location. More formal teaching is reserved for factual information, which as we have seen separates understanding from action, while more formal learning is seen in revision (largely of textbook knowledge) for postgraduate examinations.

Attempts to improve the quality of postgraduate medical teaching and learning during the late 1980s and the 1990s focused on the role of what the GMC called the 'educational supervisor' – 'normally the consultant with whom the trainee is attached, who is there to ensure that the trainee's educational needs are met' (GMC 1987). In this respect at least, the current approach to teaching and learning in postgraduate medical education is beginning to reflect more overtly a 'process' view, with the teacher being the facilitator of the learner's learning, and where some 'principles of procedure' are being drawn up to achieve this.

Much has been written about the importance of this role of educational supervisor. However, the quality of this supervision has been shown to vary markedly across clinical disciplines and within units. In the UK the **Standing Committee for Postgraduate Medical and Dental Education** (SCOPME) issued two reports in an attempt to promote postgraduate teaching (1994) and teacher development (1999). In particular they recommended that: 'Consultants and other senior hospital staff who teach doctors and dentists in specialty training should be given the opportunity to acquire the skills necessary to fulfil this responsibility' (SCOPME 1994: 2).

This was reinforced by the GMC, which said that:

> All doctors have a professional obligation to contribute to the education and training of other doctors, medical students and non-medical healthcare professionals on the team . . . Those who accept special responsibilities for teaching should take steps to ensure that they develop and maintain the skills of a competent teacher.
>
> (2001: 2)

A similar statement has recently been issued by the newly established PMETB (2004: 19):

> Those who have responsibility for teaching must develop the skills, attitudes and practices of a competent teacher and ensure that trainees are properly supervised . . . The responsibility to support learning and teaching must include clearly defined processes for selecting and training educational supervisors, trainers and other faculty staff.

There are, then, political exhortations to improve teaching in postgraduate medical education. However, little has been said about what this teaching would entail – what model of education it would represent or more particularly how it would relate to the curriculum as a whole.

Learning to practise through simulation
Also in recent times, considerable interest has been devoted to the learning of clinical practice through simulations of various kinds (Moorthy *et al.* 2005). One approach has been to develop what have been called 'skills laboratories'. These are places where people can practise, on inanimate models in a non-clinical setting, certain clinical procedures, including venepuncture, catheterization, wound closure and intubation. In some situations, animal models and human cadavers are used.

While simulation of this kind may be useful to introduce learners to the mechanics of these procedures, and certainly to familiarize them with the instrumentation that may be involved, it inevitably decontextualizes the practice of the procedure being learnt. As we have shown, particularly in Chapters 4 and 5, clinical practice always occurs in a specific context – inserting a cannula into the vein of a fit young adult requires a very different practice from doing so with a confused elderly person, not just in terms of interpersonal concerns but even of the physical actions that are involved.

An attempt to overcome the problems of the decontextualized learning of clinical procedures has been to create manikins that simulate as closely as possible real patients. Such simulators are not unlike those used in, for example, airline pilot training, and can present learners with quite complex (and even rarely experienced) situations, which through computer control can not only respond to the actions taken but also provide information to the learners to indicate what they did.

Again, while these approaches may be of some value, they still stop short of providing education in actual practice. Even the most sophisticated simulation will not lead to an actual 'death' if a fatal error is made, and there will always remain a need for further learning to take place (and to continue to take place) in the practice setting.

The educational point here is that any simulation is (inevitably) an abstraction, and it may be useful to examine this further. Medical practice can, as we have seen in this chapter, be simulated in a variety of ways, and these can be represented in the form of a typology indicating 'levels of abstraction from practice' (see the box below). The range runs from the most concrete (nearest to real practice) at the top, to the least concrete (furthest from real practice) at the bottom.

It is currently assumed in terms of learning skills and procedures that the more inexperienced the learners are, the further from practice they need to begin. However, ironically, this typology leads us to speculate that learners still gaining first-hand experience of a certain procedure may need to practise that procedure in as many concrete situations as possible (probably in real life).

Levels of abstraction from practice

Engaging in actual practice oneself
Observation of someone else's practice
Video-recording of one's own practice
Audio-recording of one's own practice
Video-recording of someone else's practice
Audio-recording of someone else's practice
Computer-controlled simulator
Skills laboratory
Narrative by oneself of one's own case
Narrative by someone else of a case
Review of a patient's case notes
Paper-and-pencil cases (PBL)
Clinical guidelines
Clinical protocols

Whereas, the learner with extensive first-hand experience may gain more through simulations (for example, in masterclasses) that are further remote from practice.

Improving practice through increased accountability: using regulation as an educational strategy

In recent years, the practice of doctors has come under much greater scrutiny than in the past. In the UK, central government has led the way in attempting to improve practice through the mechanism of increased accountability. However, as we shall show, the several confusions of terms and ideas that underpinned this enterprise have rendered it largely unsuccessful. Curriculum designers need to know about this because it is part of the context of educational strategies within which their curriculum will be enacted.

An unstated understanding

Professionals need to be accountable for their practice. Indeed, being professional carries with it the obligation to be accountable. Many see this as a fundamental characteristic of their practice (as an unarticulated 'contract' between professionals and society in which 'society would trust professionals if they could be trusted'). But until the very end of the twentieth century, this was 'never formally codified into a contract. It was unstated' (Fish and Coles 1998: 4–5). We have already illustrated the breakdown of trust that led to the need to formalize all this, and which resulted in the UK government (through the DoH) arguing that 'there is now a need to introduce reform to the NHS procedures for dealing with poor performance . . . and to extend the strong range of action already taken by the Government to achieve comprehensive quality improvement in the NHS' (DoH 1999a: 6–7). Unfortunately, again, the problem was seen as managerial rather than educational and was conceptualized as about systems rather than about changing doctors' understanding. Thus, without more debate, a managerial solution was adopted.

Appraisal for all doctors

The reform that was decided upon was for 'appraisal to be introduced for all doctors working within the NHS', which would 'be made comprehensive and compulsory' and 'form an important component of the systems required by the GMC for [the revalidation of] doctors' (DoH 1999a: 59). (However, as we showed in Chapter 3, the work of Habermas demonstrates that coercion does not achieve educational goals.) It is therefore perhaps hardly surprising that the publication in 2004 of a report from an inquiry into the homicides carried out over many years by the GP, Dr Harold Shipman, has suggested that appraisal by doctors would not provide an adequate safeguard for patients.

Designers should note too, that the concept of 'revalidation' had been introduced by the GMC at about this time for many of the same reasons identified by the DoH that led to appraisal. Revalidation was to be a five-yearly review of doctors' performance against standards set by the GMC in its publication *Good Medical Practice* (GMC 2001). Revalidation processes and the postgraduate medical curriculum will need to coexist, if not interrelate.

Several confusions

Appraisal then, as an educational strategy, is founded on confusing educational and managerial views of the problem. Indeed as the following shows, it is beginning to be clear that the attempt to marry regulatory and penal intentions with developmental and educational ones will be unsuccessful. It is also clear that a systems-level approach will not solve educational problems which ultimately must be attended to at an individual level. Appraisal is not an educational strategy and cannot do both an educational and a regulatory job.

The DoH's approach to what it called appraisal was introduced in the context of poorly-performing doctors. It nevertheless described it as:

> . . . a positive process to give someone feedback on their performance, to chart their continuing progress and to identify development needs. It is a forward looking process essential for the developmental and educational planning needs of an individual . . . It is not the primary aim of appraisal to scrutinise doctors to see if they are performing poorly but rather to help them to consolidate on good performance aiming towards excellence. However, it can help to recognise at an early stage developing poor performance or ill health which may be affecting practice.
>
> (DoH 1999a: 59)

But the DoH is now reconsidering by how much this form of appraisal can deal with the issue of poor performance let alone achieve 'comprehensive quality improvement'.

Education and accountability

It is possible, however, to develop a view of accountability which interrelates much better with educational purposes and intentions. This firstly involves conceiving of accountability in more human and humane terms, and then recognizing that the *account* at the heart of accountability can be presented in a variety of ways, some of which are more educational than others.

Onora O'Neill (2002: 19) has made this observation:

> Perhaps claims about a crisis of trust are mainly evidence of an unrealistic hankering for a world in which safety and compliance are total, and breaches of trust are eliminated. Perhaps the culture of accountability that we are relentlessly building for ourselves actually damages trust rather than supporting it. Plants don't flourish when we pull them up too often to check how their roots are growing: political, institutional and professional life too may not flourish if we constantly uproot it to demonstrate that everything is transparent and trustworthy.

How then can we be accountable for our practice? And how can that accountability be educational? O'Neill rejects the essentially scientific and agricultural research approach of 'quantifying practice' as inimical to the culture of nurturing that learners require if they are to be properly challenged to develop. But she does not pursue other solutions. We would argue for ideas that were first promoted in the literature of schoolteacher development of the 1970s, and which have ever since provided teachers and many health care professionals with better ways of giving an account of their practice.

Hoyle, writing about teacher development in the 1970s, characterized 'extended professionals' as those who:

- have a high level of competence;
- have a high degree of skill in understanding and handling the people with whom they are working;
- derive high satisfaction from personal contact with others;
- evaluate their own performance;
- attend short courses of a practical nature;

but also

- view their own work in the wider context of society;
- participate in a wide range of professional activities (e.g. attend conferences, serve on national bodies);
- have a concern to link theory and practice;
- have a commitment to some form of 'theory of practice' (Hoyle 1974).

Stenhouse, writing in the same context, adds three further characteristics of the extended professional:

- the commitment to systematic questioning of one's own [practice] as a basis for development;
- the commitment and the skills to study one's own [practice];
- the concern to question and to test theory in practice by the use of those skills (Stenhouse 1975: 144).

He argued that 'it is not enough that teachers' work should be studied: they need to study it themselves'. His notion was to develop 'the role of the teacher as researcher' (1975: 143).

This sets the scene for practitioners learning to practise and improving their practice at the same time. And it firmly locates accountability as requiring a form of *research into* one's own practice rather than a form of *record-keeping* about one's practice. Further, when learners research their own practice and give an account of that practice which draws upon every way of investigating elements of it, they come to understand it better. Such understanding then illuminates and motivates the development of their practice. We have elsewhere termed this 'insider practitioner research' (Fish and Coles 1998: 309). We also said:

> where the goal is improving understanding . . . the enterprise is essentially educational . . . That is, the intention to understand something implies the need to learn . . . The significance of this is twofold. Firstly it makes it entirely appropriate that the approaches, methods and means utilised to extend understanding are drawn from, and that practitioners see themselves as working within, the broad traditions of *educational* research. Secondly because such an enquiry will feed into accountability, research publications and professional development, it ensures that these are given an *educational* focus. That is, it will begin an important shift from seeing accountability, research and professional development as *administrative* chores to recognising their educational potential.
>
> (Fish and Coles 1998: 57–8)

We hold that practitioners are best able to be held accountable *for* their practice if they have developed more precise ways of giving an accurate account *of* their practice.

Curriculum designers, then, need to understand the importance of thinking educationally rather than managerially about the overall enterprise they are engaged in, and to seek ways of supporting the managerial needs for accountability and appraisal by promoting accounts of practice as a means of teaching, learning, assessing and only after this using them as fuel for the regulatory requirements of the system. Practitioners' accounts of their practice should be the result of their own wide investigations of their work.

Education in the practice setting provides a natural arena for this, and teachers need to encourage it in every way possible, including by engaging in it themselves. The educational thrust of the whole strategy, which we commend designers to consider embedding in any curriculum for postgraduate medicine, is best promoted via Stenhouse's research model of curriculum design.

Teaching for developing understanding in clinical settings

A major study (Coles *et al.* 2003) of curricula (in the context of cancer education) showed that in practice 'action', 'knowledge' and 'learning' were entirely integrated. When practitioners are engaged in practice (as characterized in Chapters 4 and 5) these three happen 'as one' and not as separate activities. It is only when we intentionally address people's learning (as in a curriculum or when supervising someone's practice) that the tendency to separate 'understanding' and 'action' is liable to occur.

In her story as reported in Chapter 4, Patrizia was urged by her senior, 'just do it'. Recognizing an important opportunity, she proceeded, thereby developing her practice. Her senior was there in case something went wrong or she encountered some difficulty. The same scenario is played out daily in clinical (and other forms of professional) practice – most often without those involved even noticing that it is occurring.

The learner's role then, both at undergraduate and postgraduate levels, is first and foremost to recognize opportunities in which (and through which) to learn practice and to seize them. In reality, any piece of service work that a doctor engages in can potentially become a basis for learning to practise. Learning occurs in the interstices of practice (in the moments between items of service) probably more profoundly than in the 'set piece' setting of formal teaching. The potential for learning thus occurs wherever and whenever doctors (and students) engage in practice. Earlier we argued that medical practice is, necessarily, associated with unpredictability and paradox. Those are ideal circumstances for the development of postgraduate doctors. Their education needs to be realistic. It needs to recognise and find ways of discussing, investigating and adapting to (improvising within) practice as it really is. Curriculum designers should avoid promoting educational strategies that minimize and simplify practice in order to teach it more comfortably (because the difficulties are ignored).

The teacher's role is to create a safe environment (a 'practicum', see Schön 1987a) in which learning can take place. An essential feature of learning to practise is that the learner's practice needs to be authentic. By this we mean that learners must be doing more than simply observing the teacher's practice, though early on this may be of some educational benefit and may in any case be necessary to protect patients from harm. Any observation by the learner must be accompanied by conversations and debriefing (see below) to increase the learner's understanding. A simulation (see above) is quite clearly not authentic practice.

At some point, the teacher will need to hand over practice to the learner. This can be a difficult moment for both. The teacher may believe the learner is not yet ready, while the learner may be highly confident and wish to proceed. Alternatively, the teacher might suggest too early that the learner engages in authentic practice, before the learner is ready to do so, and this might dent the learner's confidence if anything should go amiss. What is certain is that the decision to allow the learner to act must be finely judged (involving the professional judgement of the teacher) and will probably be based on very subtle 'cues' from both the teacher and the learner. An important principle should be that this is discussed between the two beforehand, talked about during, and debriefed on afterwards.

When the teacher has handed over the practice to the learner, a sufficient level of supervision needs to be maintained. However frustrating it is for teachers to watch learners' struggles, they must stay with and talk with the learner. They may also need to agree some kind of rescue package, that is, under what circumstances the teacher would take back control of the practice in question, and how this might occur.

Learning to practise occurs through 'criticality', where practice 'is constantly being reinterpreted and revised through dialogue and discussion'. 'It is precisely because it embodies this process of critical reconstruction that a tradition [of practice] evolves and changes rather than remains static or fixed' (Carr 1995: 69). Central to the process of developing understanding then, are 'professional conversations' with respected peers. Conversation here entails articulating one's thought processes and sharing these. However, people's understandings differ, so explanation and clarification are essential. Teachers need to check what the learner has understood from the conversations they have with them. In a very real sense, both the teacher's and the learner's understanding changes through conversation. Learning involves the co-construction of understanding: 'Knowledge cannot be transmitted. It has to be constructed afresh by each individual on the basis of what is already known and by means of strategies developed over the whole of that individual's life outside and inside the classroom' (Wells 1986: 236).

Conversations may be one-to-one or they may be with several others. The essence of learning to practise is that 'the collective deliberation of the many is always preferable to the isolated deliberation of the individual' (Carr 1995: 71). Practice, as we have seen, occurs in a social setting. It involves a community of practitioners. Learning best occurs where there is a sense of community and collegiality (Klass 2004).

The important feature of professional conversations is the emergence and development of practical wisdom (see Chapter 5), since 'without practical wisdom deliberation degenerates into an intellectual exercise, and "good practice" becomes indistinguishable from instrumental cleverness' (Carr 1995: 71). Practical wisdom can be developed through 'coaching' (Schön 1987a). This involves more than merely 'giving feedback'. While coaching may occur during the practice itself, it often happens prior to the action taking place, as well as afterwards. It requires the teacher to be able to put himself or herself in the learner's position, to appreciate how the learner is seeing the situation and to try to understand the learner's thinking processes and help develop them.

Even more importantly, practical wisdom can be nourished via reflection and deliberation. Reflection is 'the careful consideration of one's practice by means of systematic critical enquiry'. Deliberation, on the other hand, 'goes beyond the critical consideration of one's practice and one's thinking during it, to focus on the problematic and contestable issues endemic to practising as a professional' (Fish and Coles 1998: 68). Both are important. The second takes care of the wider issues that the extended practitioner needs to understand.

Further exploration of the use of reflective talking and writing can be found throughout de Cossart and Fish (2005), and particularly in Chapters 5, 6 and 7. They offer a table that summarizes the key differences between spoken and written reflection (p. 88), and show in Part 2 of their book how it can provide a record and thus demonstrate a pattern of the development of insightful practice.

Teaching for the 'understanding' of medical practice also requires the teacher to find ways of enquiring into professional practice and to utilize a broad range of educational processes in order to do so. In commending insider practitioner research as a central educational strategy to be promoted in any curriculum for postgraduate doctors, we are acutely conscious of the need to describe more fully what we mean by research in this context. Insider practitioner research is a form of educational enquiry, and is located within the humanistic research tradition. We are aware that many of the readers of this book, coming from a medical background, will be much more familiar with scientific forms of research that underpin clinical enquiry (as well as basic science research). However, that kind of research differs significantly from educational enquiry. We develop this argument more fully in Chapter 10.

Insider practitioner research is a form of case study (Golby and Parrott 1999: 69–71), where the 'case' in question is oneself. A highly suitable starting point is to take an incident in one's practice that was in some way or another out of the ordinary. Our unpredictable and messy practice abounds with 'critical incidents', whose significance is rendered critical by the manner in which we interpret them. This is not the same as an untoward clinical incident where things have gone wrong, but rather is more in tune with Schön's notion of 'surprise' – an incident that made one stop and think.

Our approach to researching such an incident has been described more fully elsewhere (see Fish and Coles 1998: 71–4 and Fish 1998). Briefly we suggest the following.

- First, pinpoint and then describe the incident as vividly as possible.
- Include as much 'context' as is necessary for someone else to understand what happened, what preceded the incident and what occurred afterwards.
- Ask yourself what might have happened, or what else *should* have happened.
- Try to see the incident from the perspective of the other people involved.
- Consider carefully: what are the problematic notions involved here, what are the dilemmas being posed by the incident, what is it that is essentially contestable and unresolvable? What needs further consideration? What is to be learnt from this?
- Write all this down, discuss it with others, make a record of what they say.

Conclusion and implications for designers

What then are the implications of all this for curriculum designers? They should understand the traditions of educational practice in postgraduate medicine, and they should know about and be able to select wisely from a range of educational strategies in order to promote best educational practice.

We have provided the historical context and charted the development of the educational strategies that are currently being used. These we suggest are in need of considerable 'modernizing' and extending. At worst, the teaching of practice at both undergraduate and postgraduate levels currently hardly happens at all. For the most part, however, it rests on an outmoded view of 'apprenticeship', where the apprentice learns the craft in the workplace, by working alongside 'masters'.

By contrast, we have argued that while practice is certainly learned *in* practice, learning professional practice must involve 'understanding', and that this is acquired through 'the critical reconstruction of practice' (Carr 1995). This happens when professionals engage in conversations, that is, dialogue and discussion about their practice, and inevitably results in the co-construction of understanding, where *both* teachers and learners change their practice as a result.

We have offered, as an alternative to traditional 'workplace' learning the notion of 'insider practitioner research', where practitioners (at all levels) engage in case-study enquiry of their own practice.

Thus curriculum designers should be alert to the crucial implications that learning to practise must:

- be *about* practice (that is, should be concerned with authentic, not simulated, practice);
- be *for* practice (that is, should be concerned with the development of practice);
- occur *in* practice;
- be carried out *by* practitioners (who themselves engage in the practice being taught and learnt).

This must influence every component of the main body of the curriculum.

Seen in this light, teaching and learning are both practices in their own right – educational practices that is, within the broader traditions of educational practice more generally. And as such they both share the same characteristics as medical practice – the complexity, unpredictability, uncertainty, paradox, need to take risks, inevitable fallibility and the need for judgement – that we demonstrated in Chapters 4 and 5. In addition, the main components of knowledge that underpin the practices of teaching and learning are similar to those in medicine, as discussed in Chapter 6. And, as we will see in the next chapter, the assessment of the practices of teaching and learning needs to follow the general principles we outline there.

Thus designers are going to have to work creatively to ensure that postgraduate medical education develops more rapidly in the twenty-first century. As a starting point, we offer for readers' critique the following principles that we believe should underpin their selection of such educational strategies:

- learning to practise involves a partnership between teachers and learners;
- both teachers and learners see examining their professional and personal values as fundamental to learning to practise;
- authentic practice is the key arena for learning to practise;
- conversation is central to learning to practise;
- practice involves both action and understanding;
- learning to practise requires both reflection and deliberation;
- learning to practise can usefully involve researching one's own practice;
- learning to practise involves developing sound professional judgement and practical wisdom;
- teaching and learning are both educational practices in their own right and teachers and learners need to commit themselves to developing their own.

One implication of this is that any curriculum design for practice must take into account the need to develop the practices of teaching and learning (develop the teachers who will oversee the curriculum-in-action), and we will return to this theme in the final chapter of the book. Firstly, however, we must consider assessment.

8 Getting assessment right: identifying and recording doctors' educational achievements in the clinical setting

How do *educators* see the nature and role of assessment?
What currently characterizes the activities of assessment in postgraduate medicine (and in what ways is this different from assessment in formal educational institutions)?
What ought to characterize these activities in the clinical setting?
How can such assessment provide for the gatekeeping requirements of professional education?
What are the implications for curriculum design for postgraduate medicine?

Introduction

Assessment is first and foremost an *educational* practice and part of a holistic educational process which includes teaching and learning. That is, to conceive of assessment as separate from teaching and learning is seriously to distort it by diminishing both its educational value and its validity and reliability as a means of accurate gatekeeping. This chapter is therefore a part of the previous chapter in all but physical layout. We have only placed assessment here in order to focus on and illuminate its significant details.

Given that assessment is a means of informing and shaping the understandings of both teacher and learner about the learner's progress and achievements, it is universally the case that assessment for educational purposes must come before its use for regulatory or managerial purposes. Once the educational role of assessment has been properly attended to (which includes proper documentation of progress), the rigorous use of it to chart both progression within an educational programme and also across a professional career (known within professional education as 'gatekeeping'), or its safe use to bolster a risk-management policy, will virtually be guaranteed.

Thus, those who set out to design a curriculum for practice need a sound educational understanding of assessment and its gatekeeping role. They will need to work to determine what should be assessed within the clinical setting and by whom, and how this can be capitalized upon to establish a robust gatekeeping process. This chapter seeks to support such designers. In a first section it: offers an overview of assessment generally, providing also further details of the necessary discourse for discussing these matters; reminds readers of, and elaborates upon, the role of assessment in the different design models discussed in Chapter 3; explores the nature of competence and competencies; shows how the invisible elements of clinical practice can be assessed; and discusses validity and reliability and the role of the educator's professional judgement.

In a second section, it explores and critiques the *current* practice of assessment in the education of postgraduate doctors and looks at how this has emerged. In a third section the discussion changes focus from 'is' to 'ought', by considering educational alternatives to current assessment practices. And in the final section the implications of all this for curriculum designers for postgraduate medicine are considered broadly.

An overview of assessment and its educational role

Definition of assessment and other related matters

Assessment is an all-embracing term for the educational activity of recognizing and recording learners' achievements and their development within a specific context and in the light of the quality and scope of the education provided for them. Once documented, this can provide evidence for progression within an educational programme and a career.

Assessment is therefore quite different from *appraisal*, which is normally defined as an activity in which an employer, for managerial purposes, seeks information about the progress of employees *within their jobs*. We offer this definition because it is in the discourse of most health care professions. But we acknowledge that in medicine the term 'appraisal' has been used for a kind of 'developmental' process (see DoH 1999a). This removes it from the managerial discourse and confuses it with assessment (which is always first and foremost an educational activity). Indeed, this is currently raising problems for medicine because with new moves in respect of 'revalidation', there is no term in medicine for the managerial process which is what appraisal really is but which SCOPME (1996) called 'performance review'.

We also acknowledge that in postgraduate medicine it is particularly easy to confuse appraisal with assessment, since the employee (postgraduate doctor) is *both* a learner and a practising professional at the same time. But they can be best distinguished by their differing purposes. Assessment is educational and provides evidence for the teacher and learner of success in, and where necessary of how to reshape, the educational programme. Appraisal (as performance management) is managerial and informs the employer about the suitability and efficiency of the employee (and what other educational support or development might be needed to improve that suitability and efficiency).

A further term that needs to be distinguished from assessment is *evaluation* (which is about the value of the educational programme itself). Again, assessment is related to evaluation, since the quality and worthwhile nature of the educational programme inevitably shapes the quality of the learner's achievements! Nonetheless, their focus is different, one being on the learner's achievements, the other being on the teacher's! (We deal more fully with evaluation in Chapter 10.)

Two other terms frequently connected with assessment are *outcomes* and *standards*. In terms of standards, assessment can be made against a formal, generally agreed standard (be *criterion referenced*), can compare a group of learners with each other (be *peer referenced*), or record a learner's own progress and compare it with that learner's previous achievements (be *ipsative-referenced*). The term 'outcomes' as used in association with 'standards' implies that the end result of a curriculum (as evidenced in the assessment documentation) is to produce in the learner a range of predetermined end results over which the learner has had little choice. But in fact, as we have shown in Chapter 3, this is not the purpose of sound educational practice (but rather of training). Outcomes and standards therefore should be seen for what they are, which is a means of management and regulation rather than of education. *Educational* outcomes, by contrast, cannot be fully understood in isolation from the learner (for example, what the learner was thinking at the time) and need to take account of the particular situation and context in which the outcomes were reached.

Assessments must be fair and be seen to be fair. This is often confused with the idea that they must be 'objective'. This comes from the notion that assessment is somehow 'scientific', and can be detached from the assessor, the assessee, and the context in which the assessment takes place. It is mistakenly assumed that the assessment is not valuable unless it can be rendered objective and absolute like a scientific law. As we have seen, however, not only is this not possible, it is not even desirable. Firstly, education is not a science. Secondly, as we shall see below, interpretation is an important element of educational assessment. Thirdly, the context is a vital component of assessment in the clinical setting, because it shapes the opportunities available to the learner (and these will affect what the learner can achieve). Fourthly, such an assumption distorts the respective roles of teacher and learner because rather than supporting and enlightening both teaching and learning, assessment in these terms would be quite separate from them.

This mistaken view leads also to inappropriate ideas about the *validity* and *reliability* of assessment, which is also seen in scientific terms as a means of bolstering the objectivity of assessment. In educational terms, validity is about the assessment appropriately setting out to discover that which it seeks to know about, rather than something other (where, for example, the language used by the assessor is unfamiliar to the learner, who declares no knowledge of the issue although the concepts are actually well understood). This is face validity. Content validity is about whether the assessment activity is properly wide enough to do its job; predictive validity is about whether the assessment is a good predictor of future achievement; and construct validity is about whether the assessment is organized to lead to the desired information about a learner. However, more important than these is the fact that educational assessment in the clinical setting looks at a learner's achievements over time and from a range of perspectives. This provides results whose dependability, robustness and fairness are at least equivalent to that achieved by the validity and reliability of scientific enterprises (see Moss 1994).

In relation to predictive validity and the uses of summative assessment we note in passing the dangers of conflating the idea of 'passing the assessment' with 'being competent'. Although summative assessment 'qualifies' doctors to do certain things, it is dangerous to assume that being qualified implies that one is competent in the face of all future demands. This is why indicating levels of supervision required, alongside the results of assessment ('competent to x level'), is useful (see de Cossart and Fish 2005). Even then, competence is 'a moving target' (Eraut 2003) and cannot predict someone's future practice (for all the reasons we give in previous chapters about the unpredictable and uncertain nature of practice). This suggests that a 'one-off' gatekeeping assessment has limited value.

The need for multiple perspectives to be collected about the learner's achievements in complex practice settings means that *interpretation* of the assessment evidence is necessary. In education then (as in most of the humanities) the soundness of the assessment is therefore related to the rigour with which those multiple perspectives are collected, recorded, interpreted and utilized. Thus, in all these issues, in the end, the teacher's/assessor's professional judgement has to be employed alongside the range of evidence available. And there will never be any escaping from this.

By contrast, reliability is about whether the assessment would be the same if conducted by another assessor, and whether the results would change if the assessment were re-run.

Clearly the public rightly expects a profession to have standards set in respect of the special responsibilities associated with professional practice and all members are expected to uphold these. (For medicine, of course the GMC's

Good Medical Practice provides the necessary detail and some Royal Colleges have also devised a specialty version.) Assessment (in its gatekeeping rather than its educational role) is one means of checking that people are 'up to standard', and appraisal (as performance review) is another. It should also be remembered that standards are themselves a notional and arbitrary hurdle and not 'given and absolute'. Underpinning any standards (whether this is recognized or not) is a set of values with moral and ethical dimensions which are (or *should be*) related to the profession's view of what constitutes good practice. We looked at what is meant by this in Chapters 4 and 5. While it is wise for a profession to make its values explicit and examine them carefully to be sure that they genuinely reflect their key espoused values, it is not a key role of *assessment* to check up on or police these except where professionalism itself is being considered as part of teaching and learning either *formatively* (assessment which takes place during the educational process and is used as educational feedback to teacher and learner), or *summatively* (assessment which at the end of the educational programme acts as a final gatekeeping procedure).

Broadly speaking then, 'assessment is concerned with demonstrating how well, and in what ways, a learner has profited from the learning opportunities provided, and with recording these achievements and the learner's educational progress' (de Cossart and Fish 2005: 98). The final goal of all assessment processes should be to equip the learner to become good at self-assessment.

Thus, as most educators would probably agree, assessment refers to any process in which an aspect of a learner's educational achievement or training outcome is either rigorously measured or *otherwise recognized or appreciated*. Thus, neither tests nor examinations are essential to assessment. The assessment process can be conducted by a teacher, an examiner, a colleague (peer), or learners themselves. This makes the point that measurement (the according of numbers in an assessment process) is by no means an essential element of assessment, neither does it render assessment any more scientific and object-ive than is assessment which uses written comments. Indeed, we believe that communication between teachers across time, about a learner's abilities, is better conveyed by written comment because it is less open than are numbers (or ticked boxes) to ambiguity about the learner's actual achievements.

As we have said, like medicine itself, assessment is not an exact science. Despite its presentation in percentages, graphs, curves of distribution or plain numbers, the decisions that underlie it depend upon judgements made by assessors. These are interpretations and do not represent absolute facts. They involve (and always will involve) subjectivity. That is intrinsic to the nature of education as a discipline.

So far we have talked of the more formal face of assessment (that which is made transparent and should be recorded). It should also be noted, however, that, just as no doctors can see a patient (or even, in a social context, any other human being) without automatically beginning in their heads a form of medical assessment or diagnosis, so a teacher is forming judgements which are an assessment of the learner from the very first meeting. However, these may be inaccurate, informal and subject to bias, and thus can unjustly label learners in ways that can become unfairly crucial to their progress. To be fair to the learner therefore, these informal assessments (like the doctor's intuitive diagnosis) must be confirmed by more concrete evidence formulated against public criteria (or better still, challenged by seeking evidence for their disproof – see de Cossart and Fish 2005: 98–9. These authors also offer at page 55 a table that explores further the parallels between doctors' and teachers' actions and decisions).

In education as in medicine then, evidence and logic will naturally contribute to conclusions drawn, but professional judgement will inevitably be a key component. Thus, in order to be fair and to be seen to be fair, such judgements must be part of a well-planned process, use public criteria, and involve multiple perspectives (more than one view), and they must be principled. Further, learners and all those who receive the results must be aware of what principles underlay the assessment. The role that assessment plays in the gatekeeping process for entry to various levels of a profession is straightforward once evidence of achievement and progress have been recorded on a regular basis and in a principled way.

The nature of assessment

As we have shown in the previous four chapters, the nature of assessment within professional education (like that of teaching and learning within which assessment should sit) should be determined by the character and reality of the professional practice in which the learner is engaging and the nature of the knowledge base that underpins that professional practice (see also Coles 2000).

Since this is values-based, some will see the nature of clinical practice as mainly technical (about acquiring via training and demonstrating via assessment ownership of medical skills, and scientific knowledge which can be applied to that practice). Here the assessment will check the knowledge by examination and the skills in a neutral environment from which all other confounding factors have been excluded. Success here will be interpreted as the efficient and accurate reproduction of both 'the knowledge' and 'the skills'. The documentation of this would be the kind of ticked boxes associated with competency-based assessment (which we discuss below).

Such assessment is concerned almost exclusively with the visible and assumes that this is measurable. We believe, like de Cossart and Fish, that such a view of assessment overlooks a number of highly significant matters, as follows:

- it ignores the thinking and the knowledge that lie behind the skills;
- it pretends that assessment can be context-neutral thus ignoring how, in real practice, doctors adapt their knowledge and improvise their skill;
- it is not interested in requiring them to be aware of and confront their own attitudes, values, assumptions, beliefs and personal theories which are part of the context of their practice and which drive their actions;
- it does not make central the moral and ethical dimensions of their patients' needs;
- it does not focus on how rounded a professional they are, nor on how well they collaborate with patients and other colleagues;
- above all it emphasizes only their technical accountability (slightly adapted from de Cossart and Fish 2005: 100).

As we have extensively demonstrated in Chapter 4 from the accounts of practitioners themselves, medical practice is in reality complex, messy and human, and is carried out in what Donald Schön calls 'the swampy lowlands' of practice, as opposed to the rarefied heights of pure scientific theory. Here practice includes skills and scientific knowledge, but also involves other activities, routines, and a wide range of other kinds of knowledge (all of which are dynamic and some of which are created in practice). Here, medical practice has complex decision-making processes and judgement at its core. That is why assessment must find ways of attending to the invisible as well as the visible (the understanding beneath the action, the artistry of practice, the abilities to improvise appropriately and to draw upon insight and intuition, the adaptation of knowledge and skill to individual patient care, the flexibility and open-mindedness to continue to learn and be self-critical). This means finding ways of making explicit (and thus able to be refined, developed and assessed), that which is tacit and implicit in medical practice. This involves learning through experience. Rigorous reflection on practice (which is a recognized means of serious exploration and investigation of practice) is the chief means of attending educationally to the invisible. As most other health care professions have long since acknowledged, this in turn means that the learners' very abilities in the processes of reflection and deliberation will also need to be assessed.

What role then should assessment play in the educational process? The following section seeks to provide a range of ideas to fuel the deliberative thinking of a curriculum design team for postgraduate medicine.

The role of assessment in education and gatekeeping: various views

This section firstly returns to the design models discussed in Chapter 3, secondly explores in detail the distinctions between competence and competencies which we flagged up on page 173 above, and thirdly provides ideas about some ways of assessing the invisible.

Assessment within the three models of curriculum design

In Chapter 3, following the work of Stenhouse, we offered three ways of conceptualizing the relationship between teaching, learning and assessment. In each the role of assessment was different and performed a different function for teacher and learner. For example, in the product model where teacher is active transmitter of knowledge, assessment performs the role of a test at the end of the process. (This 'summative' role is a way of summarizing what has been learnt, and inadvertently is also a way of preventing it from being used to enlighten the teaching and learning.) Success in such an assessment process often depends more on the quality of the teacher than the learner (here, failure to learn is often seen as the result of failure to teach).

By contrast, in the process model, where learners are more active and teachers are more facilitative, assessment almost naturally becomes a central part of the teaching and learning. Here it feeds into an ongoing understanding of learners' achievements, and this in turn shapes their next educational activities. Here then, assessment is essentially formative, and a number of such assessments ultimately offer a pattern of evidence across the period of learning. Analysis of these can provide a robust and fair 'summative statement' about what learners have achieved and how they have developed.

Assessment is central to learning in the third (research) model too. But here the onus is on the learners working within their own negotiated agenda, and the teacher being one learning resource among many. Thus assessment becomes a means of developing self-knowledge and charting success in using investigative approaches to learning.

Defining and agreeing the *purpose* of assessment is a vital starting point for medical educators and will help in the selection of an overall model for curriculum design. What is assessment for? Who it is for? How is it related to learning and when should it happen? These are the key questions. Responses to these should be based upon a clear educational philosophy in which the learning doctor's achievements and progress are the foremost concern, where teacher and learner work in partnership in a nurturing environment.

The choices available to anyone designing assessment are:

* formal/informal (as discussed above); continuous/final (during the programme or at the end); convergent/divergent (focusing down in detail or up on the broader picture);
* summative (at the end of the learning) and formative (integral to it);
* quantitative (using numbers as the sole evidence of achievement) and

qualitative (using a wide range of ways of recording the learner's actions and that which underlies them);
- objectivity/subjectivity (some argue that there is no such thing as objectivity);
- criterion referenced (criteria or competencies as standard)/norm referenced (average as standard or curve of distribution as standard);
- format for assessment: written/performance/oral/video/profile/portfolio/ diary.

Each choice made from the above expresses a particular sense of educational purpose, and will exclude some other possibilities. Formal assessment should never rest on a one-off process. It is about looking at the learner's achievements and progress and should be designed to help shape further teaching and learning. The learner's ability to learn should be considered during the assessment. All assessment should seek to develop the learner's ability to self-assess.

In first introducing these models we argued that decisions about which model to use should depend upon what the educator is trying to achieve. For an educator in postgraduate medicine then, there is a need (in the light of the complexity of medical practice and what the learner needs to develop) to choose an appropriate interrelation between teaching, learning and assessment, as represented by these models. This is why, despite the popularity of *competency-based* (skills-based) approaches to training, we would argue for the significance for postgraduate medicine of a *competence-based*, holistic approach to education, and now offer the arguments for why serious educators see a vital distinction between these two.

The vital distinction between competence and competencies

The competency-based approach to training
The competency-based approach to training believes that all that is needed in preparing for practice as a professional is to acquire all the skills (*competencies*) that can be listed as used in that job. Although skills are clearly a necessary part of professionals' work, alone they do not provide a sufficient basis for it. A range of educators argue that this is a naïve, rather tired and an entirely inappropriate basis for professionals in practice (Broadfoot 1993, 2000; D. Carr 1993; Eraut 1994; Wragg 1994; W. Carr 1995; Golby and Parrott 1999; White and Stancombe 2003; Talbot 2004).

The myth that has helped to spread the importance of competencies (skills) as the basis for professional practice is the myth of 'generic skills'. If skills were 'generic' (implying that they are identical across all contexts), *then* to learn skills in one context would be sufficient to ensure that they could be fully and appropriately used in all others. Were this the case, the learning of skills on a small scale would provide all that was needed to guarantee successful professional practice. However, this (conveniently) ignores the significance of the context. Once criticality is brought to bear on this notion, it takes very little thought to recognize that skills need to be adapted significantly from context to context, and that they are best adapted on a *principled* basis. In other words, it is not skills that are generic (that travel), but *principles*. These guide the adaptation of skills and are at least as important as skills in underpinning successful practice, and thus need to be attended to within the education of professionals. Competencies then, are rooted in an impoverished view of teaching, learning and assessment, being concerned only with visible behaviour and its measurement, and an impoverished view of professional work which overlooks the subtleties of sensitivity, imagination, wisdom, judgement and moral awareness.

Competencies may feed the western world's overriding obsession with measurement but at a terrible cost – that of seeing teaching and learning in terms of an industrial transaction where what is important is what will conduce to the efficient and cheap delivery of a product. Further, the myth of measurement is that it appears to render assessment clear-cut and objective, scientific and absolute. This merely covers up the processes of judgement which inevitably underpin such 'measurement'. And this in turn means that the bases of such judgements are not transparent, not public, and not able to be critiqued or developed.

Another 'selling point' of competencies is that they are simple to derive in the first place and also to teach, learn and assess. But this too hides a number of myths. For example, one key problem is that there is no end to the breaking down of skills into finer and finer detail. Other problems include the following:

- the basis on which those skills are chosen will never be clear-cut;
- the basis for their definition and level of detail is rarely made clear;
- the basis for the decision about the number of skills necessary is never made explicit;
- what will count as evidence for their acquisition is unclear (how often and in how many different contexts must they be demonstrated?);
- their hierarchy of importance is often obscure (what weighting is each given? Will learners need to pass them all, and should they pass each at the same level?);
- the significance of prior experience is rarely considered.

de Cossart and Fish summarize the competency-based approach as follows. They say it:

- may improve some basic skills in the short term (though possibly at the risk of rigidity in the longer term);
- is readily organized into a bureaucratic model for administrative purposes, thus apparently increasing efficiency (and actually increasing bureaucratic control!);
- appears to lead to objective assessment of practice (though such apparent objectivity only hides further value judgements!);
- is about improving performance (perhaps at the expense of understanding);
- undervalues theory and research;
- has no interest in theorizing about practice;
- has no interest in the moral and ethical dimensions of professional practice;
- offers professionals no inbuilt means of developing and refining practice;
- embraces the idea that professionalism can be judged only against the notion of fitness for purpose (ensures that the ends are never challenged);
- emphasizes the acquisition of basic skills at the expense of developing understanding, refining practical theoretical knowledge and engaging in scholarly activity;
- is interested in behaviour which is visible but not conduct which acknowledges the moral and ethical values, beliefs and theories which drive action;
- recognizes the need for professionals to be technically accountable (but not more than this);
- arises from a deficit model of professionalism;
- values:
  - certainties about the knowledge, skills and strategies to be a successful professional;
  - being able to analyse skills and the main characteristics of a professional down to the finest detail and being able to observe these as visible behaviour;
  - setting basic standards against which everything can be judged;
  - training;
  - measuring observable behaviour as a simple route to increasing efficiency;
  - the language and ideas of managerialism and of industrial output as equally appropriate to discussing professionalism (de Cossart and Fish 2005: 109).

Competence as the basis for educating professionals

By contrast to the above, *competence* is concerned with a holistic notion of professional practice, and the assessment of this is based upon judgements of quality, the bases of which are made explicit. It is concerned with seeing the necessary skills of professional practice in a wider context which takes account of the essence, core and complexity of what is really involved in being a professional. A competence-based approach to practice recognizes that professionals exercise judgement and wisdom which goes beyond protocols, and work in creative ways which may draw upon skills but which develops, adapts and improvises them. (The work of Carr 1993 provides details of how and why people have muddled these two concepts.)

The competence approach values:

- professional practice as involving open capacities which cannot be mastered;
- professional judgement and its complexity (the ability to choose between competing priorities, values, actions, interpretations);
- the complex and uncertain nature of day-to-day practice;
- professionals' moral responsibility to vulnerable patients/clients, and colleagues, and in addition, professional answerability in respect of their technical proficiency;
- the ability to utilize general knowledge, thinking and doing (which includes skills but far more) so that it is shaped to the specific and particular individual needs of patients;
- the development of a (personal) principled base from which to practise as a professional;
- an understanding of the importance of values and self-knowledge in respect of the individual's professional values;
- the need to attend to the moral and ethical dimensions of practice;
- an understanding of the wider issues of professionalism and the responsibilities of being a member of a profession;
- the use of a range of skills and of the importance of choosing rationally between them;
- self-knowledge and the ability of a professional to attend to their own professional development;
- the ability to influence key decisions at the level of policy and the capacity to take an active role in the development of the profession itself (de Cossart and Fish 2005: 109–10).

These then are the choices available and the reasons for choosing the broader rather than the narrower approaches to education in general and assessment in particular. Once the competence approach is chosen, the question has to be faced as to which means of assessment will do justice to the complexity of practice.

Assessing the invisible in the practice setting

The assessment of postgraduate doctors must do justice to the complexity of both the nature of clinical practice and the nature of clinical knowledge in postgraduate medicine. Much of what drives professional practice lies beneath its surface. Two key questions thus emerge:

- How shall we reveal these?
- How shall we assess them?

As we have shown in earlier chapters, there are three important aspects of our practice that drive our surface actions and conduct, and this is so whether or not they lie tacit within our practice or are explicitly recognized. These are:

- that which lurks beneath the iceberg of professional practice (our theories, beliefs, assumptions, and values);
- the knowledge we draw on while we are 'doing';
- the thinking we are engaging in while we are 'doing'.

These three 'drivers' of professional practice powerfully affect conduct in clinical settings. Awareness and refinement of them will shape the practitioner's success with patients in ways far beyond what can be achieved by learning and deploying skills alone. Patients themselves are often very aware and quick to recognize this, and it deeply affects how far they trust the knowledge, thinking and doing of those doctors.

The refinement of these three highly significant drivers depends upon the ability to surface them, and examine them. Their significance for overall success as a doctor also means that it is important to assess them. We agree that the key means to this is reflective practice that is shaped to focus sharply and educationally on these drivers of practice. We refer readers to de Cossart and Fish 2005, Chapter 5, in which the details of how to engage in reflective practice are provided.

Professional judgement, assessment and levels of supervision

Consultants have been engaged in the assessment of younger colleagues for many decades, and in all cases their professional judgement has been an inevitable part of that process, determining for example: the interpretations of conduct; the choices made about the level of current performance; and decisions made about the level of future supervision needed as a learner progresses through the system. However, in the past in many cases such judgements have not been rigorously recorded.

As is clear from Coles (2000) and de Cossart and Fish (2005), we value this use of professional judgement but believe that it needs to be better recognized as a proper part of this process. While such judgements must be principled, and backed up by evidence, no additional 'training' is required for doctors to be able to do this. Rather they need to understand the matters we have offered in this chapter. As with their clinical professional judgement, of course, their educational professional judgement will develop and be refined *in practice*. This will happen in the community of assessment practice in which medical educators already engage. (And we have already argued for the principles of multiple perspectives in assessment, which themselves will contribute to the refinement of the assessment process.)

We also made the important point earlier, that to develop assessment processes and procedures in isolation from an educational programme (curriculum) is inevitably to develop a monster – something which properly fits neither educational needs nor managerial requirements and which will, as a result, be neither valid nor reliable in either context.

How is doctors' practice currently assessed?

The historical context

As Coles reminds us: 'For much of the past one hundred years, the assessment of doctors has relentlessly pursued an "objective" (and hence psychometric) approach', attempting to measure what doctors do and 'match these measurements against agreed and observable criteria for doctors' behaviour'. As he goes on to say, this attempt has failed, so that, 'rather than pursuing the increasingly discredited "psychometric" approach to objective assessment, our future must lie in understanding and developing (rather than ignoring or dismissing) the subjective judgments we make' (Coles 2000: 1).

But medicine has not merely ignored everything that cannot be measured; worse, it has taught the complexities of clinical practice, but neither recorded what was taught nor documented what was learnt. In other words, formal assessment has been absent as an educational process and vestigial as a managerial (gatekeeping) procedure.

It is true that from about 1980 to the beginning of the twenty-first century, doctors as apprentices spent many years in 'training' and developed a repertoire of frequently-practised clinical processes and procedures. Thus the knowledge of their ability to manage a ward, run a clinic and undertake increasingly complex procedures was passed between consultants and other persons involved in their promotion, on an informal, word of mouth basis. Their achievements were only formalized in terms of assessment in the Royal College examinations which largely tested their theoretical knowledge.

But today, the time available is much shorter and more must be gained (in both depth and breadth) from each of the fewer experiences available to learning doctors. Capabilities that are built by them need to be carefully documented for subsequent teachers as well as for use by those who plan the service. And accountability now demands that all professionals collect robust and detailed evidence of their achievement at all stages, in order to ensure patient safety, to equip learners properly for their future careers, and to protect the teacher in the face of possible litigation should patients come to harm or other things go wrong with that career.

It is true that, with the reorganization by Kenneth Calman in the 1990s, it became mandatory annually for trainee doctors to present evidence of the assessments that have occurred 'in training' at a **Record of In-Training Assessment** (RITA) review. Here the RITA panel comes to a judgement of what final assessment to record. Central to this is likely to be the educational supervisor's report. However, this apparently summative assessment process, for which the postgraduate deans are held responsible, is not a direct assessment of doctors in the clinical setting, but rather an assessment of their 'record' over the year (itself not the product of a rigorous assessment process, but rather of a 'sign off' procedure which it is possible to carry out without a face-to-face discussion with the learner involved)! Clearly assessment here has not been conceived of as a central activity of a rigorous process of teaching and learning, but rather as an isolated one-off activity. It is also true that some Royal Colleges have in the past few years responded to these obvious deficits by widening their examinations and incorporating some elements of the practical within them but only in a simulated manner and never in the doctor's own practice setting.

The only possible reason for not placing assessment directly in the setting in which postgraduate doctors work seems to be that it might be difficult to carry it out because, as Coles (2000) argues, it appears to involve a subjective process which is open to bias and abuse, and which can only be made valid and reliable by means of a huge training programme for assessors. This is in fact not so. Consultants have for years successfully exercised their judgement about their juniors. The only thing they mostly did not do was record their achievements during the attachment. Such records would not be difficult to amass, and could attend to both the visible achievements in learning processes and procedures, and (through the use of reflective practice) the developing insight and judgement of learners (see de Cossart and Fish 2005 for examples of these).

New assessment practices within the Foundation Programme

Given all that we have said, readers will not be surprised to see that we are very disappointed with the Core Curriculum of the Foundation Programme. In assessment terms, it is a classic example of what happens when a design team: misguidedly begins the curriculum design process by starting with assessment (and considering it quite separately from all other aspects of the curriculum);

mistakenly assumes that knowledge, skills and attitudes will be sufficient headings to categorize the key content of medical practice and thus the key areas to be assessed; unwisely fails to recognize the real complexity of professional practice, professional knowledge and professional thinking; and evinces no understanding of the educational role of, and the principles of, assessment. We were also sad for all the reasons that readers will now understand, to see its frequent reference to 'competences' (a word we have already shown does not exist).

In the absence of such knowledge and information, it is perhaps not surprising that this curriculum has been placed on a competency base. It is clear to us that any serious and educational attempt at implementation will quickly reveal its inadequacy and no doubt it will have to be improved and developed on the ground. But it seems to us (and many knowledgeable educators) to be a sad waste of resources when the same energy could have provided a much better starting point. We also fear that the bright new doctors who have been promised this new programme will quickly realize that they have been short-changed, and so could become hugely demotivated as learners. Clearly this will be bad news for all involved in and served by medical practice in the UK.

Again, we believe that this is the result of a managerial rather than an educational approach to curriculum, and a blatant ignoring of the professional basis of the work of doctors. Our evidence for this is the crassness of the title of the national day conferences that sought to 'train' medical educators in the assessment processes. These conferences were entirely inappropriately entitled 'The tools of the trade'. We are not alone in recognizing the calculation with which this conjured up an entirely instrumental and technical rational view of assessment and undermined the professionalism of doctors at the same time! Medicine is not a trade, and patients would be ill-served if it were!

The best that we can hope for now therefore, is that this book will provide both a better basis for any new curricula that are being designed (rather than sitting them on the same faulty foundation) and that it will offer those on the ground who have to work with the Foundation Programme some solid understanding about how to develop it into something that relates properly to medical practice. To this end we offer Part 3 of this book. Meanwhile, to provide a more informed basis for using Part 3 in order to redesign the Foundation's Core, we offer here some key processes and principles of assessment for clinical practice, some of which are already in use in other health care professions!

What should be assessed in medical practice and by what means?

This is a key question for designers of an educational programme. Any response to this must be derived from the kinds of investigations we have exemplified in Chapters 4, 5, 6 and 7. As a result of these we would suggest the following as needing to be attended to in postgraduate medicine through teaching and assessment in the clinical setting:

- medical and surgical theory (all theoretical factual knowledge relevant to practice);
- educational processes (how to learn in clinical settings, how to reflect on practice);
- the principles of clinical practice (and particularly those that should guide the use of skills, processes and procedures);
- the principles of technical processes and (where relevant) operative procedures, how to learn them and how to develop them by theorizing practice;
- the principles of clinical processes and how to learn them and develop them by theorizing practice;
- clinical skills and procedures that are specific to any required specialty;
- the clinical thinking processes that lie beneath medical practice;
- the full range of knowledge (in addition to propositional knowledge and procedural know-how) that lies beneath medical practice;
- professionalism and ability to communicate and work within a multi-professional team;
- self-knowledge and an understanding of personal limitations as well as abilities;
- a knowledge of appropriate and relevant research, how to critique it, and under what circumstances it will be relevant to given cases;
- the ability to maximize the use of all learning opportunities.

This list has been adapted from de Cossart and Fish (2005: 110), who also note that very little of this would be appropriately evidenced and documented via ticked boxes.

The principles that should guide the assessment process

Any system of assessment must be coherent and principled. The following list, which is taken from de Cossart and Fish (2005), seems to sum up some of the most useful key principles for enacting assessment in clinical settings in all professions. Curriculum designers will wish to critique this list and to adapt it to their specific purposes in respect of the curriculum they are designing:

- assessment should always be a learning experience and centred first on facilitating learning;
- its purpose(s) should be clear and educational and understood by all involved;
- it should be carried out in practice by those who teach the learner in the practice setting (though it can include an external assessor as well);
- criteria should be clear and understood by all involved;
- assessment should assess that which it says it does;
- the elements to be assessed must be derived from the aims of the overall educational programme and the intentions of the individual learner and teacher;
- observation should be systematic, rigorous and take account of the complexities of practice;
- approaches to assessment that go beyond mere observation should be developed;
- evidence – of a variety of kinds – should be carefully recorded and utilized;
- multiple perspectives should be taken (assessment should be of a variety of elements of practice, and should call upon at least three assessors to do justice to the three-dimensional nature of clinical practice);
- the role of professional judgement should not be undervalued;
- simple negative inferences should never be drawn from negative situations, without first checking on how the learner construed the situation (and even the purpose of assessment) in the first place;
- what counts as evidence needs to be carefully thought through and agreed by assessor and assessee;
- learners' achievements should be seen and reported as outcomes of the interaction between the *context* and the learner (learners can only show their capabilities within what an attachment provides) (slightly adapted from de Cossart and Fish 2005: 112).

They also argue that in all assessments (formative and summative; formal and informal) the following information should be taken account of, through multiple perspectives on the learner's progress:

- the visible elements of the learner's performance;
- the impact of that performance on all others involved;
- the learner's ideas, beliefs, values, assumptions, beneath the surface of performance;
- the formal theoretical dimensions drawn upon by the learner during practice;
- how the learner has related theory and practice;
- the learner's ability to theorize their own practice;
- how the learner has capitalized on the learning opportunities provided;

- the learner's self-knowledge;
- how much input there has been from the teacher;
- how the resulting assessment judgements cross-check with those made of the learner by others (de Cossart and Fish 2005: 112).

The gatekeeping process

The principles applying to assessment generally also by definition apply to its gatekeeping (regulatory) processes. Individual assessments that have been properly recorded in the ongoing educational programme will feed into both a summative process for that attachment, and a gatekeeping purpose related to readiness to progress beyond the programme. At this stage, rigour involves cross-checking the evidence and judgements made and what emerges, in terms of larger patterns of development. Here judgement needs to be used to consider the balance of different purposes of assessment and different ways of looking at criteria. It should also be remembered that virtually all research into learning shows that it happens in fits and starts, involves plateaux of various kinds (which are actually important in the learning process), and thus does not proceed incrementally.

Documenting assessment

It will have emerged from all that we have said that the rigorous documentation of the learner's achievements (or lack of them) is a vital part of the assessment process. We have also shown that tick boxes, lickert scales, and numerical representations of the learner's progress are insufficient for several reasons. They do not do justice to the complexity of real practice, they do not provide clear and unambiguous evidence of actual achievements, and they do not inform later teachers of the detail of the learner's progress and achievements. They also offer no means of contextualizing the skills and procedures involved, and do not attend to the learning opportunities available and how well or poorly the learner used them.

We accept, as does Eraut, that the public would be 'distinctly uneasy if evidence of authentic performance did not play a major part in the assessment of professional competence' (Eraut 1998: 135). But, the development and refinement of a doctor's conduct depends upon making explicit all the complexities that have driven the visible actions. This is why there is a need to develop the use of reflective accounts of practice; narratives of practitioner development; even recordings of practice, together with proper critiques of these. (de Cossart and Fish 2005 offer a glimpse into the detail of these in Chapter 11.)

It is fairly traditional within professional education for the learner to have responsibility for keeping a portfolio of work which demonstrates educational achievements within the practice setting (and is not just a repository for CVs and courses attended). It should contain a mixture of sections in which a range of kinds of evidence of developing understanding and insight are demonstrated. Some who wish to avoid engaging in these complex practices argue about the possibilities in this of breaching confidentiality and of fuelling litigation. Naturally therefore, proper research ethics need to be adopted in relation to narratives and other written accounts, and they need to be kept confidentially and only the insights should be fully shared. An increasing number of examples of educational portfolios in various layouts are available, and are valued by the teachers and learners who use them.

What are the implications of all this for curriculum designers in postgraduate medicine?

We have already established that all concepts within education are problematic and values-based. We have recognized that it is only possible to offer a broad definition of teaching, learning and assessment, that ideas about them and about professional priorities change and develop and that such practices evolve as a result of being used and discussed. This is why curriculum designers have to be able to work at the level of principle, have to offer in the curriculum document the principles of assessment it recommends, and have to provide a rationale explaining what values they are based upon.

It must also by now be clear that educational choices have to be made in response to the evolving needs of the medical profession and its patients, society and the government, and that this is why educational programmes should, even must, be eternally developing.

This means that there will be and there needs to be proper and healthy ongoing contention within a profession about the nature of practice generally, the nature of the practice of that profession, the nature of the knowledge which underpins it, the nature of assessment itself, and how practice currently does, or shortly should, relate to these choices.

This debate is already well attended to in all educationally mature health care professions, and now needs to be begun and sustained in medicine. This means eschewing the current unquestioned assumption that in medicine, educational matters can be 'got right' and cast in tablets of stone. It means abandoning the consequent futile search for 'the correct curriculum which will contain perfected assessment procedures'. It also means that the current worrying refusal to put any assessment in place in the clinical setting until this perfection has been reached cannot continue. It also means that the endless search for the 'ideal' assessment approach that will precisely show us someone's competence will always be fruitless. Indeed, assessments of learners are like X-rays. They can only be indicative, and we must not read too much into them, or at least not into one alone. This is because, like X-rays, there are no assessment methods that are 100 per cent accurate, every method has false positives and false negatives, and any method tells you only about the learner's achievements (patient's condition) at the time, but this will not necessarily predict how they will be in the future. Indeed, we too often read too much into and make far too many high-stakes decisions about an individual's future on the basis of assessments of only marginal validity and poor predictive value.

What we offer here, therefore, is fuel to enable colleagues to engage in an informed way in these debates. Clearly, our own presentation as writers is itself influenced by our own educational and professional values (which we have already indicated in earlier chapters). Readers will therefore need to take this into account as they critique what we have offered, and seek to build their own personal educational philosophy.

It should also be noted that a coherent system of assessment crystallizes for learners and the public the priorities and values of those who set it up, and who, as a result, inevitably promote a particular set of educational and professional values. Curriculum designers need to remember how powerful will be the influence of the assessment system they set up.

9 From problematic to procedural matters: setting the regulations for supporting and managing the curriculum on the ground

Introduction

In Chapter 1 we showed how those who are currently engaged in developing medical education have as their starting point the effective and efficient management of a curriculum. We pointed out that this is to begin at the wrong end. Professional matters must come first. And they bring with them many issues that are problematic and require careful deliberation. Management issues are not even pertinent for consideration until these have been settled. The point here is that the managerial systems and regulations are there to support properly the 'live' success of the educational enterprise on the ground. Thus *they need to be sensitive to, and facilitative of* that enterprise, and not the other way round. This is why the temptation to tackle, as a first priority, the *easier* managerial decisions about curriculum design must be resisted. We have cited the Foundation Programme as an example of the yielding to this temptation, and shown how such a move can distort the curriculum.

That is why we have offered an overview of what is involved in good practice in curriculum design in Chapter 2, rehearsed the understanding necessary to sound educational practice in Chapter 3, and provided readers with the key evidence and ideas that will fuel their deliberations about the problematic aspects of curriculum design in Chapters 4 to 8. We have also made the point that the matters discussed in Chapters 4 to 8 are problematic precisely because they relate to the key *educational* decisions that have to be made by designers. We have said too that educational matters are always values-based and therefore do not yield to simple decision-making but rather that the combined expertise of the team has to generate and weigh the possible pros and cons of various choices in the light of the general and specific contexts for which the curriculum is being shaped.

Key procedural matters

There are five areas that a design team needs to attend to in order to provide key managerial regulations and systems to support the curriculum-in-action on the ground. These are:

- *serious educational support for the teachers and learners* such that they understand the educational thrust of the programme, are sympathetic to or share its values and philosophy, and recognize and can enact the educational activities it calls for;
- *the administrative and educational structures* that need to be in place to provide for the smooth running of the educational activities;
- *the recruitment and selection regulations* that provide a framework for ensuring that the best candidates to benefit from the programme are appointed to it;
- *the regulations for educational progression and provision for non-progression* which support the educational thrust of assessment and use the *results* of this for deciding who should progress through the programme and at what speed, and for attending to the career pathway of those who are in difficulties;
- *the quality assurance procedures*, which should support the educational development and refinement of both the programme and the educational context in which, and for which, it takes place.

The first of these, the educational support for teachers and learners, is an educational not a management enterprise and we offer a section on this in Chapter 12.

We shall take the four management issues in turn and consider three aspects of them that the design team will need to have in mind as they document them. These are as follows.

- What might be the *main elements* of these structures, systems and policies that a design team might need to consider?
- In what ways might these managerial systems need to be *sensitive to and facilitative of the educational decisions* and intentions of the programme?
- How should such systems relate to and *take account of present organizational structures*?

Administrative and educational structures

The main elements

The main administrative and educational structures that curriculum designers need to attend to in the definitive document include the following:

- the contracts between health care providers and deaneries as educational providers, including the processes for the approval of programmes and any necessary commissioning of placements;
- mapping the principles and values of the curriculum to *Good Medical Practice* (GMC 2001);
- structures for ensuring compatibility with EWTD and Hospital at Night Policies;
- a statement about how the curriculum links to appraisal;
- the structure of the educational staff on the ground (tutors, clinical supervisors etc.);
- the roles and responsibilities of those educators;
- the roles and responsibilities of the learners;
- the responsibilities of the employers;
- systems for:
  - transfer into and out of the programme;
  - deferring the start of a programme;
  - temporary or permanent withdrawal and for time out and study leave;
  - overseas applicants;
  - candidates with disabilities;
  - those needing additional educational support;
- policies to ensure equity of treatment and absence of discrimination;
- policies relating the programme to clinical governance;
- guidelines for handling complaints.

Most of these are relatively self-explanatory and are offered as an *aide mémoire*. However, the following points need to be made about the first two.

In respect of the contracts between health care (Trust) providers and each deanery, the **Chief Executive Officers** (CEOs) of the Trust as heath care providers are required to contract with the deanery to provide the educational resources for the medical staff in educational programmes within that Trust. The agreement in respect of any curriculum for postgraduate doctors will need careful documentation (and this may be checked as part of quality assurance procedures). Such documentation should indicate a commitment from the Trust on the one hand and the deanery on the other to provide the necessary educational resources for the smooth running of the curriculum-in-action, and therefore requires both the CEOs and the deanery staff as well as the clinicians to understand that curriculum and its implications in some detail (see Playdon 2004b: 388). The definitive document should recognize the need for such contracting and require the local personnel responsible for enacting the curriculum on the ground to ensure that the contract covers their requirements.

Playdon also notes that where deaneries operate by means of 'management-by-network', Trusts operate by 'management-by-committee', and that 'both cultures need to be robust for curriculum implementation to be successful'. She recommends that for successful implementation:

- the management structures and processes should be demonstrably 'sufficient' to support it;
- the different cultures of Trust and deanery need to be recognized;
- the two cultures should be brought closer together by appointing the director of medical education/clinical tutor as a full member of the Trust senior executive committee; appointing the medical education manager as a full member of the Trust's senior human resources committee; and establishing a Strategic Education Group within the Trust;
- a CEOs' forum should be established, where Trust CEOs meet deans and Strategic Health Authority CEOs (Playdon 2004b: 388–9).

Curriculum design teams need to be alert to these matters and may need to make some reference to them in the definitive document.

In respect of the mapping exercise in which the curriculum is matched to the dimensions of *Good Medical Practice*, it should be noted that provided there is a section in the curriculum document that expresses the values and principles upon which the entire curriculum is based, then only this section needs to be used to demonstrate that the values of the GMC document have been attended to. This should make the mapping exercise a relatively simple one in which the results can be set out in a table.

Sensitivity to and facilitation of the educational decisions

We cannot emphasize enough that all 12 systems and policies listed above are there not for their own sake, nor is their role to bolster or boost the management power base, but rather to ensure the smooth running of the curriculum. For example, policies that are unsympathetic to the crucial facilitative relationships between teacher and learner (or whose language is drawn from managerial rather than educational discourse) should be reconsidered, and may need to be expressed differently. Structures that do not recognize the significance of education should be revisited. Educational roles and responsibilities need to be expressed in the educational discourse of the curriculum itself, and not inadvertently promote the language of (for example) training or management.

Relationship to present organizational structures

Many, if not all, these systems and policies are already in place on the ground in support of the current educational situation, and clearly it is important to utilize these and/or adapt them in respect of the above list, and not to invent more new ones than necessary. But it is important to check that their role is compatible with and sensitive to the educational philosophy of the curriculum being promoted. In terms of preparing for quality assurance procedures, it is also important to explain in the definitive curriculum document who is responsible for overseeing that all these systems and policies are in place, which ones need to have been generated at Trust and which at deanery level, and where the documentation about them can be found. An eye should also be kept on the requirements and principles of PMETB.

Recruitment and selection regulations and criteria

The main elements

The main components here are the regulations that set down:

- the application processes;
- the criteria for selection;
- the processes involved in selection (usually a paper exercise or interview).

If the curriculum is at national level, there may also have to be agreements about when, where and how recruitment is permitted to take place nationwide.

The statement about the application process will probably need to set down the minimum qualifications necessary to gain entry to the programme. A sound application for the programme would be one that demonstrated knowledge of the overall structure together with some of the details of the relevant curriculum. Equity of opportunity and anti-discriminatory policies will need to govern all recruitment processes. However, this process should be in the hands of those who will teach and should, in a curriculum for practice, focus on the candidates' practical and professional attributes.

The criteria for recruitment should indicate the kinds of candidate who would most benefit from the curriculum. To determine these, it is necessary to revisit the educational aims within the curriculum and recognize and examine the starting points that they assume. From this a list of attributes required of learners at the start of the programme will be able to be deduced.

Sensitivity to and facilitation of the educational decisions

Again it will be clear from the above that these decisions cannot be made until the curriculum is substantially written, and they need to reflect the values, priorities and educational philosophy as well as the aims of that curriculum.

Relationship to present organizational structures

While fitting into the Trust procedures for interview for posts, the processes involved in recruitment to the programme should ensure that those involved in the selection process will inevitably and properly use their professional judgement. We are very concerned about the straightjacket which human resources regulations wraps round the human process of recruitment, which is a much more sensitive and professionally-focused process than traditional interview protocols assume.

Recruitment and selection regulations and criteria must also be sensitive to all relevant requirements and principles of PMETB.

Regulations for educational progression and provision for non-progression

The main elements

This section is about how to manage the assessment process both educationally and managerially. The main elements here are:

- the educational role of assessment (which should come first and be part of the section on assessment in the definitive document);
- what counts as evidence of failure (this should also be part of the main section on assessment);
- the regulations for progression;
- provision for a mid-term review of progress (an assessment board, its constitution, terms of reference and procedures);
- principles to guide the remedial provision for struggling learners identified at the mid-term review;
- constitution, terms of reference and procedures for a final assessment board;
- provision for the learner still in difficulty, including career guidance;
- processes for reporting and recording the gatekeeping results of the educational programme (RITA processes).

Needless to say these have to be very clear in their formulation and expression.

Sensitivity to and facilitation of the educational decisions

Again, we would emphasize that once assessment has fulfilled its proper educational purposes of informing teachers and learners about the educational achievements of the learner, then and only then can it validly fulfil the managerial needs of regulating progression, of providing the evidence for learners in difficulty, and of documenting and recording the decisions.

Relationship to present organizational structures

It remains to be seen how and to what extent current structures (like the RITA process) will need reconsideration in the light of the new medical curricula being developed. Our view is that this should arise from the practice of the new curricula rather than being revised in advance of seeing how the new assessment approaches work out.

Regulations for progression must also be able to demonstrate compatibility with the principles of PMETB in relation to what they call 'assessment in the workplace'.

Quality assurance procedures

Account has been taken in this section of the normal arrangements for quality assurance as required in postgraduate education by the Quality Assurance Agency. It is not yet clear how PMETB will fulfil this role for postgraduate medical education.

Quality assurance is concerned with the overall quality of the education provided within the curriculum-in-action on the ground. It is about reassuring the public and specific consumers about the rigour and standards of an educational enterprise (the curriculum-in-action). It may be seen merely as an administrative and managerial matter, or it can be linked more directly to education and seen as a developmental activity which is supported by administrative procedures. This makes more central the process of educational evaluation, which is a separate activity, and which we address more fully in Chapter 10.

When quality assurance is conceived of only as an administrative enterprise, terms like 'inspection', 'examination' and 'validation' come into play. Here, the concerns are technical, and the questions are about what is visible and therefore measurable. However, as we shall see, there has always been a blurring of the educational and the managerial, and a variety of issues were traditionally attended to during a hospital review visit, even where educational expertise was not included in the visiting team! For example, questions about living conditions are asked alongside questions about the aims of the curriculum and whether it has succeeded in terms of these goals.

Quality assurance then, is here seen as essentially investigative in terms of scientific research. Again, we would see this as another example of distorting the nature of education (which is not scientific). Quality assurance seeks data which provide clear-cut (simplistic) evidence for coming to precise conclusions about the success of an educational programme as if the main marker of such success is immediately visible. Such a way of auditing important public and institutional matters may appear to be a necessary – but is by no means a sufficient – approach to understanding and improving professional practice (which is why the following chapter is focused on educational evaluation).

Educators are clearly accountable for the quality of the education they provide. But in reality they should be answerable for the moral and ethical as well as the technical aspects of it. Quality assurance should therefore be about deepening the educational understanding (of practitioners and of the public) in respect of the achievements and complexities of the educational enterprise. Teachers seriously improve their practice in the light of enhanced educational understanding, not in response to mandates from outside.

Real commitment to improving quality (as opposed to going through the motions) requires recognition of the following. Quality:

- cannot be inspected into an enterprise;
- does not lend itself to systemization;
- cannot be externally imposed;
- is not susceptible to top-down models;
- will never come from tight prescription.

Quality comes from a real and shared commitment to improvement through seeking increased understanding between educators and those who evaluate education.

The main elements

Administrative procedures have long been in place in respect of quality assurance, and any new curriculum will have to consider how these should be utilized and to what ends. For example, Royal Colleges have a range of hospital inspection committees, and deaneries conduct inspection visits to Trusts. While the future of these arrangements is not yet clear and PMETB will no doubt be providing guidelines and principles in respect of quality assurance, the traditional tasks associated with quality assurance will no doubt still have to be carried out. These include:

- ensuring that programmes of education enable postgraduate doctors to meet the standards required by Colleges (and PMETB);
- collecting data and views on the standards of education offered by programmes;
- recognizing posts;
- checking the suitability of Trusts as educational institutions (though it should be noted that this is not as simple as it seems);
- checking the suitability as educators of those who teach;
- checking the standard of education against requirements of the Colleges, the Deaneries, the GMC and PMETB.

In the past the purpose of visits has been:

- to ensure that the post provides the necessary education and supervision;
- to help improve the facilities and support available for consultants in order to improve the education of postgraduate doctors;
- to ensure that there are suitable facilities for audit;
- to ensure that the curriculum is suitably enacted on the ground;
- to ensure that study leave is available where appropriate;
- to ensure, in collaboration with other agencies, that the following facilities are acceptable:
  - library
  - educational facilities
  - living accommodation
  - meals.

In the past, visits have included the following procedures:

- a confidential meeting with the learning doctors;
- inspection of clinical facilities;
- inspection of educational facilities;
- inspection of accommodation;
- a meeting with consultants;
- a meeting with the Chief Executive;
- a meeting with the surgical and/or medical tutor.

A report was written on each visit. It was confidential to the Royal College/ deanery, the specialty tutor, the regional adviser, the postgraduate dean, the CEO of the hospital, the GMC and the **Specialist Training Authority** (STA) when appropriate. Its substance may already have been conveyed to the hospital. The visitors' recommendations were submitted to the College inspection committee and final decisions on recommendations following a visit usually rested with that committee. The report was not normally divulged to the health authority but the hospital/Trust could disclose the report if they so wished.

Sensitivity to and facilitation of the educational decisions

Some of the above matters are far more educational and far more complex than has been acknowledged in the system described. It is to be hoped that curriculum designers will have a better understanding than previously about the complex and values-based nature of education and of the appropriate grounds for determining its success or otherwise. A section in the definitive curriculum document needs to list the activities seen as appropriate to assure the quality of the education, and to provide the rationale for these. Readers are referred back to Chapter 3 for help with this matter.

Relationship to present organizational structures

As will be obvious from the above, it is not yet clear how future requirements for quality assurance will relate to the present system as described above. For the detail of what is involved in educational evaluation, which might properly be seen as part of good quality assurance (but requiring separate and educational expertise), readers should now proceed to Chapter 10.

PART 3
Curriculum development in medicine: a way forward

10 Shaping an evaluation policy: some principles, values and practices for developing and refining a curriculum

> How can and should the curriculum be kept under review and developed?
> How can rigorous and robust educational evaluation be designed as part of the curriculum?

Introduction

The purpose of curriculum evaluation is to facilitate educational development. It thus has a crucial role in curriculum projects, and involves the teachers and learners, those people running the curriculum, those planning it, and those who have a wider interest in the curriculum's success at a policy-making level. This chapter begins by locating evaluation within purposeful enquiry generally and educational research in particular. Readers seeking more practical advice may wish to focus initially on pages 211–223, but are encouraged to return in due course to the context, with which we begin.

In Chapter 2 we showed that curriculum design is a postgraduate specialty of education, and that curriculum development is the process of making that design manifest in educational settings. Curriculum evaluation is central to that process. We argued that curriculum design results in a curriculum document, and we discussed in some detail a framework not just for the document itself but also to guide the deliberation that needs to underpin its creation. Curriculum evaluation then, in fact begins at the very start of the curriculum design stage. The discussions that go on in a well-founded curriculum project will inevitably engage in evaluation of the ideas and propositions that are being considered. In Chapter 9 we also indicated that quality assurance would need to take account of some aspects of curriculum evaluation.

All this means that in reality, curriculum 'design', 'evaluation' and 'development' are (or rather ought to be) closely interrelated. At one level they are not three separate or distinct entities. Indeed, we strongly urge people involved in a curriculum project to see them as one whole. Unfortunately, this is often not the case. Frequently (as we have so painfully seen in the Foundation Programme initiative in the UK which was under development while we were writing this book) the design phase is conceived of as preceding development in the field, and curriculum evaluation is not considered (except at local level) to be part of either design or development but rather, is carried out separately from both. Properly conducted, evaluation can help to show how and in what ways a curriculum project is proceeding at all stages.

Curriculum evaluation then, is educational in nature, and certainly not regulatory. We see it as a process of enabling a curriculum project to proceed in an orderly and educationally proper manner. It can help the process of critique necessary for the curriculum design to be placed on a sound footing, and it can provide evidence of how that design is being translated into practice.

Curriculum evaluation is properly educational in another sense. As we argued in Chapter 3, education is primarily concerned with values – the values of teachers and learners, those of the managers and leaders of educational initiatives, and those too of the people engaged in curriculum design and development. The notion of values lies, in fact, at the very centre of the word evaluation itself. Values are central to education, and central too to evaluation. It is not difficult to see therefore, that a primary concern of curriculum evaluation is to identify and to deliberate on the values that underpin a curriculum project at all stages.

Having thus located curriculum evaluation as a distinctive aspect of education we go further to suggest that in fact it is a form of educational enquiry – curriculum evaluation looks at an educational project in a particular way for a particular purpose. However, before we embark on a discussion of the nature, purpose and practice of curriculum evaluation we see a necessity to consider the nature and purpose of educational research more generally.

We believe that it is important to examine critically the nature of educational research at this point since medical readers of this book will inevitably come to this chapter from a particular (and some might consider partisan) viewpoint – that of a background in scientific research. More especially from our point of view, we believe it is important to see the place of educational enquiry within the larger and more general tradition of research as a whole so as to clarify (make clear and be clear about) what educational research can, and, perhaps even more particularly can't, do, and why it must necessarily be significantly different from other forms of research.

In doing this we hope to establish why we believe it is important for all researchers, in whatever discipline, to recognize that all forms of research reflect the special nature of the particular focus of their enquiry, and that is why they inevitably differ one from another. Put more bluntly here, you cannot carry out curriculum evaluation (or any other form of educational research for that matter) through randomized controlled trials, as though a curriculum (or any other educational initiative) is amenable to scientific enquiry.

The nature and purpose of educational research

Our sources

In compiling this section we have drawn substantially on the work of Michael Golby and Allen Parrott (1999) in their monograph *Educational Research and Educational Practice*. In summarizing what they say, we have inevitably been selective and truncated much of the argument they present in their valuable document, so we urge readers who wish to take their thinking further in this matter to refer directly to the monograph itself. In addition, we have drawn on the work of Carr (1995) and Pring (2000), who are educationists writing about the philosophical basis of educational research.

The wider research traditions

As we have already intimated, our starting point in this discussion is that different research traditions are necessary for different forms of enquiry. The kinds of enquiry needed to conduct research into, say, molecular biology or clinical genetics will differ from those that address educational topics and initiatives. This is because the nature (ontology) of what is being researched differs across disciplines, as do the kinds of knowledge (epistemology) that the research will reveal and deal with. Both of these must determine the research approach (methodology) adopted. Similarly the purposes of the research will be different depending on what is being researched and the way the enquiry is being conducted. In short we are stating that there is no single entity that we can call 'research'. There is no single research methodology that applies to every kind of enquiry. Thus, researchers adopt an enquiry paradigm, and they do so whether they realize it or not.

For the scientist (and we use that term here to refer to those who are engaged in research into natural phenomena, for example physics, chemistry and biology – and their offshoots in the field of medical research), a positivist approach has been adopted, certainly in the western world, since the days of Francis Bacon.

The positivist paradigm asserts that the external world – 'the world of factory-built machines and monetary exchanges, of high-speed travel and Clapham bus timetables, of market economies and percentage points' is the 'real' world. (Golby and Parrott 1999: 290) So dominant has the positivist paradigm become, and so widespread its effects on people since the so-called scientific and industrial revolutions, that any alternative is considered to be inadequate and even 'unscientific'. One result is that those who (like us) hold a different view of research appear almost apologetic in defending their position. While we see no need to apologize, we nevertheless accept the need to give a clearer account of what we do and how we approach both educational research and curriculum evaluation. As Golby and Parrott (1999: 28) put it:

> as soon as we enter the world of genuine enquiry, in which people are claiming to have derived some kind of knowledge about some kind of reality using some kind of method, we have to ask questions about their deep-seated beliefs and pre-conceptions, and, of course, about our own.

The positivist paradigm

The term 'positivism' was coined by Auguste Comte (1798–1857) to describe scientific method. It arose out of the intellectual challenges following the Renaissance period in European history. 'Scientists' (as they later became known), such as Galileo with his telescope, began to reveal some of the mysteries of the universe, which until then had been regarded as the province of God and thus the concern of only a restricted group of enquirers. They began to question the more submissive paradigm of the mediaeval period that was based on wonderment and obedience to higher powers. They believed that, as a result of their work, the world could be revealed to mortal man. The shift in thinking was from addressing the question 'why?' to answering the questions 'what, when and how?'

This movement in western thought led to the development of what have become known as Baconian empiricism and Cartesian rationalism. Within these two belief systems, knowledge became associated with certainty, which in an otherwise uncertain world gave people a sense of control over not just their environment but also, even their destiny. Central to these beliefs (which became an entire value system in itself) was that the world was a huge machine made up of matter that could be divided into its constituent parts, and of motion that obeyed mathematical laws. Eventually, it was believed, science would establish the laws that govern everything in the world.

The overarching values of scientific researchers were bound up in the notion that the findings of such research revealed 'the truth' about nature, and that this truth could be determined only through 'objective' enquiry, that is by the researcher being a dispassionate and objective observer of nature, with the 'knower' necessarily detached and separated from 'the known'.

The emergence of the social sciences, and 'the paradigm wars'

Comte's view of positivism was that these 'scientific' approaches ought to be utilized in understanding the human condition – 'society'. He believed that 'if social scientists could develop the same kind of positivist certainties or laws as their counterparts had done in cosmology and physics, a "technology" of society itself would become possible' (Golby and Parrott 1999: 31).

This led to what became known as 'the paradigm wars', since not everyone involved in researching social phenomena considered the positivist paradigm to be pre-eminently and unquestionably appropriate, and their arguments became as much philosophical as they were methodological. Research, not just in relation to the human condition, became a moral and ethical matter. Many writers and artists of the eighteenth and nineteenth centuries challenged, and in some instances railed against, what they saw as the inevitable and unacceptable human costs of industrialization, and some philosophers vigorously questioned the positivist view that assumed an exclusive hold on reality and truth.

Those engaged in purposeful enquiry into social phenomena began to explore alternative approaches. Kant (1724–1804), for example, rejected the empiricist and dualist views of Bacon and Descartes of a detached and separate mind – a *tabula rasa* waiting to be written on – in favour of a view of the mind that had a structure and function of its own that could exert some influence over, and even create, its own reality.

The challenge to positivism from within

Ironically, it was not only artists, philosophers and the emerging social scientists who began to challenge the apparently impregnable edifice of positivism. So did empirical scientists themselves. Among the most prominent were people such as Einstein, whose theory of relativity undermined Newton's laws of physics, and Heisenberg, whose indeterminacy principle stated that there could never be an entirely separate or detached observer, since the observation process itself will always have some effect on what is being observed.

In the 1930s Karl Popper's views further challenged the absolutism and essential certainties of positivism, and suggested that all knowledge was tentative. Nothing could ever be said to be 'true'. There were no timeless and universal laws of nature. Scientific enquiry, he believed, fundamentally lay in relentless criticism.

Thomas Kuhn, who in the 1960s popularized the notion of 'paradigms', supported Popper's ideas. He suggested that all 'discoveries' were nothing more than the product of the way in which the discoverer has gone about the process of discovering. This led to the view that our understanding of the world is limited by the paradigm within which we view it. Thus what had been held to be 'scientific breakthroughs' were no more than shifts in the researchers' paradigmatic thinking. In short, knowledge was never 'true' and fixed for all time but had to be seen as a 'construction' rather than a 'discovery', and to a great extent a social construction (Golby and Parrott 1999: 39). Even today, some physicists argue that physics, perhaps the most fundamental of all the sciences, does not follow rules but is part of a 'dappled world' (Cartright 1999).

Positivist and non-positivist paradigms compared and contrasted

Golby and Parrott offer a table that summarizes these matters by indicating the positivist and non-positivist views of: the nature of reality (ontological assumptions); the nature of knowledge (epistemological assumptions); and the nature of enquiry (methodological assumptions) (see Table 10.1). They make the point that such a table can only be 'suggestive of ideas', but the detail they offer within each section provides a vivid encapsulation of the essential differences and similarities involved. Incidentally it also demonstrates the basis of the paradigm wars. They do however, direct the reader to further exploration of all this, which can be found in Lincoln and Guba (1985) (see Golby and Parrott 1999: 45b and 104).

The emergence of a paradigm for educational enquiry

It is one matter to show in what ways the positivist paradigm is inadequate as a form of social enquiry (such as educational research), and even to demonstrate in what ways the positivist and non-positivist paradigms differ from one another. However, that tells us little about what would be an appropriate approach for educational research and curriculum evaluation.

We recognize and acknowledge that social scientists from different backgrounds (sociologists like Becker *et al.* 1961; anthropologists like Sinclair 1997); and policy researchers like those who provided the evaluation report for The Open University (2001) quite legitimately conduct enquiries into educational matters. However, their research cannot claim to be strictly educational. While it may be *about* education, it is not necessarily *for* education. Social scientists generally might conduct research into educational situations to find out more about them but educationists conduct research for educational reasons. This raises two broad questions for us here: what makes an enquiry distinctively educational; and what elements of educational enquiry can contribute towards a paradigm for curriculum evaluation? Along with other writers (see especially Golby and Parrott; W. Carr; and Pring) we see several broad contributions.

Table 10.1 Three basic assumptions of positivist and non-positivist paradigms

The nature of reality (ontological assumptions)

Positivist paradigm	Non-positivist paradigms
Reality is single, tangible, fragmentable into measurable parts/particles/atoms/quarks etc.	Realities are multiple, perspectival, complex Wholes are greater than the sum of parts
Consists of matter and motion obeying 'laws'	
Objectively 'out there' and discoverable	Subjective meanings help to create reality
Subjective meanings and 'mind' are always caused, not causal	Mind as real as matter – causal and caused simultaneously

The nature of knowledge (epistemological assumptions)

Positivist paradigm	Non-positivist paradigms
Knowledge is absolute, universal and quantifiable	Knowledge is time-bound and context-bound, constructed
Abstract and context-free generalizations	Concrete and particular, never static
Built up incrementally as 'facts' which confirm 'theories' or 'hypotheses'	Different ways to know, no such thing as an objective fact free of theory or free of values
Knower separate from what is known	
	Knower interconnected with known

The nature of enquiry (methodological assumptions)

Positivist paradigm	Non-positivist paradigms
Search for new facts, generalizations and laws	Search for understandings, meanings, insights
To discover simple causal relationships and provide explanations. To isolate key variables. To provide quantifiable evidence which reveals some aspect of reality	To explore complex connections and interrelationships. To provide 'thick' or in-depth descriptions. To gain quality awareness of some aspect of reality

The 'interpretivist' approach

Weber (1964) held that sociology was 'a science which attempts the interpretive understanding of social action'. This view, held by many social scientists over the past 50 years, suggests the importance of interpreting and understanding people's actions rather than explaining and quantifying them. Beneath such interpretation lie values. Indeed 'values are inseparable from facts and interpretation as an inescapable aspect of description and explanation' (Golby and Parrott 1999: 43).

This view has led to what some call a 'science of interpretation' (hermeneutics) and others term 'phenomenology' (the idea that human consciousness is just as 'real' as physical objects). Forms of enquiry such as anthropology, as well as sociology and ethnography, base much of their methodological approach on these beliefs, and give rise to the social sciences as we know them today – sociology, psychology, anthropology, economics, political science etc. (In this regard some aspects of psychology, such as behaviourism and experimental work in perception and cognition, can be regarded as positivist forms of enquiry rather than social science, though other elements, such as social psychology and psychopathology, are more 'naturalistic' and interpretive.)

The interpretivist approach is not without either its problems or its critics of course. The main argument is that the researcher can never be 'objective'. He or she is the primary 'instrument' of the enquiry. His or her subjective views, beliefs and values will inevitably intrude, not only by distorting their interpretation of the data but actually determining the very data that the researcher obtains.

Since the context for human enquiry is the human situation, research of this nature is often carried out in natural settings rather than in the controlled environment of the laboratory. This means that 'variables' cannot be held constant. There can be no prediction of what might happen. The research 'plan' may not work out, or even be possible.

Questions of validity and reliability are often asked of social enquiries. Some researchers, like Lincoln and Guba (1985), argue that these are tenets of the positivist paradigm and should not apply in the non-positivist arena. They prefer to use terms such as 'credibility' instead of validity, 'dependability' for reliability, and 'confimability' for objectivity.

Perhaps the greatest challenge to the interpretivist approach relates to the 'problem of generalization'. In what ways can research into social situations (with all their context specificity) ever be generalized to other people or situations? Lincoln and Guba (1985) counter this by speaking of the need to establish the data's 'transferability' – the extent to which findings in one area (and the ways of obtaining those findings) can be adopted and utilized to aid interpretation and understanding in another. In this regard Golby and Parrott speak about the 'intelligibility' of research findings, for they say that social enquiry 'is not principally a matter of looking [at something] but, inseparably from looking, a matter of inspecting the lens through which we look' (Golby and Parrott 1999: 74). Enquirers into social phenomena must therefore be acutely aware of their own beliefs and values.

Nevertheless, many educational researchers recognize the importance of the interpretivist approach. They obtain data in educational settings, and in doing so they inevitably interpret what they collect. Interpretation is necessary but it is not sufficient to turn a social enquiry into educational research. And the educational values they espouse must be made explicit at all stages of any enquiry (see Chapter 3 for a fuller account of ours).

The critical approach

Wilfred Carr (1995) argues that the interpretivist approach has yet a further weakness in relation to educational enquiry: social researchers who adopt such an approach are likely to be motivated largely by intellectual curiosity. This is no great error for research generally but it has a serious flaw when the object of an enquiry is education. Educators exist to improve the understanding of others. Educational researchers are not simply interested in what is happening in an educational setting, or even why. They are interested in learning. And to achieve this, there is a need for 'criticality':

> Educational enquiries in the critical paradigm aim . . . to do more than increase awareness of the many different understandings which exist in a given situation, though this may be a necessary starting point. They aim to improve the practice of education by helping practitioners to alter their actions as a result of critical and self-critical reflection.
>
> (Golby and Parrott 1999: 53)

Similarly, Carr argues that educational research ought to be conducted within the critical paradigm because educational practice is not just a moral endeavour (doing good for others, making their lives better and more fulfilling through greater understanding) but it is also what he calls a 'social practice' which is 'historically located, culturally embedded and hence, always vulnerable to ideological distortion':

> Educational practice is always [to be] interpreted as 'problematic', not in the sense that it gives rise to practical problems to which theoretical solutions can be applied, but in the sense that the purposes it serves, the social relationships it creates, the form of social life it helps to sustain, can all be critically reconsidered in terms of the way in which they either assist or impede genuine educational progress and change.
>
> (Carr 1995: 50)

Carr distinguishes between two forms of educational enquiry that he calls 'empirical' and 'critical'. He sees the major characteristic of the empirical approach as being 'to improve the rationality of education through the practical application of knowledge it has itself produced'. We suggest that he has in mind here the contribution of the broad range of social sciences. On the other hand we believe that the purpose of critical educational enquiry is:

> . . . to improve the rationality of education by enabling educational practitioners to refine the rationality of their practice for themselves. Thus, a critical educational science [*sic*] would not produce theoretical knowledge about educational practice, but the kind of educative, self-knowledge that would reveal to practitioners the unquestioned beliefs and unstated assumptions in terms of which their practice was sustained.
>
> (Carr 1995: 117–18)

In short, we believe that educational practice changes for the better when educators understand their practice more clearly, and that happens when they review it critically. Educational research in general (and curriculum evaluation in particular) can play a central role in this.

The participatory approach

Others writers like Heron (1996) and Reason (1996), argue that educational enquiry should not simply be conducted *on* education (as seen in a positivist/empiricist approach which applies knowledge gathered through research to educational phenomena), nor should it be just *about* education (as in the interpretivist approach, even though this increases our understanding of educational matters), nor should it be simply *for* education (as when the critical approach helps to emancipate educators from their unquestioned beliefs) but that it should be undertaken *with* educational practitioners:

> In this respect all participants in a project have the same status as 'co-enquirers' and do not divide into researchers and research subjects, or investigators and informants. It is not the researcher who provides all the thinking, and the research subjects who contribute all the actions; all participants are expected to be critical and self-critical actors and practitioners operating in both roles.
>
> (Golby and Parrott 1999: 54)

The major resource of educational practitioners is, of course, the academic world. However, educational researchers in these institutions have often adopted an empirical (if not positivist) approach to research, or have been more focused on research about educational provision. Partly (and particularly in the UK) this has resulted from the ways in which research effort can be accounted for, notably through the so-called 'research assessment exercise' which 'measures' the research output of academic departments. The problem here, of course, is that this inevitably 'measures the measurable' which may not always be the most valuable. The research 'output' that supports a curriculum project may be difficult (if not impossible) to measure even though it may 'count for a great deal' in terms of educational progress through the refinement of the curriculum.

It is now becoming clear that this traditional role of academic institutions 'to conduct research, to discover new knowledge, to promulgate the findings, and for researchers to apply these to their practice' (Fish and Coles 1998: 312) has failed to influence developments in practice (Haines and Jones 1994).

Stenhouse's observation of curriculum development was that 'most of the work done in this area has relied on . . . [external] research workers rather than teachers', and that these researchers were 'more interested in building a theory of teaching and reporting observations in a form addressed mainly to the research community, than in improving the classrooms they have studied' (Stenhouse 1975: 156). His view was, in contrast, that academics ought to be 'helping schools to undertake research and development in a problem area and to report this work in a way that supports similar developments in other schools' (1975: 223). He added 'a research tradition which is accessible to teachers and which feeds teaching must be created if education is to be significantly improved' (1975: 165).

Eraut similarly argues for a close partnership between academics and professional practitioners. What he sees as the barriers to linking the academic world and the world of practice 'are most likely to be overcome if higher education is prepared to extend its role from that of creator and transmitter of generalisable knowledge to that of *enhancing the knowledge-creating capacities* of individuals and professional communities' (Eraut 1994: 57).

An overview of curriculum evaluation

Put together, these various contributions to curriculum evaluation can be summarized in this paraphrase of Golby and Parrott's view of educational research: Curriculum evaluation:

1   . . . should be *about* curriculum, i.e. it should specifically focus on the educational elements of a curriculum project, and on the nature of curriculum itself;
2   . . . should be *for* development of a curriculum, i.e. it should be focused on bringing about development;
3   . . . should be educational for the evaluators, i.e. the people conducting the evaluation should increase their understanding not just about the curriculum being evaluated and of curriculum matters more generally but of educational phenomena even more widely;

4   . . . should be educational for those who are the focus of the evaluation, i.e. the people who are involved (at all levels) in the curriculum project should come to a greater understanding of the educational basis of their work (after Golby and Parrott 1999: 60–4).

Evaluation and curriculum models

Curriculum evaluation then, is best seen as a branch of educational research, and as such it draws on the variety of research traditions that are to be seen in that more general field of educational enquiry. In curriculum evaluation, it is the practice of those engaged in a curriculum project that is the focus of enquiry. And, as with any educational research, the purpose of curriculum evaluation is increased understanding – specifically about the development of the curriculum. Curriculum evaluation is an educational process.

In principle, the way one evaluates a curriculum will depend on (and flow directly out of) the view one takes both of curriculum and of enquiry more generally. In Chapter 3 we discussed the notion of curriculum as a 'product', a 'process' and as 'research'. Each of these views has influenced and directly determined its own particular approach to curriculum evaluation.

The evaluation of a curriculum as 'product'

The 'product', or objectives, view of a curriculum cashes out as an outcomes approach to evaluation – the curriculum is judged in terms of what is achieved, chiefly the performance of learners. The literature on this is peppered with bold statements: 'What one really wants to know about a given curriculum is whether it works' (Gagné 1967: 29). The curriculum 'must describe an observable behaviour of the learner or a product which is a consequence of learner behaviour' (Popham 1969: 35). Evaluation is 'concerned with securing evidence of the attainment of specific objectives of instruction' (Bloom 1970: 28).

The contention is that if the curriculum can specify in great detail what the learner is expected to be able to do as a result of some teaching, then it can be evaluated in terms of whether or not the learner's behaviour can be shown to meet that expectation.

As we argued earlier, while a 'product' curriculum might prove to be of some value where the ends of the educational enterprise (the outcomes) can be determined with accuracy in advance, and where the means for achieving those ends are somewhat straightforward, for a practitioner to learn much of what counts as professional practice it has serious limitations. The characterization we gave to such a curriculum was that it might be appropriate where someone needed to be 'trained' to carry out a specific task in a specific situation in a specific manner. However, we noted that there were very few situations in medical practice (or indeed educational practice) where this is the case. Even in the setting of, say, emergency medicine, where actions may need to be taken speedily, and where everyone involved might be expected to act in the same way, nevertheless a doctor's judgement is likely to be required at any moment as situations of uncertainty arise. Similarly, in an apparently 'technical' specialty such as surgery, judgement is central to the practitioner's actions.

'Process' evaluation

The second model we presented in Chapter 3 viewed a curriculum as a process. This was particularly evident in curriculum projects in schools during the 1960s, which was also a time when curriculum evaluation began to emerge as a discernible approach (see Stenhouse 1975: 98–122). Here we list some of the key proponents in these developments.

Stake's model
Stake (1967, 1995) was one of the pioneers in process evaluation, which he argued was necessary to reflect 'the complex and dynamic nature of education, one which gives proper attention to the diverse purposes and judgements of the practitioner'. In 1967 he offered a model of curriculum evaluation (see Stenhouse 1975: 108) that distinguishes between what he calls the antecedents of a curriculum (those things that are in place before a curriculum is introduced), the transactions of a curriculum (what happens when the curriculum is introduced), and the outcomes of a curriculum (what the results are when a curriculum has been introduced).

This model recognizes that what is intended may not be what is observed, so antecedents, transactions and outcomes might not happen as planned, intentions and outcomes may indeed not be 'congruent'.

While the relationship between antecedents, transactions and outcomes may be 'logical' in the curriculum planners' intentions, the relationship between them when observed in practice will be contingent on many factors associated with both the practice and the observer.

Stake later (1974) went on to suggest that curriculum evaluation needed to be 'responsive', that is to reflect more what happens when a curriculum is introduced than merely to evaluate its intentions, and in his later writing (1995) emphasized the need for case study research to investigate this.

Parlett and Hamilton's illuminative evaluation
In the 1970s two UK educationists proposed an approach to curriculum evaluation which they termed 'illuminative':

> The aims of illuminative evaluation are to study the innovatory pro-
> gramme; how it operates; how it is influenced by the various school

situations in which it is applied; what those directly concerned regard as its advantages and disadvantages; and how students' intellectual tasks and academic experiences are most affected. It aims to discover and document what it is like to be participating in the scheme, whether as teacher or pupil; and, in addition, to discern and discuss the innovation's most significant features, recurring concomitants, and critical processes.

(Parlett and Hamilton 1972)

Two concepts are central to this approach: 'the instructional system' and 'the learning milieu'. The instructional system relates to the curriculum specifications and how these may be modified in practice (thus reflecting Stake's notion of the congruence between what is intended and what is observed). The learning milieu relates to 'the social-psychological and material environment in which students and teachers work together', and the instructional system interacts with this because 'the introduction of an innovation sets off a chain of repercussions throughout the learning milieu. In turn these unintended consequences are likely to affect the innovation itself, changing its form and moderating its impact' (Parlett and Hamilton 1972).

Stenhouse's criteria for educational evaluation

Stenhouse was somewhat sceptical about evaluators who 'aspire to "tell it as it is", and . . . [who] often write as if that is possible if they allow for some distortion due to their own values. But there is no telling it as it is. There is only a creation of meaning through the use of criteria and conceptual frameworks' (Stenhouse 1975: 116–17). He proposed five criteria 'which might be used in the estimate of a curriculum or an educational practice':

- *meaning* – to disclose the meaning of a curriculum rather than to assess its worth by observing classrooms;
- *potential* – to identify the potential of a curriculum and to estimate in what ways this is realized in practice;
- *interest* – to identify the problems that a curriculum raises in practice;
- *conditionality* – to explore the factors which are likely to make for success or failure in realizing the potential of the curriculum in relation to the problems that are being faced;
- *elucidation* – to show in what ways the response to the curriculum throws light on how innovation is possible either generally or in a particular place (summarized from Stenhouse 1975: 118–19).

A research model of curriculum evaluation

The third model we presented in Chapter 3 viewed a curriculum as research – learners learning by engaging in enquiries of their own, with teachers supervising them, and where the roles of teachers and learners become blurred.

Stenhouse suggests that any curriculum project ought to be seen as a research enquiry in its own right. He saw a clear role for teachers, not as the subjects of evaluation carried out by external evaluators but as important and central figures in the evaluation process itself. His vision was of teachers as researchers:

> All well-founded curriculum research and development, whether the work of an individual teacher, of a school . . . or a group working within the co-ordinating framework of a national project . . . rests on the work of teachers. It is not enough that teachers' work should be studied: they need to study it themselves.
>
> (Stenhouse 1975: 143)

He recognized the problems surrounding 'objectivity' in such an approach but argued:

> any research into classrooms must aim to improve teaching . . . There is no escaping the fact that it is the teacher's subjective perception which is crucial for practice . . . Accordingly we are concerned with the development of a sensitive self-critical subjective perspective and not with an aspiration towards an unattainable objectivity . . . Illusion may be destroyed when disclosed. Assumptions and habits will be changed. The problem is one of awareness.
>
> (Stenhouse 1975: 157–8)

This could be achieved, suggested Stenhouse, through collaborative research between teachers and 'full-time' research workers, adding that 'it may also involve research-trained personnel in taking consultancy roles in teacher groups, and support roles in schools and classrooms'. He reported that in one enquiry:

> one of the important roles [of the] outside researchers was to interview pupils in order to compare the teachers' and the pupils' perceptions of particular sequences of teaching . . . Substantial perceptual disparities emerged. Teachers and pupils were then able to discuss these and attempt to resolve them, and in many cases the outside researchers were able to withdraw from the task of pupil interviewing

having helped teachers to establish an open dialogue with their pupils about their teaching.

(Stenhouse 1975: 162–3)

An approach to evaluating a curriculum for practice

Drawing together the threads of our discussion so far, not just in terms of curriculum evaluation but taking account of our earlier thinking in this book regarding the nature of curriculum generally and of a curriculum for practice more particularly, we now present an approach to curriculum evaluation. We do so in terms of the evaluation's purposes, the criteria to be used, a conceptual framework, and a review of evaluation methods and procedures.

Purposes

As we have shown, our perspective on curriculum evaluation follows the traditions of educational research and the key concepts in curriculum evaluation that we have outlined above, but it goes further.

To reiterate, the purpose of curriculum evaluation is to facilitate the design and development of a curriculum. Thus we see curriculum design, development and evaluation as needing to be closely interrelated.

Evaluation cannot begin too soon. It should be built into the design and development processes from the very beginning. Too often, curriculum evaluation is grafted onto the curriculum development process, frequently towards the end, often missing the design phase, and most often while development in the field is under way. This is a grave error. Curriculum evaluation is part of the total process of curriculum design and development.

Evaluation of curriculum design

Curriculum design most commonly involves a group (or groups) of people meeting to discuss the curriculum, and results in the publication of a curriculum document. As we showed earlier, Stenhouse has noted that a curriculum should be 'an attempt to communicate the essential principles and features of an educational proposal in such a form that it is open to critical scrutiny' (1975: 4). This, then, establishes a clear purpose for curriculum evaluation during the design phase of a curriculum project. The question being addressed here is: is it right?

To achieve this purpose the curriculum evaluator needs to have access both to the meetings of the groups involved in curriculum design and the records of their deliberations (usually the minutes of the meetings). In addition, the evaluator ought to be able to speak with, or preferably interview, the people concerned. (We deal below in more detail with issues concerning interviewing.)

Sometimes there are discrepancies between what is written in curriculum documents and what people say are the purposes and intentions of the curriculum. The comments people make about the curriculum's documentation can expand on the curriculum's intentions and even illuminate the processes that led to the decisions that were made and that resulted in the documents being written in the way they were. On occasions what people say about 'the curriculum on paper' may reflect ambitions that have not been realized, and the evaluator can gain great insights into the curriculum by exploring the reasons for this.

A common omission from the deliberations of a curriculum design group is some form of 'situational (or needs) analysis'. As we showed in Chapter 2 this requires an enquiry into current educational provision, and clearly requires educational research of some kind. In addition, a situational analysis for a curriculum for practice ought to look into not just what constitutes practice at present but into the possible results of the enactment of those changes that are desired within the proposed curriculum.

Following the traditions of educational enquiry discussed above, and in particular the involvement of the people concerned so that they learn through the evaluation, the evaluator would, in the course of the evaluation, engage the people concerned in a deeper deliberation than hitherto of the matters they are discussing. In this way, the evaluator would, in common parlance, provide 'feedback' but would do so in such a way that the discussion of the curriculum design moves to a higher educational plane. The evaluator's specialist knowledge of the educational (and in particular the curriculum) literature is a major contribution to the discussion of the curriculum design group. The evaluator will, in the course of the evaluation, become aware of the educational writing that is made available to the people involved. Often, where there is no curriculum expert chairing the design team, this lacks rigour. The specialist evaluator, in the absence of such an expert, is in a position to offer more appropriate writing.

Typically, the contribution of the evaluator at the design stage is to focus people's attention on the educational values they are espousing (orally and in writing). In addition, as a curriculum document begins to emerge from the group, the evaluator (alongside a curriculum expert in the chair, or in the absence of one) ought to be in a position to guide the group through a framework for the document such as the one we outlined in Chapter 2.

Evaluation of the curriculum development phase

While we see danger in separating curriculum design and curriculum development, there comes a point in a curriculum project when the curriculum is translated into practice. The purpose of curriculum evaluation now is to show how and in what ways the translation into practice is effective. The question being addressed of the curriculum now is: is it working?

We saw above, particularly from the work of Stake, that the curriculum's intentions may not be realized in practice. Curriculum research (see, for example, Coles 1985) shows that this notion requires amplification.

We believe that a useful framework for curriculum evaluation represents a curriculum as comprising three facets: 'the curriculum on paper', 'the curriculum in action' and 'the curriculum that people experience' (Coles 1985). This suggests that, in practice, there is no single curriculum that is being evaluated, only perspectives – different views of the curriculum as seen from the vantage point of the various people involved. This is shown in Figure 10.1 where each perspective is represented as a circle.

The *curriculum on paper*, which currently is concerned with purposes, intentions and occasionally reasons for these, represents the design phase that we have already discussed above. At present it is often little more than a list of topics to be covered – sometimes a syllabus – with perhaps some statements as to how these are to be taught, though it sometimes appears in the form of policy statements about purposes and content.

Interestingly, the curriculum on paper is not always written down, or at least not as fully as is suggested in the phrase: 'that's what the curriculum is

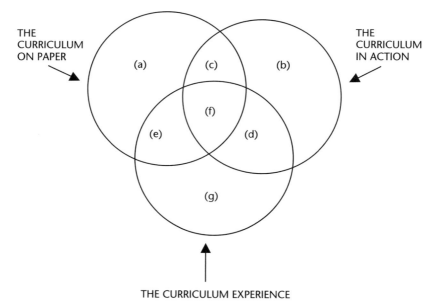

Figure 10.1 A curriculum evaluation framework (after Coles 1985: 259).

"on paper" '. This suggests that the curriculum on paper may include inten-tions and aspirations so far unacknowledged, some which have not been clearly articulated and fully recorded.

The *curriculum in action* represents what actually happens when the curri-culum 'goes live'. It includes teaching sessions, the activities of learners, and committees that meet to discuss the curriculum's activities. Some of these activities are planned, others occur informally. The task of the curriculum evaluator is to 'capture' in some way the essence of all this.

The range of people involved is great – teachers as well as learners (together and apart), administrators, planners, programme directors and policy-makers. In short, anyone associated with the curriculum can be considered to be a source of insights into how the curriculum works in practice.

A key question for the evaluator will be to see in what ways the curriculum design is being translated into practice. Some aspects of the curriculum on paper may never become the curriculum in action and never be experienced (see area 'a' in Figure 10.1). However, some aspects of it may be experienced though never be part of the curriculum in action (area 'e'), for example when the people involved have informal discussions with the curriculum planners or perhaps read the curriculum documentation and come to recognize certain intentions behind the curriculum that have never been realized in the formal actions that followed its introduction.

Similarly, some aspects of the curriculum in action may never have been intended (areas 'b' and 'd') in that they did not appear in the curriculum on paper. This may be because those responsible for the teaching for example decided, quite independently, that they would teach certain topics in certain ways that were never written into the curriculum.

In some curriculum projects the design is introduced in a limited way in selected contexts – sometimes referred to as 'pilot sites' – and these can be a useful focus for the evaluation, particularly to check on the feasibility of the curriculum design. Having said this, pilot sites are often atypical in certain ways:

- they may have been volunteered;
- they are often 'small scale';
- they can be specially resourced;
- they could be the focus of an evaluation.

These factors may make the evaluation findings rather more 'unique' than is useful, and care may be needed for extrapolation to what the situation might be when the curriculum is more widely introduced.

The third circle of our diagram represents the *curriculum that people experi-ence*. The essence of this representation of the curriculum is that people's experience differs. What the planners consider ought to be happening may well differ from what the teachers experience, which again may differ from that of the learners.

The curriculum that people experience may have been intended (areas 'e' and 'f') though only part of that became the curriculum in action (area 'f'). Some of the curriculum that is experienced was part of the curriculum in action that was never intended (area 'd'). Other aspects of the curriculum in action (areas 'c' and 'b') may never be experienced in practice (for example, if students or trainees fail to turn up to a teaching session).

This leaves an aspect of the curriculum that people experience (area 'g') but that was never intended, nor enshrined in the curriculum in action. Over 30 years ago in 1971, Snyder proposed the concept of 'the hidden curriculum'. This refers to the observation that whatever is planned to occur within a curriculum, and whatever activities do occur, the people involved may get from it something quite different, and that this 'hidden' curriculum exerts a powerful influence over people. For example, students may come to believe that their task in developing their clinical practice is to rote learn textbook knowledge – a view most likely promoted by their previous experience of coping with formal examinations, but which may be at variance with the aims and intentions of the curriculum (on paper and in action).

These three aspects of the curriculum – on paper, in action and as experienced – are contained within (and are most probably constrained by) the cultural, historical and ideological matrix in which it is located. A fundamental role of the evaluator is to unearth, explore and fully appreciate the significance of this, and to determine its impact on the curriculum.

As with the evaluation of the design phase, the role of evaluators during the development of the curriculum in the field is one of 'giving feedback' as they go along – that is, engaging as fully and as widely as possible the people concerned with the curriculum project in what the evaluation is indicating. Where possible, as we have argued above, the process of curriculum evaluation (including data collection and interpretation) ought also to be carried out by those who are experiencing the curriculum at first hand as well as those responsible for its design.

Evaluation findings during the development phase may even indicate the need for further design work. Indeed, our view is that curriculum change is never completed. There is no such thing as the perfect curriculum. A curriculum must always be taken to be 'problematic', not so much that it is always a problem but that it ought continuously to be deliberated upon. And the evaluator's role in this is simply crucial. *How then ought evaluators to go about curriculum evaluation? What methods and procedures need to be employed?*

Methods of procedure in curriculum evaluation

Ethical considerations

We begin this final section of the chapter by very properly considering the ethics of curriculum evaluation. Quite fundamentally, it is important for the evaluator to clarify and discuss as widely as possible the purposes of the evaluation and the methods used. It may be that someone they encounter as part of the evaluation is unaware of the role of the evaluator, so it is important to declare this early on. This is even more important as and when some potential 'data' emerge. At this point the evaluator should acknowledge the value of such information and ask permission to record it in some way for subsequent use. The negotiation that may take place at this point can be delicate and should be handled sensitively. Confidentiality, and at least anonymity, should be ensured.

The ethical stance of the curriculum evaluator is crucial. Evaluators exercise great power and must be careful not to abuse this. The **British Educational Research Association** (BERA) published ethical guidelines for all educational research, and readers are directed towards these for further information (see www.bera.ac.uk). The areas of research that need to be considered include:

- the purpose of the research;
- costs and hoped-for benefits;
- privacy and confidentiality;
- selection, inclusion and exclusion;
- funding;
- review and revision of the research aims and methods;
- information for the respondents;
- consent;
- dissemination;
- impact of the research findings.

Working to a steering committee

Curriculum evaluation must be steered, as we indicated in Chapter 2. We have consistently argued that evaluation continuously feeds curriculum development. However, the connection between the two cannot be left to chance. This is why there needs to be a steering committee to transform the researched findings brought to it by the evaluators into a coherent presentation about the state of the curriculum as it evolves, capable of influencing its ongoing development.

Such a committee would comprise members of the original design team, teachers and learners on the ground, and those whose task is to manage the educational programme being developed. It will need to be led by someone with experience of a full range of curriculum matters – from initiation, through design and implementation to evaluation itself. The person leading the steering committee would necessarily be drawn from the curriculum design group.

The work of the steering committee would revolve around that of the evaluators who, forming their own team of educational researchers experienced in curriculum work would present their findings to the steering committee at regular intervals. The committee would critically discuss these findings, recommend areas for further investigation, on occasions challenge the evaluation team, and support the researchers in writing reports for the curriculum designers. On occasions, reports may need to be made from the steering committee to the design team. They also may need to report to the people on the ground (where necessary directly and without recourse to the curriculum designers, if matters are unearthed of a local nature that require particularly sensitive handling, re-emphasizing the ethical nature of the work being undertaken).

Data collection

How then can the evaluator obtain data about the various elements of the curriculum outlined above? Chiefly there are five broad methods:

- the study of documents;
- observation;
- interviews;
- surveys;
- reports.

We will not give extensive details of these here. They are the methods of educational research more generally. Rather we point readers towards some of the published literature (see, for example, Delamont 1992; Cohen *et al.* 2000).

Documents   Curricula often attract a mass of documentation. We have already indicated that these include a curriculum plan and minutes of meetings. To these can be added: programmes, timetables, class lists, assessment forms, results sheets and feedback forms.

Observation   Observation can be made of planning meetings, teaching sessions (whether these are formal or informal) and the activities of the people involved – to observe what actually happens, not just the planned actions but the unplanned ones.

Interviews   Interviews are a generally accepted research method in educational enquiry, and can be structured, semi-structured, unstructured and formal or informal. Informal and unstructured interviews may well provide the greatest insights into the nature of a curriculum. In this sense, the interviews are more like conversations with the people involved. There is an ethical issue here: is it right to obtain research data when the person with whom you are holding a conversation is unaware that research is your purpose? It is important that people know who you are (as a curriculum evaluator) and what your purpose is within the organization (curriculum evaluation). We do not condone the notion of 'curriculum evaluator as private detective'. Curriculum evaluation is not an 'undercover operation'.

It is an ethical obligation to send the person with whom you are having this conversation a copy of the notes that you have made, partly to check on their accuracy but also to establish that they can be used with the person's agreement.

Surveys   These often take the form of questionnaires. Care is needed in their construction. Surveys do not always meet the criteria for educational research described earlier in this chapter. While they may inform the researcher they rarely educate those being researched.

Surveys are probably best employed following the gathering of information (and insights) using other methods. Then, the survey could check with a wider group of people what the evaluator has interpreted through the study of documents, through observations, and through interviews. This role for the questionnaire is the opposite to its traditional one in survey research.

Reports   These are a crucial part of any curriculum evaluation. Reports can be prepared for a wide variety of people, and should be structured to meet their particular needs. We have argued strongly for wide involvement of everyone concerned with a curriculum, but also for use of the steering committee as a sounding board. Reporting back to the committee at all stages of the evaluation will help refine what is presented more widely and ensure that it is fully sensitive to the developing context of the whole enterprise. Some reports will simply feed back to people the evaluator's perceptions of what has been read, observed or talked about. Other reports, probably to the planners and policy-makers, can usefully explore the educational underpinnings of the conclusions being drawn.

Conclusion

In this chapter we have explored the nature of curriculum evaluation. We locate this more generally within the traditions of contemporary educational research. We took as our starting point the wider discussion of research, so as to enable readers more familiar with the more dominant research approach in medicine (the randomized controlled trial) to see not just that there are other research traditions than this but that educational research, and thus curriculum evaluation, has its own identity as distinct even from other social sciences that attempt to conduct enquiries into human situations. The general principle we see operating here is that the research methodology adopted must reflect the nature of the object of that research and the forms of knowledge that are likely to emerge as research findings.

Educational research is concerned with the improvement of educational initiatives, and centrally involves teachers and learners as well as managers, planners and policy-makers. Since education is primarily values-driven, so too is educational research, both in terms of its processes (as seen in the necessary ethical considerations) and the focus of the research – the values underpinning people's actions.

We have argued that curriculum evaluation has its traditions. We reject the notion that anything very useful can be gained merely by measuring the learning outcomes of an educational endeavour. Rather, we argue that much more is to be learnt about a curriculum by enquiring into its processes, and that curriculum design and development are most likely to be effective with the involvement of curriculum specialists in collaboration with those people responsible for the curriculum. We see the role of the external evaluator as an outsider who becomes an insider, who at all stages engages the people involved. In this way, curriculum evaluation is central to the effective introduction of a curriculum project.

11 Some principles of change: the problems of curriculum development and ways forward

Introduction

In this chapter we look at ways in which a curriculum for practice can be introduced. As part of this process we will review some of the literature on innovation and change. In offering these ideas we have constantly in mind two matters. Firstly, we draw heavily on the arguments we made earlier in this book, and in particular our discussion of curriculum design in Chapter 2 and the foundations of educational practice in Chapter 3. Secondly, we are very conscious of the current curriculum development initiatives occurring within postgraduate medical education as we write – the Foundation Programme and the development of specialty education programmes.

While we acknowledge that the documentation for F1 and F2 that emerged finally in April 2005 (DoH 2005b) is to remain in place for several years, a curriculum always remains 'work in progress', and we have seen enough of the ways in which this has been developed to fear that it will ultimately prove to be unsuccessful as a sound curriculum. We conclude the chapter with an alternative approach to the development of a curriculum, which is based on a more reasoned and educational perspective rather than managerial dictate.

Models of change

Change and 'the stable state'

The human species functions best in situations of relative stability. The mind interprets a confusing world as threatening, and attempts to make sense of it. We have a strong sense of identity – who we are, what our name is, a sense of being. We locate ourselves in time and place. We hold identifiable possessions. We value certain things. We hold certain beliefs, one of which is that our world is in a state of relative stability (Schön 1971). And this is still the case today despite the depredations of postmodernism and its view of the world as essentially fragmented.

Yet change is all around – and even within – us. Not only does our world change and everything in it but we too are constantly changing – developing new ideas, growing older. Change is inevitable.

Reactions to change can vary. People may hanker after a former time; others revolt against all that is past. Some pursue mindless diversions. Generally we adopt a stance of 'dynamic conservatism' (Schön 1971), that is: we accept change but in balance with making sense of our experience within a relatively stable perception of our world and ourselves. By how much this dynamic conservatism is a natural response (our biological 'hardwiring' that enables us to function on a day-to-day basis in the light of our ever-changing world) is unclear, yet it has important implications for any educational change. Education after all is synonymous with learning and hence development, and in particular is central to our discussion here about the introduction of a new curriculum.

The 'centre-periphery' model of change

The dominant approach to change within western society over the past hundred years or so (in which change is deliberately and calculatedly introduced endlessly by those in charge) has been popularly called 'top-down', and is sometimes known as the 'centre-periphery' model (Schön 1971). As seen in commerce, the main concern here is getting the product 'right' and then marketing it (Stenhouse 1975: 219). The object of the change is said to be 'diffused' through this process.

In this model, an innovator devises some innovation, and then makes it available to others. The 'diffusion' of innovation, in this model, has three elements:

- the innovation to be diffused exists, fully realized in its essentials, prior to its diffusion;
- diffusion is the movement of an innovation from a centre out to its ultimate users;
- directed diffusion is a centrally managed process of dissemination, training and provision of resources and incentives (Schön 1971: 81).

The success of this model, according to Schön: 'depends first upon the level of resources and energy at the centre, then upon the number of points at the periphery, the length of the radii or spokes through which diffusions takes place, and the energy required to gain a new adoption'. Central to this approach is a well-developed infrastructure:

[the] scope [of the centre-periphery model] depends . . . on . . . the level of technology governing the flows of men, materials, money and information . . . [and the centre's] capacity for generating and managing feedback. Because the process of diffusion is originally regulated by the centre, the effectiveness of the process depends upon the ways in which information moves from periphery back to the centre.

(Schön 1971: 82)

The essential characteristics of 'leadership' in this model, that reflect a military style of command-and-control, are that the leader's place is at the 'centre' and exhibits:

- a clear sense of purpose (sometimes called 'vision');
- the ability to see how the necessary change 'fits' with broader issues (sometimes called 'the wider picture');
- forcefulness (to be able to make people do what you want them to);
- resilience and stamina (to endure the difficulties).

At the periphery, people's role is more submissive – one of implementing the proposed change. These 'implementers' merely act on what is required of them. It is assumed that the rationale for the change is self-evident – that people will see the logic in it; that others will want what the people at the centre believe they need.

Schön's analysis of innovation (while being apposite to and reminiscent of what drives the Foundation Programme) is not primarily focused on education. The work of Havelock (1973) is more directly related to curriculum development. His name for the centre-periphery model, which shares many of its fundamental characteristics, is '**Research, Development and Diffusion**' ('R, D and D'). In this model the innovation is researched by the centre, which then more fully develops it, prior to the innovation's diffusion to those who must take it up:

[This] is sometimes called 'the agricultural model' (even in the curriculum literature) and it is often accepted as a pattern for dissemination and implementation in medicine and in education, where, as in agriculture, ideas have to reach geographically dispersed users.

(Stenhouse 1975: 219)

Schön identifies serious practical weaknesses in the centre-periphery model, which lead to what is often called 'innovation without change':

When the centre-periphery system exceeds the resources or the energy at the centre, overloads the capacity of the radii, or mishandles feedback from the periphery, it fails. Failure takes the form of simple ineffectiveness in diffusion, distortion of the message, or disintegration of the system as a whole . . . Once the new centres [at the periphery] are established, for better or worse, they pursue their disparate paths.

(Schön 1971: 83–4)

The 'proliferation of centres' model

A variant of the 'centre-periphery' model involves what Schön calls 'the proliferation of centres'. This approach maintains the basic centre-periphery structure, but more clearly differentiates primary from secondary centres and provides these secondary centres with a more strategic role than merely being the recipients (and adopters) of the innovation: 'Secondary centres engage in the diffusion of innovations; primary centres support and manage secondary centres . . . Each secondary centre now has the scope of what would have been the whole system' (Schön 1971: 84).

Current curriculum development within postgraduate medical education in the UK (and elsewhere) closely reflects this 'proliferation of centres' model. The 'centre' (the DoH) has devised a curriculum and now requires that it be implemented. At the 'secondary centres' level are organizations known as postgraduate medical and dental deaneries, headed by postgraduate deans who are given the task of implementation. Since they themselves are not physically (and possibly not philosophically) able to carry out the operational tasks required, the work of implementation is devolved to others locally (within hospitals who are known in the UK often as 'clinical tutors'), thereby setting up 'tertiary' centres.

Leadership in this model is thus divided. At the centre the same characteristics are needed as described above for the centre-periphery model. In the secondary centres those appointed to lead the innovation need to be in tune with the beliefs and values of the people at the primary centre, and to accept, probably unquestioningly, not only the innovation itself but also the means whereby it will be introduced.

This requires a mindset of these leaders to 'get things done' which is expressed in management-speak as follows. It involves being 'task orientated' and 'focused'. Such leaders need to have the qualities of 'efficiency' and 'effectiveness'. They require 'strategic judgement', and often engage in 'organizational development' and 'systems thinking' to 'make things happen'. Such a leader is not his (or her) own agent. He or she is implementing someone else's master plan. (This is what Habermas calls the technical approach to education, see above, pp. 75–77.) There are risks involved of course, but the leader's task is 'risk avoidance'. Success is seen through 'performance management' and 'quality assurance'.

As perhaps can be imagined, there are potential weaknesses in this model, which again reflect its strong command-and-control nature:

> The limits to the reach and effectiveness of the new system depend now on the primary centre's ability to generate, support and manage the new centres ... [This] makes the primary centre a trainer of trainers. The central message [being communicated] includes not only the content of the innovation to be diffused, but a pre-established method for its diffusion. The primary centre now special-ises in training, deployment, support, monitoring and management.
>
> (Schön 1971: 85–6)

Schön expresses strong warnings of potential failure in the proliferation of centres model of the implementation of innovation as follows:

> The process [of failure] has a pattern something like the following:
>
> 1 A primary centre emerges.
> 2 It develops a diffusion system. The primary centre replicates itself in many secondary centres. The primary centre specialises in cre-ation and management of secondary centres and in maintenance of the overall network.
> 3 The diffusion system fragments. The centre looses control. The network disintegrates. Secondary centres gain independence (or they decline, or one of them assumes the role of primary centre).
>
> (Schön 1971: 90–1)

Social change models

The major cause of failure with the centre-periphery model is that it sees people as machines – the very notion of 'hub and spokes' reflects a wheel. It is a technical solution to a human problem, in which people are expected to react rationally – to acknowledge 'that the change is a good idea, so let's adopt it!' However, people do not react to change with a 'rational-logic'; more often with an idiosyncratic 'psycho/social-logic'.

In other words, innovations must demonstrate that they recognize the nature of the social context in which the innovation is to be taken up. Ques-tions need to be asked about that context *before* the innovation is even con-sidered (see Chapter 2). These questions include: What is happening there at the moment? What organizational values and structures underpin what is happening? What are the beliefs and values associated with the current practice? What are the social practices that determine what happens there?

This thinking is reflected in alternatives that have been proposed to the centre-periphery (R, D and D) model. Any model of change must recognize the importance in it of social interaction where: 'the focus shifts to the diffusion of ideas [rather than the introduction of "worked up" proposals]. It stresses not the marketing of products but the flow of messages from person to person'. Nevertheless, such a model still rests on the concept of 'a centre' that is seen as 'having a product or message which is to be diffused throughout the system'. Havelock's preferred alternative to a centre-periphery model is a 'problem-solving' one, which starts 'from the problems and needs which are defined by the client . . . or diagnosed by a "change agent" by direct study of the client's situation' (Stenhouse 1975: 220).

Grant (1993) argues for just such a model of change for medicine, which she suggests reflects the needs of doctors and is based on research carried out through interviews with medical practitioners (Gale and Grant 1990). This holds that the management of change ought to include the following:

- thorough consultation;
- talking to people and explaining the changes;
- teamwork;
- ensuring that the need for change is agreed;
- ownership of the change;
- the use of demonstration projects;
- constraints of time;
- predicting potential barriers to change.

Grant concludes:

> The desires for thorough consultation and for people to have changes explained to them personally mean that agreed change will be a long process. The desire for wide ownership of the change and the preference for demonstration projects also imply that slow and steady progress is preferred to untested radical change.
>
> (1993: 90–1)

The role of leaders in these 'social change' models is not greatly different from that in the proliferation of centres model discussed above. While at the centre, leadership is one of command and control, at secondary centres it is one of acceptance of need for change (and of the change itself) coupled with the necessary charisma to 'get people on board'. Here, the emphasis is on creating 'ownership' of the change by the people most affected by it. It is a matter of 'overcoming resistance' and of finding appropriate 'attractors':

> Those who seek to change an organisation should harness the natural creativity and organising ability of its staff and stakeholders through

such principles as generative relationships, minimum specification, the positive use of attractors, and a constructive approach to variation in areas of practice where there is only moderate certainty and agreement.

(Plsek and Wilson 2001: 749)

Schön concludes that: 'under *these* circumstances, the [solution] is to set in motion and guide a change of related processes of social learning' (1971: 108).

Each of these alternatives to the centre-periphery model has its attractions but all of them share the same difficulty. There remains an emphasis on innovations providing solutions (solutions that are other people's that come from outside, from someone else's practice) (Stenhouse 1975: 220). Largely they are the solutions to the innovators' perception of the problems facing the practitioners. The innovations are not located within (and perhaps more importantly derived from) the practice of the individual or practice communities that are faced with dealing in some coherent way with their own situation.

Towards an educational model for curriculum change

Unintended change

We are acutely conscious that in the case of the current developments being introduced in postgraduate medical education in the UK, the primary centre (the DoH) has replicated itself in the secondary centres (postgraduate deaneries), and that these have then attempted to replicate themselves in the tertiary centres (postgraduate medical education centres within hospitals). The danger is that the tertiary centres:

- may either decline or become ineffectual in implementing the innovation;
- may take on the role of being a primary centre (by assuming its values and implementing the plan that the primary centre intended);
- or, as Schön puts it, 'gain independence'.

The problems here are twofold. Firstly, the 'system' has become highly complex and difficult to manage, so a management approach will inevitably fail. The danger (as Schön pointed out over 30 years ago) is that the system fragments, both the primary and secondary centres lose control, and the network disintegrates.

Secondly, the leaders at the local (tertiary) level are principally medical practitioners, with considerable educational experience and even holding educational qualifications (which is less the case at the primary or the secondary level). Quite probably they will have been involved in other educational innovations, and certainly in constantly rethinking their own teaching. They will hold certain educational values (as we have discussed in Chapter 3), and may therefore 'reinterpret' the innovation in the light of all of this. What they actually do (which may not be what the 'centre' might want them to do, or even believe they are doing) will be determined as much by their background and their interpretation of what is proposed, and by what they believe to be achievable, as by the proposals of the people at the centre.

For all of these reasons their view of the innovation may be radically different from that held at either the primary or the secondary centre. Indeed, their view of professional practice (whether medical or educational) is likely to reflect what we have argued for in this book. So it is likely that some (perhaps even significant) development will occur locally, *despite* the efforts of the centre.

It is interesting to note that when innovation *does* succeed even where there is a centre-periphery (or multiple peripheral centres) approach, it is often for other reasons than those intended or prescribed by the innovators. Schön (1971: 107) observes that in these very particular circumstances:

- the innovation does not by any means entirely antedate the diffusion process; it evolves significantly within that process;
- the process does not look like the fanning out of innovation from a single source; many sources of related and reinforcing innovations are likely to be involved;
- and the process does not consist primarily in centrally managed dissemination of information.

Curriculum development as educational practice

Our perspective on the problem of curriculum change is not one of improving communication between innovators and practitioners, but of developing the educational practice of practitioners themselves within their practice communities.

In Chapter 3 we argued that 'education can only be realized in practice', and noted that 'the practice of education is an ethical activity undertaken in pursuit of educationally worthwhile ends and which seeks to realize morally worthwhile virtues'. However, we also said that 'these educational ends and virtues can *only* be realized through, and exist in, *virtuous action*, and they are themselves being continuously developed'.

Curriculum development is an educational practice of a particular kind. It is concerned with the practice of developing a curriculum, and it has the same nature as any other professional practice. This includes it being complex, unpredictable and often uncertain. Nothing about curriculum development is ever straightforward. A curriculum can never be fixed and for all time. There is never a curriculum 'plan' that can simply be 'implemented'.

Like any other form of professional practice, curriculum development entails risk. Indeed, it is through taking risks that creative solutions emerge to apparently intractable problems. In short, curriculum developers must use their professional judgement, and to do so their judgement needs to develop in terms of the practical wisdom that underpins any ethically driven practice.

As with any educational enterprise, what curriculum developers do (and say), and indeed what they choose not to do (and say) will be driven by the values that they espouse and enact. It is for this reason that a thorough clarification of the values underpinning any curriculum development both lies at the heart of these initiatives and comprises an early task for designers and developers.

Curriculum development occurs then, like the development of any professional practice, through iteration, involving dialogue and discussion. A curriculum needs constantly to be under review, and this is why evaluation, which we described fully in the previous chapter, is simply central to the whole process of curriculum design and development. It provides the fuel for the process.

Leadership for curriculum development

It follows then, that the kind of organization that deals with curriculum development must not be hierarchical in the commonly accepted way of many organizations. It requires a much 'flatter' structure, where there is full involvement in and great respect for all those engaged in its work. The people involved will have a much greater sense of equality – of shared power – in their input to decision-making, and in their actions in transforming the curriculum design into practice. Such an organization needs to be 'business-like' (there are administrative tasks to undertake) but it cannot be based on a managerial model.

In such settings, the leadership approach adopted will be much less 'task' or 'goal' orientated, less focused on 'getting things done', and far less committed to 'strategic' matters. Rather, leaders who are developers will be committed to engaging their colleagues in deliberation about what ought to happen (emphasizing the moral imperative bound up in the word 'ought'). They will understand that the 'ends' of any curriculum development are essentially (and eternally) 'debatable', as are the means for achieving that development. They will know that 'the collective deliberation of the many is always preferable to the isolated deliberation of the individual' (Carr 1995: 71), and that development occurs within communities of practice (see Lave and Wenger 1991). These leaders will make judgements that are 'professional' (not strategic), will recognize that education, like medicine, is eternally 'problematic'.

They will encourage autonomy (naturally within the parameters of the profession).

Leadership for curriculum development, then, requires an educational orientation. In a world dominated by 'command and control', such an approach may be in conflict with those who manage educational organizations (whether at the primary, secondary or tertiary levels). It is a disturbing fact too, that these managers, seeing their role (as we have described above) as 'getting things done', are likely to opt for a minimalist view of development, not allowing for the time necessary, nor sanctioning the iteration required. Those who are able to influence this must have the insight to ensure that educational development can occur through the means we have been describing, by 'creating an environment in which excellence . . . will flourish' (DoH 1999b). Indeed, as Stenhouse so succinctly puts it: 'communication is less effective than community in the utilization of knowledge' (1975: 223).

12 Developing a curriculum for postgraduate medicine at the local, intermediate and national level

Introduction

In this final chapter we return to our overall concern with how to develop a curriculum for practice. With some confidence we can now summarize this entire enterprise as involving: designing a curriculum; developing a curriculum; developing the curriculum designers and developers; developing evaluation and the evaluators of a curriculum; and developing the teaching, learning and assessment of practice (and the teachers and learners who engage in it). We can also confidently claim that, like all professional practices, the practice of curriculum design and development is best learnt by engaging in it in a knowledgeable and thoughtful way.

We now demonstrate the nature of curriculum design and development as circular, in addition to being dialectical. That is, we shall show how progress can be achieved at three levels (the local, the intermediate and the national), which need to interact with each other such that the local level influences the intermediate and national levels, and issues raised at the national level lead back to the local. Readers will note that following Ryle's ideas about the primacy of practice (see above, pp. 134–5), we believe that curriculum development must begin in the practice setting. Here, we believe, both the educational and management structures described in Chapters 9 and 11 should be used to encourage the development of 'centres of excellence' of postgraduate medical educational practice on the ground. This will mean that the teachers involved will begin to understand the quality of what can be achieved and will own the educational enterprise. Further, as we shall see, this should have a powerful impact at intermediate and national level.

Beginning curriculum development at local level means developing firstly an understanding of medical practice as it exists in the given context *on the ground*, and then developing or evolving the educational practice of doctors as teachers (their curriculum-in-action) so that it is sympathetic to the needs of such practice. This also involves considering how the context (including the organizational structures) can recognize and support such postgraduate medical education. The second (intermediate) level will then evolve in response to what is needed by the teachers and learners themselves at local level as they become the key developers and begin to uncover what they need in order to be properly prepared to enact their new or developing educational practices. Thus a curriculum for teaching the teachers and learners will be developed at intermediate level and the overall design of the curriculum at national level, together with the necessary supporting management structures, can then be adjusted properly to support the all-important education at local level (the curriculum-in-action).

It should be noted that although for the sake of clarity we have presented these matters in a linear way, they in fact depend on frequent interaction between levels throughout the process of development. It will be a matter of the professional judgement of those involved as to when, where and how these interactions take place. This is because, as we have argued throughout the book, these activities (curriculum design, curriculum development, curriculum evaluation, teaching, learning and assessment) are all educational practices, and each should be recognized as a practice within the overall professional practice of education. They thus share the same characteristics as medical practice, and require the exercise of professional judgement, because of their complexity, unpredictability, uncertainty, paradox, the need to take risks, the inevitability of 'fallibility', and the need to find the 'best' rather than the 'right' answer to what are often *indeterminate* problems. It should be remembered too that the knowledge that underpins these practices is also like medicine. That is, it is complex, and contains the full range of knowledge we describe in Chapter 6.

As we have shown, the practices of professionals are developed through linking action and understanding (that is, through the critical reconstruction of practice) and this happens largely through discussion and dialogue, often informally. But if we are to facilitate development at the local level and encourage it to influence development at the intermediate and national level, then we need to plan (and manage) that development. This involves both developing curricula to develop those practices (which itself requires the expertise of curriculum design and development experts), and developing supporting cultures wherever that educational practice is located.

It remains then to look at each level in some detail.

Developing a curriculum for postgraduate medical practice at the local level (starting with practice)

As we have already seen, the first stages here are to carry out a situation analysis. This should be designed to recognize the complex realities of medical practice, observe and analyse the quality of the current educational processes and the teachers' and learners' underlying models of learning and assessment, and to look at the level and kind of support available within the cultural context.

Broadly this means conducting enquiries (evaluations) into the nature of the medical practice that is to form the substance of what is to be taught, learnt and assessed, considering the nature of the knowledge that underpins medical practice, and investigating that practice (looking at what is taught, learnt and assessed, how, and by whom), and analysing and interpreting its nature in the light of an understanding of what makes for sound educational practice. (We have provided the understanding needed for this in the early part of the book.)

It also means analysing the organizational culture at local level, in terms of how well it interacts with the cultures of the intermediate and national level, as well as how well it understands and provides active support for the teachers and learners. Playdon (2004a, 2004b) provides an excellent source both for methods of identifying and exploring 'the management structures and processes that could support or disable curriculum innovation', and for analysing them (2004b: 388).

She asked senior managers (including chief executives, directors of medical education, directors of human resources, medical directors, and medical education managers of Trusts where a new curriculum for medical practice has just been piloted) to complete an 'Education Management Audit Questionnaire' (which had been developed out of a project for educational governance for PGMDE and which had been running successfully in the Kent, Surrey and Sussex Deanery for three years). She also interviewed them for up to an hour using a tape recorder, and validating the transcripts with them. By these means she was able to see to what extent they understood the particular curriculum she was concerned with (which was the curriculum for SHOs in surgery, as developed and piloted in two deaneries by the Royal College of Surgeons between 2001 and 2004, and called the 'General Professional Practice of Surgery').

She identified a gap in management culture between the Trusts and the deaneries, which she saw as 'a potentially valuable source of new ideas and creativity' (2004b: 388). But she also pinpointed problematic aspects of this, and the need to set up new committees and management structures within Trusts, to ensure better understanding of educational matters across management. Further, she costed the planning time for consultants and tutors, the educational contact time and the educational support for all involved, and pointed out the need for:

- making appropriate preparations and providing a long lead-in time;
- gaining the support of the Trust directorate and the clinical team;
- providing teacher education for those involved in the implementation;
- recognizing that not all consultants may be teachers in future;

- providing financial support for the additional administration required;
- ensuring a coherent management approach to the implementation (Playdon 2004b: 390).

How, then, should those developing the curriculum at the local level proceed? The following activities seem to us to be vital, and indicate the cyclical nature of the work involved:

- engage as many people as possible from among those who will be affected by the curriculum to be involved in the situation analysis and its interpretation;
- identify or redefine through this the overall educational aims of the curriculum;
- explore the values and assumptions that underpin those aims;
- undertake and evaluate small-scale 'pilot tests' of possible teaching, learning and assessment situations and activities that might feature in a curriculum;
- report the findings of all of this to the national group;
- have representatives from the local level on the national curriculum design group (and its sub-groups);
- receive the draft written curriculum, discuss it widely, and report back;
- be involved in discussions nationally about the redraft, and in the rewriting of the next draft;
- receive the redraft, discuss it widely and report back;
- be engaged in pilot tests and report back.

Given the work to be done here, the complex nature of the educational implications of all this, and the resulting need for expert educational and curriculum development support at the local level, it is simply amazing to us that many deaneries have prepared for (or continue to prepare for) the Foundation Programme by offering a mere couple of hours discussion to each key educator and setting up some assessment 'training' in isolation from the rest of the educational activities. Worse, a number of deaneries appear to be choosing this (rather vital) moment to rid themselves of the presence within their teams of educators with specialisms in educational practice and curriculum development. We believe that this will only add to the spectacular problems of 'implementation' that we expect to see emerging in the rest of this first decade of the twenty-first century. What curriculum development support, then, could and should deaneries be offering?

Developing a curriculum to support local education in postgraduate medicine (teaching the teachers, and others)

As Stenhouse (1975) reminds us, and as the research literature of curriculum implementation within schools shows, there can be no sound curriculum development without teacher development (teacher education). As the resource base and the management of postgraduate medical education stands at the moment, this is the inevitable responsibility of the postgraduate deaneries whom we have characterized as at the intermediate level of curriculum development.

We believe that they would need to include the following in order fully and responsibly to support curriculum development. Without so doing, they would put the entire enterprise of curriculum innovation at risk and be responsible for the waste of considerable financial resources. They might also prompt questions about whether deaneries rather than universities are the appropriate organizations to oversee this work.

We believe that – if medicine is to catch up with all other professions – the following should be developed to support curriculum development in *postgraduate* medicine at this intermediate level:

- at regional level an educational *strategy* is vital;
- an 'educator development' strategy needs to be developed for three levels of staff:
  1 educational supervisors, for whom educational understanding should be provided at the level of the postgraduate certificate in education (which as a first level qualification can lead on to work at postgraduate diploma and masters level);
  2 local 'lead' educators (for example, clinical tutors and programme directors) for whom we believe a masters degree in medical education will need to be recognized as essential;
  3 regional leads (for example, associate deans for programmes, evaluation, teacher training and so on) whom we believe should be in possession of a doctorate in medical education;
- an evaluation strategy needs to be developed between the intermediate and the national level, to support the local evaluators;
- ways need to be found of making all of these happen, for example by influencing chief executives for whom supporting curriculum development fully should become a key target, and the success of which should be reported regularly to the **Strategic Health Authority** (SHA).

Were the local and national levels to begin to operate in this way, it would have a profound impact upon the national level curriculum, and that in turn would become a powerful support to these developments.

Developing a national curriculum framework for postgraduate medicine (supporting education in practice)

The following are our suggestions for procedures that need to be instituted at national level. Readers should bear in mind as they consider them that, as we have said before, curriculum design and development will never produce a perfect, completed master plan. Rather it is a matter of continual development, refinement and evolution. With this is mind we offer the following suggestions:

- establish a national curriculum framework redevelopment group (that includes educationists with expertise in curriculum design and development);
- develop a strategy for curriculum development (that is in line with the model we are proposing here);
- resource that strategy (funding the local and regional action);
- liaise with central government (e.g. through PMETB) for resources (including realistic timescales), and influence central government's thinking about curriculum development.

Coda

It is something of a shock to record that as far as postgraduate medicine is concerned, the ideas that we have presented in outline in this chapter are as yet only distant ideals! They deserve exploration at a greater length than is possible here. But we believe that they can and should become a reality.

Indeed, it would probably alarm the public to know that as yet, in respect of preparing for and developing postgraduate curricula, medicine is way behind all the other professions that we are familiar with (education, health care and social practice).

In the face of media and government concerns about medicine, it is ironic that few have yet grasped that it is sound *understanding* (which has been developed by rigorous education) that drives action and is the chief means of ensuring safe patient care and high-quality medical practice.

The resources spent currently on systems to ensure risk management and professional behaviour (those protocols which practitioners neither own nor obey; neither rate nor remember), should be spent instead on developing and refining postgraduate medical education. It is time that the onus of education is placed once more not on checking visible behaviour, but on developing and refining the professional judgement of practitioners and the values that underpin their conduct.

Finale

For further ideas about curriculum design and development we now refer readers back to the beginning of this book, believing that T.S. Eliot's (1965) words capture the essence of educational development:

> We shall not cease from exploration
> And the end of all our exploring
> Will be to arrive where we started
> And to know the place for the first time.
> (section V of 'Little Gidding'): *Four Quartets*)

Appendix: A response to the consultation on *Curriculum for the Foundation Years in Postgraduate Education and Training* (November 2004)

We welcome the opportunity to give a commentary on this consultation document. We are educationists who teach at postgraduate level and have specialist qualifications and considerable experience in curriculum design and development. Further, we have been working in the field of medical education for a combined total of 50 years. Our detailed comments are given in the attached table but we wish to make the following general points in relation to these.

1. Curriculum design is a postgraduate specialty of education in the same way as medical specialties are in medicine. Yet we can find no evidence of input from people with this level of expertise in the design of the F2 curriculum. Many may feel uneasy about the present document but only a curriculum design specialist understands exactly what is wrong with it.

2. The traditions of curriculum design and development for professional practice at higher education level are both extensive and well documented in the UK and the USA. Within this lie well-established and well-honed methods for ensuring the proper internal logic of a curriculum document. Addressing the headings in our table will achieve this.

3. A significant number of people in the UK have extensive practical experience of curriculum design and development. Many also know first hand the rigour required by the Quality Assurance Agency (and before it the Council for National Academic Awards which accredited much postgraduate education for professional practice settings). Tapping into this experience and advice, as we have here, would assist in selecting a design format that is appropriate for Foundation Programmes.

4. Other health care professions have developed experience in curriculum

design by turning to the advice of those with educational expertise in this field. Medicine should do the same.

5. We limit our response here (though there is more we could add) to offering a framework for presenting a curriculum document, which we have derived from our own considerable experience of how to adapt the general principles of curriculum design to the specific case of professional postgraduate practice (see Table A.1). A version of this framework, and an elaboration of our argument, is soon to be published in our forthcoming book (Fish and Coles 2005).

6. We are aware of the recent publication by the Postgraduate Medical Education and Training Board of a set of standards for curriculum development. While we see these as a beginning, we are clear that they do not go anywhere near far enough to support the rigorous and sound development of curricula for postgraduate medicine.

7. A curriculum is an educational proposal for a programme of learning. Experts agree that the main criteria for determining the worth of a curriculum document are that it should 'communicate the essential principles and features of an educational proposal in such a form that it is open to critical scrutiny and capable of effective translation into practice' (Stenhouse 1975: 4). The F2 curriculum document urgently needs development on both counts: (a) the communication of the essential principles and features for critical scrutiny and (b) being capable of effective translation into practice.

Additional design work involving greater rigour is needed if this document is to provide a meaningful basis for the next stage of further development of Foundation Programmes in the field.

Professor Colin Coles, University College, Winchester
Professor Della Fish, King's College, London
January 2005

Fish, D. & Coles, C. (2005) *Medical Education: Developing a Curriculum for Practice*. Maidenhead: Open University Press.
Stenhouse, L. (1975) *An Introduction to Curriculum Research and Development*. London: Heinemann.

Table A.1

Sections needed in a curriculum document	Areas that need to be addressed	Where found in current document	Further work indicated
A: Introductory matters	Statements of how, and on what basis the curriculum was designed		
A.1 Situational analysis	Description of the context for which the curriculum is intended	In part in the introduction	Much more detail needed on how the practice of a FP doctor will differ from that of a current PRHO or year one SHO. What is to be expected of a FP doctor's practice?
A.2 Those involved in the design	Lists of those involved with designations and allegiances, indicating expertise in curriculum design matters	Two lists (pp. 100/1).	Indicate designations and expertise in curriculum design matters, and provenance of working party. Show link between committee and working party
A.3 Definitions of key terms, including agreed principles, processes and values	Statements of: what makes for good practice in medicine; criteria for sound educational practice; the educational philosophy underpinning this curriculum and its underlying values; the professional philosophy that the curriculum is to cultivate and the underlying values	Not found	Much more needed, e.g. on the nature of clinical practice and the forms of knowledge that underpin it, criteria for sound educational practice, educational philosophy and professional philosophy and the values underpinning these
A.4 Rationale for the curriculum	The arguments, reasons and priorities that led to the key decisions in designing this curriculum, and how these are justified and defended	Not found	Much more needed to show why key decisions were made in designing this curriculum, and their justification

Continued overleaf

Table A.1 Continued

Sections needed in a curriculum document	Areas that need to be addressed	Where found in current document	Further work indicated
A.5 Criteria for recruitment to the programme and the process of recruitment	Statements about what kind of person ought to be recruited to the programme, and what that means	Not found	Much more needed on what is expected of medical graduates entering the programme
B: The organisation of the curriculum	Statements of how, and on what basis the curriculum is organised		
B.1 General overall educational aims	Statements about what kind of person the curriculum will create	In part on pp. 3, 4, 5	Links needed to A.1 and A.3 above. Stated aims 'low level' (primary school). Should be related to higher education postgraduate study/professional development
B.2 Specific intentions, objectives, agenda	Statements of the capabilities, characteristics, knowledge, and capacities to be developed by the curriculum	In part in many places in the document	Shown throughout the document as 'competencies' (which are not the same as, and do not summate into, 'competence'). Emphasis entirely on knowledge, skills and attitudes. These are not the same as clinical practice and do not automatically 'translate' into practice. This section needs to link to B1 (see comments above)

B.3 Chosen ways of seeing teaching and learning	Statements of the kinds of activities that learners ought to engage in to learn those things, and what ought to be the role of the teachers	In part on pp. 9–12. Useful list of learning opportunities but needs to go much further	Postgraduate study, especially learning to practise, differs from adult education. Document needs to say how informal learning (in the interstices of practice) can occur. Simulated clinical situations not mentioned, nor how these will need to be re-learnt in actual practice. Needs to show roles of learners and teachers
B.4 Content/syllabus, balance of breadth and depth, structure of the content	Statements of what the learners are required to achieve	In part on pp. 5, 14–37, 44–47, 51–80. Emphasises largely content (the document is therefore chiefly a syllabus rather than a curriculum)	Needs to be consolidated into one section, and show how complex relationship between 'theory' and 'practice' is dealt with.
B.5 Assessment, including its role and processes	Statements of what role assessment ought to play, and how learners' achievements will be identified and recorded	Pages 38–41, Part III: Appendices pp. 81–99, and Part IV: Annex A pp. 102–105	All of this needs to be amalgamated and made an integral part of curriculum (and its document). Unclear how assessment relates to rest of curriculum (i.e. was designed by a separate group). Assessment strategy unfocused. Appears to relate more to regulation than learning, does not detect practice and the knowledge that underpins it (as it occurs as 'set piece' situations). Unlikely to detect poor performance. Does not link directly to intended curriculum aims. Anticipated time required (p. 41) unrealistic and assesses only a fraction of trainee's practice

Continued overleaf

Table A.1 Continued

Sections needed in a curriculum document	Areas that need to be addressed	Where found in current document	Further work indicated
B.6 Regulations for progression/how failure will be managed	Statements of rules and regulations that ensure fairness and equity	None found	Urgently needed
B.7 Evaluation	Statements of how the curriculum's success will be shown, both in terms of ends and means	None found	An evaluation strategy is urgently needed to inform all stages of curriculum design and development
C: Management of the curriculum	Statements of the provision for the management of the curriculum		
C.1 Administrative structures	Statements of how the programme is to be managed	None found	Urgently needed. Who is to do what to (a) complete this design, (b) translate the design into action?
C.2 Support for teachers and learners	Statements of what procedures and processes will be in place to support the work of teachers and learners as they engage in refining the curriculum	Teacher support briefly shown p. 42. No learner support found	Needs much more detail and indication of resource availability. This is a hugely important aspect of this curriculum design. E-learning will merely inform, not educate, the educators. Learner support strategy urgently needed
C.3 Quality control procedures	Statements of the quality control procedures	QA is mentioned (e.g. pp. 103/5). No QC procedures found	QC section needed

© Colin Coles and Della Fish, January 2005

References

Anwar, R. (2004) Opinion, *BMA News*, 19 June.

Astal, B., Kelly, H. and Devaux, T. (1998) *The Report of the Luke Warm Luke Mental Health Inquiry*. London: Lambeth, Southwark and Lewisham Health Authority.

Aylin, P., Tanna, S., Bottle, A. and Jarman, B. (2004) Dr Foster's case notes: how often are adverse events reported in English hospital statistics? *British Medical Journal*, **329**: 369.

Becker, H.S., Geer, B., Hughes, E.C. and Strauss, A. (1961) *Boys in White*. Chicago: University of Chicago Press.

BERA (2004) www.bera.ac.uk.

Bloom, B.S. (1970) Toward a theory of testing which includes measurement – evaluation – assessment, in M.C. Wittrock and D.E. Wiley (eds) *The Evaluation of Instruction: Issues and Problems*. New York: Holt, Rinehart & Winston.

BMJ (2004) Endpiece: no hands, *British Medical Journal*, **329**: 374.

Brigley, S., Golby, M., Johnson, C. *et al.* (2003) Report of an evaluation of the pilot project: implementing The General Professional Practice in Surgery. Paper presented to the RCS England, 29 October.

Broadfoot, P. (1993) Educational assessment: the myth of measurement (inaugral lecture given at the University of Bristol, 25 October), in P. Woods (ed.) (1996) *Contemporary Issues in Teaching and Learning*. London: Routledge in association with the Open University.

Broadfoot, P. (2000) Assessment and intuition, in T. Atkinson and G. Claxton (eds) *The Intuitive Practitioner: On the Value of Not Always Knowing What One is Doing*. Buckingham: Open University Press.

Carper, B. (1978) Fundamental patterns of knowing in nursing, *Advances in Nursing Science*, **1**: 13–23.

Carr, D. (1993) Questions of competence, *British Journal of Educational Studies*, **41**: 253–71.

Carr, W. (1995) *For Education: Towards Critical Educational Inquiry*. Buckingham: Open University Press.

Carr, W. and Hartnett, A. (1998) *Education and the Struggle for Democracy: The Politics of Educational Ideas*. Buckingham: Open University Press.

Cartwright, N. (1999) *The Dappled World: A Study in the Boundaries of Science*. Cambridge: Cambridge University Press.

Chang, R.W., Bordage, G. and Connell, K.J. (1998) The importance of early problem representation during case presentations, *Academic Medicine*, **73**(10 suppl): 109–11.

Cohen, L., Manion, L. and Morrison, K. (2000) *Research Methods in Education,* 5th edn. London: Routledge Falmer.

Coles, C. (1985) A study of the relationships between curriculum and learning in undergraduate medical education, PhD thesis, Faculty of Educational Studies, University of Southampton.

Coles, C. (1990) Is problem based learning the only way? in D. Boud and G. Feletti (eds) *The Challenge of Problem Based Learning.* London: Kogan Page.

Coles, C. (2000) Developing our intuitive knowing: an alternative approach to the assessment of doctors, in P. Bashook, S. Miller, J. Parboosingh and S. Horowitz (eds) *Credentialing Physician Specialists: A World Perspective.* Chicago: The Royal College of Physicians and Surgeons of Canada and The American Board of Medical Specialties.

Coles, C. and Mountford, B. (1978) Relevance in medical education: an evaluation of students' introduction to clinical medicine, in D. Brook and P. Race (eds) *Aspects of Educational Technology XI.* London: Kogan Page.

Coles, C., Fleming, W. and Golding, L. (2003) *Curricula for Cancer: A Practice Focused Approach.* London: Cancer Research UK.

Cox, K. (1999) *Doctor and Patient: Exploring Clinical Thinking.* Sydney: University of New South Wales Press.

Cunningham, W. and Wilson, H. (2003) Shame, guilt and the medical practitioner, *The New Zealand Medical Journal,* **116**(1183): 629–35.

de Cossart, L. and Fish, D. (2002) Membership of a profession: part two: the nature of professional knowledge in medical clinical practice, *Mersey Deanery Newsletter,* **14**(2).

de Cossart, L. and Fish, D. (2005) *Cultivating a Thinking Surgeon: New Perspectives in Teaching, Learning and Assessment.* Shrewsbury: tfm Publishing Ltd.

Delamont, S. (1992) *Fieldwork in Educational Settings: Methods, Pitfalls and Perspectives.* London: Falmer Press.

DoH (Department of Health) (1999a) *Supporting Doctors, Protecting Patients: A Consultation Paper on Preventing, Recognising and Dealing with Poor Clinical Performance of Doctors in the NHS in England.* London: Department of Health.

DoH (Department of Health) (1999b) *A First Class Service: Quality in the New NHS.* London: Department of Health.

DoH (Department of Health) (2002) *Unfinished Business – Proposals for Reform of the Senior House Officer Grade.* London: Department of Health.

DoH (Department of Health) (2003) *Modernising Medical Careers.* London: Department of Health.

DoH (Department of Health) (2004) *MMC: The Next Steps – The Future Shape of Foundation, Specialist and General Practice Training Programmes.* London: Department of Health.

DoH (Department of Health) (2005a) *The Curriculum Framework for the Surgical Care Practitioner.* London: NHS Modernization Agency and Department of Health.

DoH (Department of Health) (2005b) *Curriculum for the Foundation Years in Postgraduate Education and Training*. London: Department of Health.

Dyson, R. (2003) *Why the New NHS will Fail*. And what should replace it. Chelmsford: Matthew James Publishing Ltd.

Eliot, T.S. (1965) *Collected Poems*. London: Faber & Faber.

Eraut, M. (1994) *The Development of Professional Knowledge and Competence*. Lewes: Falmer Books.

Eraut, M. (1998) Concepts of competence, *Competence to Practice: A Special Issue of The Journal of Interprofessional Care*, **12**(2): 127–41.

Eraut, M. (2000) Non-formal learning and tacit knowledge in professional work, *British Journal of Educational Psychology*, **70**: 113–36.

Eraut, M. and du Boulay, B. (2000) *Developing the Attributes of Medical Professional Judgement and Competence*, www.cogs.susx.ac.uk/users/bend/doh/reporthmtl. hmtl. Brighton: University of Sussex.

Fish, D. (1998) *Appreciating Practice in the Caring Professions: Re-focusing Professional Development and Practitioner Research*. Oxford: Butterworth-Heinemann.

Fish, D. (2003) Education in a community of professional practice: a new approach to curriculum design, in C. Coles, W. Fleming and L. Golding (eds) *Curricula for Cancer: A Practice Focused Approach*. London: Cancer Research UK.

Fish, D. (2004) The educational thinking behind the Royal College of Surgeons of England's first curriculum framework, *Annals of the Royal College of Surgeons of England*, **86**(7): 312–15.

Fish, D. (2005) The anatomy of evaluation, in M. Rose and D. Best (eds) *Transforming Practice through Clinical Education, Professional Supervision and Mentoring*. Edinburgh: Elsevier.

Fish, D. and Coles, C. (eds) (1998) *Developing Professional Judgement in Health Care: Learning through the Critical Appreciation of Practice*. Oxford: Butterworth-Heinemann.

Fish, D. and Twinn, S. (1997) *Quality Clinical Supervision in the Health Care Professions: Principled Approaches to Practice*. Oxford: Butterworth-Heinemann.

Freidson, E. (1994) *Professionalism Reborn: Theory, Prophecy and Policy*. Oxford: Polity Press.

Fromm, E. (1978) *To Have or to Be*. London: Jonathan Cape Ltd.

Gagné, R.M. (1967) Curriculum research and the promotion of learning, in R.E. Stake (ed.) *Perspectives of Curriculum Evaluation*. Chicago: Rand McNally.

Gale, R. and Grant, J. (1990) *Managing Change in a Medical Context: Guidelines for Action*. London: British Postgraduate Medical Federation.

Gawande, A. (2002) *Complications: A Surgeon's Notes on an Imperfect Science*. London: Profile Books.

GMC (1987) *Recommendations on the Training of Specialists*. London: General Medical Council.

GMC (1993) *Tomorrow's Doctors: Recommendations on Undergraduate Medical Education*. London: General Medical Council.

GMC (1997) *The New Doctor: Recommendations on General Clinical Training*. London: General Medical Council.

GMC (2001) *Good Medical Practice*. London: General Medical Council.

Golby, M. (1993) Educational research in *Educational Research: Trick or Treat? Exeter Society for Curriculum Studies*, **15**(3): 5–8.

Golby, M. and Parrott, A. (1999) *Educational Research and Educational Practice*. Exeter: Fair Way Publications.

Grant, J. (1993) Managing change in a medical context, in C. Coles and H.A. Holm (eds) *Learning in Medicine*. Oslo: Scandinavian University Press.

Greenhalgh, T. (1998) Narrative in an evidence based world, in T. Greenhalgh and B. Hurwitz (eds) *Narrative Based Medicine*. London: BMJ Books.

Grundy, S. (1987) *The Curriculum: Product or Praxis?* London: Falmer Press.

Haines, A. and Jones, R. (1994) Implementing findings of research, *British Medical Journal*, **308**: 1488–92.

Havelock, R.G. (1973) *Planning for Innovation through Dissemination and Utilization of Knowledge*. Ann Arbour, MI: Ann Arbour Center for Research on Utilization of Scientific Knowledge.

Heron, J. (1996) *Co-operative Inquiry*. London: Sage.

Higgs, J. and Titchen, A. (2002) Knowledge and reasoning, in J. Higgs and M. Jones (eds) *Clinical Reasoning in the Health Professions*. Oxford: Butterworth-Heinemann.

Higgs, J., Andressen, A. and Fish, D. (2004) Practice knowledge – its nature, sources and contexts, in J. Higgs, B. Richardson and M. Abrandt Dahlgren (eds) *Developing Practice Knowledge for Health Professionals*. Edinburgh: Butterworth-Heinemann.

Hoyle, E. (1974) Professionality, professionalism and the control of teaching, *London Educational Review*, **3**(2): 3–18.

Hunter, K. (1996) 'Don't think zebras': uncertainty, interpretation, and the place of paradox in clinical education, *Theoretical Medicine*, **17**: 225–41.

Klass, J. (2004) Will e-learning improve clinical judgement? *British Medical Journal*, **328**: 1147–8.

Knaus, W.A., Draper, E.A., Wagner, D.P. and Zimmerman, J.E. (1986) An evaluation of outcome from intensive care in major medical centers, *Annals of Internal Medicine*, **104**: 410–18.

Lave, J. and Wenger, E. (1991) *Situated Learning: Legitimate Peripheral Participation*. Cambridge: Cambridge University Press.

Leape, L.L. (1994) Error in medicine, *Journal of the American Medical Association*, **272**: 1851–7.

Lincoln, Y. and Guba, E. (1985) *Naturalistic Inquiry*. London: Sage.

Little, M. (1995) *Humane Medicine*. Cambridge: Cambridge University Press.

Margetson, D.B. (1999) The relation between understanding and practice in problem-based medical education, *Medical Education*, **33**: 359–64.

McLure, M. (2003) *Discourse in Educational and Social Research*. Buckingham: Open University Press.

Moorthy, K., Vincent, C. and Darzi, A. (2005) Simulation based training, *British Medical Journal*, **330**: 493–4.

Moss, P.A. (1994) Can there be Validity without Reliability? *Educational Researcher*, **23**: 5–12.

O'Neill, O. (2002) *A Question of Trust*. Cambridge: Cambridge University Press.

Oakeshott, M. (1967) *On Human Conduct*. Oxford: Clarendon Books.

Parlett, M. and Hamilton, D. (1972) *Evaluation as Illumination: A New Approach to the Study of Innovative Programmes*, occasional paper of the Centre for Research in the Educational Sciences, University of Edinburgh. Edinburgh: University of Edinburgh.

Phenix, P.H. (1964) *Realms of Meaning*. New York: McGraw-Hill.

Playdon, Z.J. (2004a) *Improving Education, Improving Patient Care: A Management Enquiry into the Pilot Implementation of General Professional Practice of Surgery in four NHS Trusts*. London: The Royal College of Surgeons of England.

Playdon, Z.J. (2004b) The management evaluation of general professional practice [in] surgery (GPPS), *Annals of the Royal College of Surgeons of England*, **86**(9): 388–90.

Plsek, P.E. and Greenhalgh, T. (2001) The Challenge of Complexity in health care, *British Medical Journal*, **323**: 625–8.

Plsek, P.E. and Wilson, T. (2001) Complexity, leadership and management in healthcare organisations, *British Medical Journal*, **323**: 746–9.

PMETB (2004) Appendix 1: key principles and standards for postgraduate medical education training programmes, in *Modernising Medical Careers: The Next Steps*, London: Department of Health.

Pollock, A.M. (2004) *NHS plc: The Privatisation of Our Health Care*. London: Verso.

Popham, W.J. (1969) Objectives and instruction, in W.J. Popham, E.W. Eisner, J. Howard and L.L. Tyler (eds) *Instructional Objectives*. Chicago: Rand McNally.

Pring, R. (2000) *Philosophy of Educational Research*. London: Continuum Books.

Reason, J. (1992) *Human Error*. Cambridge: Cambridge University Press.

Reason, P. (1996) Reflections, in Y. Lincoln and P. Reason (eds) *Qualitative Inquiry*, **2**: 15–28.

Reid, W.A. (1978) *Thinking About the Curriculum: The Nature and Treatment of Curriculum Problems*. London: Routledge & Kegan Paul.

Rikers, R.M., Loyens, S.M. and Schmidt, H.G. (2004) The role of encapsulated knowledge in clinical case representations of medical students and family doctors, *Medical Education*, **38**: 1044–52.

Ryle, G. (1949) *The Concept of Mind*. Harmondsworth: Penguin.

Sackett, D.L., Richardson, S., Rosenburg, W. and Haynes, R.B. (1997) *Evidence-based Medicine: How to Practise and Teach It*. Edinburgh: Churchill Livingstone.

Schmidt, H.G. and Boshuizen, H.P.A. (1993) On acquiring expertise in medicine, *Educational Psychology Review*, **5**(3): 205–21.

Schön, D. (1971) *Beyond the Stable State: Public and Private Learning in a Changing Society*. London: Temple Smith.

Schön, D. (1983) *The Reflective Practitioner*. New York: Basic Books.

Schön, D. (1987a) *Educating the Reflective Practitioner*. London: Jossey-Bass.

Schön, D. (1987b) Changing patterns of enquiry in work and living (The Thomas Cubitt Lecture), *Journal of the Royal Society of Arts*, **5367**: 226–33.

Schwab, J.J. (1973) The practical 3: translation into curriculum, *School Review*, **81**: 501–22.

SCOPME (1994) *Creating a Better Learning Environment in Hospitals 1: Teaching Hospital Doctors and Dentists to Teach*. London: Standing Committee on Postgraduate Medical and Dental Education.

SCOPME (1996) *Appraising doctors and dentists in training: A SCOPME working paper for Consultation*. London: The Standing Committee on Postgraduate Medical and Dental Education.

SCOPME (1999) *Teacher Development in Hospital Medicine and Dentistry*. London: Standing Committee on Postgraduate Medical and Dental Education.

Sinclair, S. (1997) *Making Doctors: An Institutional Apprenticeship*. Oxford: Berg.

Snyder, B.R. (1971) *The Hidden Curriculum*. New York: Knopf.

Stake, R. (1967) *Perspectives of Curriculum Evaluation*. Chicago: Rand McNally.

Stake, R. (1974) Responsive evaluation (revised), in *New Trends in Evaluation*. Göteborg: Institute of Education, University of Göteborg.

Stake, R. (1995) *The Art of Case Study Research*. London: Sage.

Stenhouse, L. (1975) *An Introduction to Curriculum Research and Development*. London: Heinemann.

Sylvester, R. (2005) The man who thinks NHS funding needs radical surgery, *The Daily Telegraph* 13.08.95.

Talbot, M. (2004) Monkey see, monkey do: a critique of the competency model in graduate medical education, *Medical Education*, **38**: 587–92.

Tallis, R. (2004) *Hippocratic Oaths: Medicine and its Discontents*. London: Atlantic Books.

The Open University (2001) *Evaluation of the Reforms to Higher Specialist Training 1996–1999, Executive Summary*. Milton Keynes: The Open University Centre for Education in Medicine, Walton Hall.

Weber, M. (1964) *The Theory of Social and Economic Organisation*. New York: The Free Press.

Wells, G. (1986) Conversation and the re-invention of knowledge, in A. Pollard (ed.) (2002) *Readings for Reflective Teaching*. London: Continuum Books.

White, S. and Stancombe, J. (2003) *Clinical Judgement in the Health and Welfare Professions: Extending the Evidence Base*. Maidenhead: Open University Press.

Williams, G. (1980) *Western Reserve's Experiment in Medical Education and its Outcome*. Oxford: Oxford University Press.

Wilson, T. and Holt, T. (2001) Complexity and clinical care, *British Medical Journal*, **323**: 685–8.

Wass, V. (2005) The changing face of assessment: swings and roundabouts, *British Journal of General Practice*. (June): 420–422.

Wragg, E. (1994) Look on my works ye mighty, and despair, *Times Educational Supplement*, 25 November.

Index

Related books from Open University Press
Purchase from www.openup.co.uk or order through your local bookseller

---

QUALITY, RISK AND CONTROL IN HEALTH CARE
Ellie Scrivens

> With better governance a key issue in the NHS boardroom, this book provides a comprehensive underpinning to future developments.
>
> Roger Moore, Chief Executive, NHS Appointments Commission, UK

> This book provides a much needed integration of different streams in the quality movement, examining the need and methods for control and accountability as well as the continuous improvement approach.
>
> John Ovretveit, The Karolinska Institute Medical Management Centre, Stockholm, Sweden

> This excellent book is both informative and challenging . . . [it] helps us work our way through the contradictory and often inconsistent health maze that is bound by quality, risk, control, governance, trust, regulation, private activity, accountability, assurance and outcome.
>
> Adam Graycar, Cabinet Office of South Australia

This book explores the concepts of trust, control and risk management as key components of organisational accountability in the public sector. It explores how the concept of risk management has been introduced into the public sector and how this has impacted on the definition of governance in the National Health Service. It also addresses the concept of controls assurance by placing it in the context of developments both in local health care management and central government.

Key questions that are addressed include:

- How can devolved public sector organisations be held accountable?
- What is the relationship between risk, control and governance?
- How do private sector ideas about governance translate into the provision of public health services?

Quality, Risk and Control in Health Care is essential reading for health policy makers, health practitioners and professionals, as well as students and academics in the fields of health policy, health services management, social policy and public policy.

Contents
Foreword – Preface – Acknowledgements – The search for good quality health care: establishing principles for control – Controls and Assurance – The emergence of internal control: control in private businesses – The modification of internal control: control in government departments – Standardizing internal control: controls in the National Health Service – The case for change – New governance and intelligent accountability – References – Index.

200pp   0 335 20711 1 (Paperback)   0 335 20712 X (Hardback)

RESTRUCTURING THE MEDICAL PROFESSION
THE INTRAPROFESSIONAL RELATIONS OF GPS AND HOSPITAL CONSULTANTS

Juan Baeza

- What is the relationship between general practitioners (GPs) and hospital consultants in the United Kingdom?
- How does government health policy impact upon GPs and hospital consultants?
- What influence does the medical profession have upon policy makers in the United Kingdom?

The medical profession occupies a dominant position within the British health care system and as such is able to influence the development and implementation of health policy. The main division within the medical profession lies between general practitioners and hospital consultants.

This book provides a comprehensive analysis of British health policy over the past twenty-five years. Drawing on data from case studies, it provides empirical evidence of the impact of recent health policies upon the National Health Service (in general) and the medical profession (in particular). The case studies provide an analysis of the impact of the 1991 NHS reforms, as well as examining the ongoing influence of the post 1999 NHS reforms upon these intraprofessional relations. What emerges is that the relationship between GPs and hospital consultants is transforming from a collegial to a more managerial relationship. This book sheds light on the resulting development of intraprofessional relations between GPs and hospital consultants within the NHS.

Restructuring the Medical Profession is key reading for undergraduate and post-graduate students, researchers and professionals in the fields of social policy and health policy. It is also of interest to health service practitioners, health service researchers and health policy makers.

Contents
Acknowledgements – Restructuring professional relations: Health reform and the medical profession – Reforming professional relations – The politics of the medical profession – New public management enters primary care – Health care quality – Transforming intraprofessional relations? – Intraprofessional futures – Appendix: Methodology – References – Index.

200pp   0 335 21627 7 (Paperback)   0 335 21628 5 (Hardback)

PATIENT SAFETY
RESEARCH INTO PRACTICE
Kieran Walshe and Ruth Boaden (eds)

In many countries, during the last decade there has been a growing public realization that healthcare organisations are often dangerous places to be. Reports published in Australia, Canada, New Zealand, United Kingdom and the USA have served to focus public and policy attention on the safety of patients and to highlight the alarmingly high incidence of errors and adverse events that lead to some kind of harm or injury.

This book presents a research-based perspective on patient safety, drawing together the most recent ideas and thinking from researchers on how to research and understand patient safety issues, and how research findings are used to shape policy and practice. The book examines key issues, including:

- Analysis and measurement of patient safety
- Approaches to improving patient safety
- Future policy and practice regarding patient safety
- The legal dimensions of patient safety

Patient Safety is essential reading for researchers, policy makers and practitioners involved in, or interested in, patient safety. The book is also of interest to the growing number of postgraduate students on health policy and health management programmes that focus upon healthcare quality, risk management and patient safety.

Contributors
Sally Adams, Tony Avery, Maureen Baker, Paul Beatty, Ruth Boaden, Tanya Claridge, Gary Cook, Caroline Davy, Susan Dovey, Aneez Esmail, Rachel Finn, Martin Fletcher, Sally Giles, John Hickner, Rachel Howard, Amanda Howe, Michael A. Jones, Sue Kirk, Rebecca Lawton, Martin Marshall, Caroline Morris, Dianne Parker, Shirley Pearce, Bob Phillips, Steve Rogers, Richard Thomson, Charles Vincent, Kieran Walshe, Justin Waring, Alison Watkin, Fiona Watts, Liz West, Maria Woloshynowych.

Contents
*List of contributors – Preface – Introduction – **Part 1: Perspectives on patient safety** – Clinical perspectives on patient safety – Sociological contributions to patient safety – Psychological approaches to patient safety – The quality management contribution to patient safety – Technology, informatics and patient safety – Patient safety and the law – **Part 2: Approaches to evaluating patient safety** – Developing and using taxonomies of errors – Incident reporting and analysis – Using chart review and clinical databases to study medical error – Techniques used in the investigation and analysis of critical incidents in healthcare – Learning from litigation: The role of claims analysis in patient safety – Ethnographic methods in patient safety – Evaluating safety culture – **Part 3: Patient safety in practice** – Patient safety: education, training and professional development – Pathways to patient safety: The use of rules and guidelines in healthcare – Team performance, communication and patient safety – Conclusions – and the way forward – References – Index.*

256pp   0 335 21853 9 (Paperback)   0 335 21854 7 (Hardback)

Open up your options

 Education

 Health & Social Welfare

 Management

 Media, Film & Culture

 Psychology & Counselling

 Sociology

Study Skills

for more information on our
publications visit **www.openup.co.uk**

OPEN UNIVERSITY PRESS

McGraw - Hill Education